CREOLIZATION

CREOLIZATION

HISTORY, ETHNOGRAPHY, THEORY

Charles Stewart, Editor

Walnut Creek, CA

 Left Coast Press, Inc.
1630 North Main Street, #400
Walnut Creek, California 94596
http://www.lcoastpress.com

Library of Congress Cataloging-In-Publication Data

Creolization: history, ethnography, theory/Charles Stewart, editor.
    p.cm.
  Includes bibliographical references and index.
  ISBN 13: 978-1-59874-278-7 (hardback: alk. paper)
  ISBN 13: 978-1-59874-279-4 (pbk.: alk. paper)
  1. Creoles—Ethnic identity. 2. Creoles—History. 3. Creole dialects—
Social aspects. 4. Creole dialects—History. I. Stewart, Charles, 1956-
  GN549.C73C74   2007   305.8—dc22   2006031604

06 07 08 09 4 3 2 1

Printed in the United States of America

The paper used in this publication meets the minimum requirements of American National Standard for Information Sciences—Permanence of Paper for Printed Library Materials, ANSI/NISO Z39.48—1992.

Left Coast Press Inc. is committed to preserving ancient forests and natural resources. We elected to print *Creolization* on 30% post consumer recycled paper, processed chlorine free. As a result, for this printing, we have saved:

    4 Trees (40' tall and 6-8" diameter)
    1,798 Gallons of Wastewater
    723 Kilowatt Hours of Electricity
    198 Pounds of Solid Waste
    389 Pounds of Greenhouse Gases

Left Coast Press Inc. made this paper choice because our printer, Thomson-Shore, Inc., is a member of Green Press Initiative, a nonprofit program dedicated to supporting authors, publishers, and suppliers in their efforts to reduce their use of fiber obtained from endangered forests.

For more information, visit www.greenpressinitiative.org

Cover design by Andrew Brozyna

Contents

Acknowledgments

Conversations with Stephan Palmié planted the seed out of which this volume has grown. I thank him for his support and advice at all stages of this project. Discussions with David Armitage while we were at the National Humanities Center alerted me to important work done by historians on creolization and spurred me to begin to imagine a collaborative, interdisciplinary investigation of the concept and its genealogy. The opportunity to actually do this came when the ESRC's Transnational Communities Programme, directed by Steven Vertovec, provided funding to host the conference "Creolization and Diaspora: Historical, Ethnographic, and Theoretical Approaches," at University College London in 2002. I salute my Department at UCL for contributing resources that helped make this conference a success. David Armitage, Catherine Hall, Daniel Miller, and Kit Davis chaired the various sessions, and Ulf Hannerz presented a final summation.

Leading up to this conference I convened a seminar series with Steven Vertovec entitled "Considering Creolization" (Oxford University, 1999); a workshop with G. P. Makris on "Europe through Its Diasporas" (EASA Biennial Conference, Krakow, 2000); and a panel with Stefan Senders on "Time Out of Place: The Temporalities of Diaspora" (AAA Annual Meetings, Chicago, 1999). I thank all those who participated at these events. Much to my benefit, Ulf Hannerz, Peter Hulme, Nancy Stepan, and Robert Young each took the time to discuss creolization and related ideas with me as the project developed. I am indebted to the British Academy and the Getty Research Institute for their support during the completion of this volume.

Charles Stewart

1 Creolization: History, Ethnography, Theory

Charles Stewart

CREOLIZATION HISTORICIZED

The concept of creolization has a rich and varied history stretching back to the sixteenth century. Even if the word did not appear until later, the idea arose implicitly the moment the term "creole" was coined in the early colonial period.[1] "Creole" denoted the offspring of Old World progenitors born and raised in the New World. How did creoles become creoles? This was the question of creolization at the outset. What transformations did creoles undergo, and how did they differ from their Old World relatives? These questions could also be posed in relation to creoles in other parts of the world, such as Mauritius and Réunion in the Indian Ocean.

By and large creolization had negative connotations at first. Emigration to a distant environment was thought to transform Europeans into a different sort of people. As the historian Antonello Gerbi observed: "The distinction was not ethnic, economic, or social, but geographical. It was based on a negative *jus soli*, which took precedence over the *jus sanguinis*" (1973:182). During the run up to independence, as several of the early chapters in this volume document, societies in the Americas appropriated and recast creolization as a more fortunate process productive of cultures and individual abilities distinct from, and possibly superior to, those found

I am especially grateful to Nancy Stepan for her suggestions that enriched this introduction.

in the Old World. New World societies embraced their local identity, thereby valorizing the process of creolization. The term "creole" obviously continues to have positive connotations for self-identifying creoles in Trinidad, Cape Verde, Mauritius and elsewhere.

As Philip Baker and Peter Mühlhäusler (this volume) show, "creole" came to be applied to mixed languages, or nonstandard versions of an accepted language, from the late seventeenth century onward. In the mid-twentieth century, linguists reached a consensus view of creole as a type of language that emerged when pidgins (contact languages facilitating trade between Europeans and locals) were learned as mother tongues by subsequent generations. Creolization thus refers to the linguistic restructuring in the domains of grammar, phonology, lexicon, and syntax involved in the formation of creoles.

Historians, linguists, and anthropologists have attempted to understand the social conditions of plantation slavery in which creole languages took shape and out of which creole societies grew (Brathwaite 1971; Chaudenson 2001; Mintz 1971; Trouillot 1998; Vaughan 2005). These studies point to the cruel and painful social circumstances of creolization. Françoise Vergès (this volume) presents a particularly evocative picture of the conditions of deprivation under which creolization occurred on Réunion.

Some anthropologists have been attracted by the creole linguistic model of a creole continuum (or postcreole continuum) of intermediate languages (mesolects) found in countries such as Guyana or Jamaica (see Eriksen, this volume). Mesolects typically span from the standard form of a European language, the acrolect, to the most fully creole basilect. Hannerz (1987), drawing on Drummond's study of Guyana (1980), applied this model of a linguistic continuum to the apparent continua of cultural repertoires in world societies generally. Urban elites tend to travel and absorb globally circulating cultural forms (such as knowledge of kung-fu films) to a greater degree than town-dwellers who, in turn, incorporate more of these exogenous forms than do remote villagers. Granted that different societies draw on roughly the same globally available stock of culture, the cultural continua developing in different places form by similar processes, and using common materials. For Hannerz, "this world of movement and mixture is a world in creolisation" (1987:551). The entities that we once called "cultures" are all becoming subcultures (Hannerz 1992:218).

The tributaries of the term become further complicated if we consider the contributions of Creole intellectuals, primarily from the French Caribbean island of Martinique. This body of thought began with the reflections of the novelist and essayist Édouard Glissant collected in his volume *Le Discours antillais*, (*Caribbean Discourse*, 1989 [1981]). There he generalized the Caribbean experience of creolization as a globally occurring process. All cultures have absorbed and continue to absorb influences from other cultures. Since no one has been spared creolization, no one can assert "purity" of origins as a pretext for domination (1989:140). In later writings Glissant has elaborated his view of creolization as an unending, fluid process that cannot be reduced or essentialized, and he applied ideas such as diffraction and transversality to capture the creative, unpredictable results of cultural contact (Dash 1998:155; Glissant 1995).

The succeeding generation of Martinican writers declared "a world evolving into a state of Creoleness."[2] At first blush this seems to agree with Glissant and independently to converge on Hannerz's position. Yet, as Mary Gallagher explains (this volume), the insistence on "Creoleness" (*créolité*) has turned creolization from a process into a static quality. Caribbean Creoles—and primarily French Carribbean Creoles, at that—become the forerunners and the prophets of world Creoleness. They participate in a temporally complex condition of cultural knowledge validated simultaneously by their historical emergence from the plantation past and by their current dedication to expressing this inward authenticity through the medium of art.

* * *

The foregoing should make it clear that the concept of creolization is at once fascinating, fertile and potentially very confusing. Those who approach it from one or another of the disciplinary approaches or literary currents mentioned above, or with the normative meaning from a particular historical period in mind, are in for some surprises should they encounter it outside their own familiar territory. The present collection offers the opportunity to understand this diversity, while also providing clues as to how these various strands of meaning may historically relate to one another. This volume, at one level, presents a collective effort to historicize creolization.

HISTORY, ETHNOGRAPHY, AND THEORY

The historical and ethnographic studies in this volume enable one to evaluate the thorny issue of whether the terms "creole" and "creolization" can be extended for use in current theories of globalization (for example, those of Hannerz 1987, 1996a,b; see Hall 2003 and Palmié 2006). In contemporary theory it is not clear if the concept denotes anything different from the apparently synonymous terms "syncretism" and "hybridity" (Stewart 1999). All these terms, currently used in positive senses to describe the resilience, creativity, and inevitability of cultural mixture, had extremely pejorative meanings in the past. In the cases of syncretism and hybridity, various writers have examined these pasts and reappropriated the terms through a positive reevaluation of the political significance of mixture.[3]

Faced with a similar proposition in the case of creolization, scholars have baulked at releasing the term from certain of its historical meanings. Sidney Mintz, the doyen of Caribbeanist anthropologists and social historians alike, has criticized Hannerz and his fellow travellers for borrowing creolization "from a geographically and chronologically specific New World setting, without serious attention to what the term meant, or to what historically specific processes it stood for." Today's globalization does not bear comparison with the Caribbean where, "people . . . subject to the original processes of creolization were—among other things, and with their children—manacled for life." Historical Caribbean creolization involved the loss and refashioning of cultural materials—becoming "hemispheric Americans of a new sort" (1996:302; see also Mintz 1998). The historical realities of creolization are, on this view, too extreme to serve as models of contemporary cultural mixtures such as eating a Big Mac in Tokyo, belonging to the Madonna fan club in Singapore, or even moving from Nigeria to the United Kingdom and becoming naturalized as a British citizen.

Contemporary ethnographers of the Caribbean such as Aisha Khan (2001, 2004) have offered another set of reasons why the Caribbean experience of creolization cannot usefully serve as a model for a world in creolization. In Trinidad, for example, local opinion assumes creolization to involve genetic mixture between the two oldest exogenous populations of the island: the black descendants of African slaves and whites of European descent (Khan 2001:280). As relative latecomers, the Sino- and Indo-Trinidadian populations did not figure in the original creole equation. Numerous ethnographic studies document the ambivalence that has greeted recent Indo-Creole cultural productions such as Chutney Soca, or the phenomenon of *douglas*—mixed Indo-Afro offspring (Khan 2004; Munasinghe 2001; Puri 1999; Stoddard and Cornwell 1999). East Indians apparently remain sidelined from the creole game. This situation undermines the image of total creole openness assumed by cultural theorists. If the world is in creolization the Caribbean, paradoxically, might have some catching up to do.

The reservations articulated by Mintz, Khan, and others reveal the challenges that history and ethnography can pose to theory. Creolization belongs to "middle range" theory; it is a found object, as is "taboo" or "shaman," each of which also initially had particular social and historical contexts of use but which have now been applied to many different time periods and societies. The ongoing comparative theoretical use of these terms inevitably grates on the sensibilities of specialists on Siberian and Polynesian societies, much as the use of creolization irritates Caribbeanists. Stephan Palmié (this volume, a; see also Palmié 2006), in fact, presents an articulate plea for not allowing the Caribbean signature term "creolization" to float out freely in general theory. One can see the virtue of high theoretical neologisms such as Derrida's *différance*, which avoid this sort of historical or ethnographic challenge altogether.

Unlike "totem," "taboo," or "shaman," "creole/ization" arose within the West, and it has the Latin roots to show for it. Creolization did not depend on the writing of academics in order to travel. As Miguel Vale de Almeida shows (this volume), sailors, traders, and slaves spread it along their routes, and its uptake as an ethnonym or language denominator meant that the term has always been available in many parts of the world over the centuries. Simply put, "creole" and "creolization" have meant lots of different things at different times. As with all natural language development, trying to control it is like putting one's finger in a dike that has already burst. Can the Caribbean exercise copyright over the meaning of creolization? Even should such a copyright be attempted, which strand of meaning and which century in the Caribbean would it generalize— the sixteenth or the seventeenth, when to be a creole meant purity of descent, or the twentieth, when it meant mixture? The word and the concept existed at early stages outside the Caribbean—in Latin America and in Portuguese colonies and in vastly separated areas such as the Indian Ocean. The term "creole" has itself creolized, which is what happens to all productive words with long histories.

This observation underscores the fact that new usages can be unpredictable from the point of view of the past precisely because they do not take shape according to rule-governed trajectories. One of the earliest creole linguists, Hugo Schuchardt (Baker and Mühlhäusler, this volume) made this point when he criticized the view, widely held in the late nineteenth century, that a set of "exceptionless" rules governed all historical sound changes among the various Indo-European languages. The neogrammarian proponents of this "sound-change law" (*Lautgesetz*) assumed a Darwinian evolution of languages toward greater complexity (Alter 1999:123; Wilbur 1972:90). Their conception in terms of a "family tree" (*Stammbaum*) and language "families" paralleled contemporaneous nationalist notions of unmixed populations speaking discrete mother tongues. Schuchardt interrupted this ethno-racial idyll by asserting that sound changes are better explained as the results of external influences such as language contact, social pressure and conscious imitation in the name of fashion. These unpredictable contingencies could not be swept aside as inconsequential exceptions to neogrammarian rules, which held that language changed according to mechanical, physiological processes (at the level of the individual) motivated by time alone (Schuchardt 1972 [1885]:51]. Schuchardt's observations on historical linguistics—largely ignored during his lifetime—surely grew out of his familiarity with contemporary creole languages (Fought 1982:429).

The semantics of creolization have similarly proceeded in multiple directions only intelligible post hoc, as is the case with history generally. To use one part of this history to negate other parts implies that development should be regular proceeding from a certain point in the past. The various essays assembled here expose the striking diachronic plurality of creolization thereby making the concept a platform for multiple theoretical departures.

Hannerz's use of creolization to propose a continuum model of global flows and accommodations represents just one application of creolization in social theory. A different theoretical extension from the concept would be that of Kobena Mercer, who drew on the linguistic restructuring involved in the formation of creole languages. Writing with the Black British diaspora in mind Mercer applied creolization as part of a Bakhtinian dialogical struggle over meaning in the following influential passage:

> Across a whole range of cultural forms there is a "syncretic" dynamic which critically appropriates elements from the master-codes of the dominant culture and "creolises" them, disarticulating given signs and re-articulating their symbolic meaning. The subversive force of this hybridising tendency is most apparent at the level of language itself where creoles, patois, and black English decentre, destabilise and carnivalise the linguistic domination of "English"—the nation-language of the master-discourse—through strategic inflections, re-accentuations and other performative moves in semantic, syntactic, and lexical codes. Creolising practices of counter-appropriation exemplify the critical process of dialogism. . . . (1988:57; quoted in Hall 1990:236 and Young 1995:25)

The analysis of resistance in diaspora situations has not been built upon further with specific reference to the idea of creolization. In social science usage "creolization" seems, rather, to have flattened out into an expressive buzzword used in concatenation with "syncretism," "hybridity," or "mixture"—as, indeed, it already is in the passage from Mercer. Papastergiadis (2000:128) equates it with "transculturation" and "hybridization," and one of the editors of a French volume on *créolité* describes this as "every space of cross-breeding or mixture" (Cottenet-Hage 1995:20).[4] The creole idea has become more of an epigrammatic than an analytic concept: "We are all Caribbeans now, in our urban archipelagos" (Clifford 1988:173).

More than a decade ago, referring to his own appropriation of the creolization idea, Hannerz recognized that "linguistic sources of inspiration have not always served cultural analysis well, and whenever one takes an intellectual ride on a metaphor, it is essential that one knows where to get off" (1992:264). The ideas of creolization as continuum and as a synonym for mixture may well have run their various courses. Thomas Hylland Eriksen (this volume) reconsiders what the term might usefully mean by contrasting it with other terms such as "hybridity" and "syncretism" and also by considering decreolization, whereby creolized forms assimilate back to standard acrolectal versions. The other essays in this volume likewise show that the concept of "creolization" may have yet other rides to offer. There is more to the idea than just "mixing," and there are other suggestive models to be drawn on besides the linguistic continuum example used by Hannerz.

CREOLIZATION AND "RACE"

Creolization can give us at least one different metaphor to ride if we situate the development of the term in the history of ideas about "race." The word "creole" first arose in Portuguese (*crioulo*) sometime in the sixteenth century, although it was first attested in Spanish in 1590 with the meaning of "Spaniard born in the New World."[5] By the early 1600s a Peruvian source records it with the meaning of "black born in the New World." It came to mean any plant, animal, or person born in the New World but of Old World progenitors. The concept did not originally indicate mixture. In fact, from the earliest colonial period down to today in various parts of Latin America and the Caribbean, "creole" has often designated a person of "pure" Old World parentage (Stephens 1983, 1999).[6]

"Creole" was an oppositional term; it distinguished blacks born into slavery in the Americas from African-born slaves transported to the New World and known variously as Guinea Blacks, Saltwater Blacks, or *bozales/boçais* in Spanish and Portuguese.[7] Applied to Europeans, "creole" distinguished those locally born from those born in the Old World, who in Spanish were sometimes referred to as *peninsulares* (that is, hailing from Iberia), and in Portuguese as *renóis* (from the Realm) or *marinheiros* (sailors; Vale de Almeida, this volume). With the cessation of slave importation in the early nineteenth century the opposition of creole to *bozal*, ceased to be relevant. So the terms *criollo/crioulo* began to hold more significance for contrasting types of European-descended people. Increased intermarriage among blacks, whites, and Indians created a temporary situation in which the putatively pure "creole" became a contrast category with the mixed "mestizo."

The rise of independence movements in the Americas, often led by creoles, required forging a unified national identity as "local" as opposed to the European, colonial power. Various nation-building strategies accordingly embraced and valorized *mestizaje*. Palmié (this volume, a) quotes Simón Bolivar's rallying speech on the eve of the independence of Gran Colombia exhorting that "we are not Europeans, we are not Indians, but a mixed species of aborigines and Spaniards." The term *criollo* now became compatible and overlapping with *mestizo*. Not only had intermarriage proceeded apace, but claiming to be purely Spanish while revolting against Spain became incoherent as a strategy (Earle 2001:134). "Creole" came to designate someone who was *local* in birth and allegiance, a tack that was also quite useful for expropriating land from Indians, as Cañizares-Esguerra contends (this volume). It is worth noting that in postcolonial Mexico the identity term *criollo* carried, and still does carry, overtones of eliteness in contrast to *mestizo* (Arrom 1951:173).

The foregoing shows how historical contingencies have fractured and inflected the meaning of "creole" so that it denotes different things in different places. In Haiti, which won independence early, and expelled the white population, *créole* could refer only to black people, whereas on Martinique, which remained within the French orbit, the same word referred to white people, as it did in Louisiana. In Mauritius, according to Chaudenson (2001:6), creoles are those who cannot claim the term "white" following the "one drop" rule. It is evident that the historical development of "creole" as an identity in the postcolonial period is quite complex. Certainly there can be no disputing that the historical concept offers plenty of support for those who apply it today in the sense of mixture.

This focus on mixture has, however, obscured the appreciation of creolization as structuring the opposition between metropolitans and colonial-born subjects in the early colonial period. If a Spanish couple had one child born to them in Spain, and a second child born in South America, this second child would be marked as creole. What was the import of this distinction? How could the one child, who shared the same parents, be different from its sibling? The distinction was not a neutral one. Creoles were thought to be lazy, disease ridden, promiscuous—in short, their relocation to a different climate zone, or hemisphere, had caused them to become physically denatured and morally degenerate. This transformation resulted from astral and climatic influences, and not necessarily on account of intermarriage, or genetic mixing, with blacks or Indians.

The environmental explanation for human difference produced at this time already had a long pedigree in the West beginning with the

Hippocratic treatise on *Airs, Waters, and Places* dated to around 430 B.C.E. (Jouanna 1996:82). In this text, composed a couple of generations after the Greek defeat of the Persians, the author drew attention to the effect of climate on peoples by contrasting Asians and Europeans. In the author's view the lack of variation in the Asian climate caused the people to be cowardly, mentally flabby, unwarlike, and subject to tyranny (Chapter 12). By contrast, in Europe the climate varies seasonally, and this variation stimulates people to be mentally sharper, more courageous, and inclined to democratic forms of polity. An account of the Scythians, a people who lived north of the Black Sea, illustrated this environmental determinism.[8] The author asserted that the cold, moist climate induced such a lack of sexual desire in Scythian men that they became completely impotent and ultimately transgendered.[9] Athens, needless to say, had the perfect climate for fostering an attractive and intelligent population. Centuries later Vitruvius made exactly the same claims for Rome at the height of the Empire (Sassi 2001:113ff).

As the age of exploration got underway this classical environmental approach to difference still existed, although somewhat submerged by Christian explanations for human difference. On the one hand, there was the view that all people, no matter how physically different, were created by God, lived under divine protection, and were potential brethren in Christ. On the other hand, there was the harsh European view that darker-skinned people, especially Africans and New World Indians, bore the curse of Ham, Noah's middle son, who committed the sin of looking upon his father's naked body (Chaplin 2002:159; Hannaford 1996: 91).[10] Some saw the dark skin of these people as the symbol of their inferiority, a demonic darkness related to evil, sin, and the Devil.

The ancient environmental approach was potentially blasphemous because, if pushed hard enough, it could imply the emergence of entirely new forms of being (species), and this notion ran counter to the idea that the present variety of life forms on earth were all created by God and eternally fixed.

The renaissance of Greco-Roman philosophy and science breathed new vigor into environmental determinism. The prime example would be Jean Bodin's volume on history (1945 [1566]), in which he explained that people in the northern latitudes needed to be more active in order to generate body heat. This made them superior to the inhabitants of the tropics and grounded his assertion that empires would usually spread from north to south (Glacken 1967:438; Hannaford 1996:156). The Romans, for example, successfully subdued the Carthaginians but did not realize success north of the Danube (Bodin 1945 [1566]:93). Inhabitants of the temperate north, furthermore, lived in moral virtue, whereas those in the south suffered proliferating vices. Bodin's vocabulary implicitly reconciled Hippocrates with Christianity.

Environmental determinism continued to be entertained into the eighteenth century, when Montesquieu substituted the Ottomans for the Hippocratic Scythians in his *Spirit of the Laws* (1748; Arnold 1996:21). The Abbé du Bos observed that Portuguese long-settled in Africa became black and speculated that if a colony of Africans were settled in England they would turn white (Glacken 1967:558). Edward Long, in his *History of Jamaica*, confidently stated that just as Englishmen who settled in China or Africa became Chinese or African, so settlers in Jamaica were undergoing permanent physical alteration (Chaplin 1997:242). Perhaps the most influential of all eighteenth-century writers on this topic was the French naturalist Buffon, who observed that New World flora and fauna were smaller than their Old World counterparts. He attributed this to the climate in the Americas, which was "antagonistic to the increase of living nature." The Native American was, in his view, "[f]eeble and small in his organs of generation; he is also much less sensitive and, and yet more fearful and cowardly; he lacks vivacity, and is lifeless in his soul . . ." (cited in Gerbi 1973:5f.). These opinions about the effects of living in the New World fueled allegations of creole weakness well into the nineteenth century, thereby supporting the maintenance of Old World rule over the American colonies.

Predictably, New World creoles reacted against allegations of their degeneracy. In the English colonies of North America settlers contended that their bodies and constitutions remained thoroughly English (Chaplin 1997). In this volume, Joyce Chaplin points out that English colonists never adopted the word "creole" to refer to themselves, nor did those in the homeland apply this label to them. The absence of the term can be interpreted as reflecting their successful resistance of a discourse that forecast that long-term residence in North America would turn them into Indians. In the run-up to revolution they began to call themselves "Americans"—this, rather than "creole," was their term of self-identification as New World "locals."

In Latin America, discussions over the deleterious effects of New World residence proceeded into more elaborate detail. From the 1590s to the mid-seventeenth century various humanists and clerics published claims that the climate of New Spain was "inferior" to that of Europe and induced "inconstancy, lasciviousness, and lies, vices characteristic of the Indians and which the constellations make characteristic of Spaniards who are born and bred there."[11] Latin American creoles replied that the skin color of blacks and Indians was the result of the curse of Ham; European-descended people would not become black.[12]

The Spanish émigré doctor, Juan de Cárdenas, writing in Mexico in 1591, detailed the many physical differences between creoles and Europeans.[13] The creoles apparently aged sooner, went grey faster, suffered painful menstrual cramps, and had more stomach problems than Europeans did. Cárdenas explained these conditions, and any changes in appearance or complexion among Creoles, by casting them as "accidental" rather than "essential" changes. According to medieval Eucharistic theology, the accident (outward appearance) of bread, or wine, could remain constant while the essence to which it referred could alter (for example, from bread to the body of Christ). Cárdenas reversed the stability of accident and essence. In his formulation the white, European *essence* of creoles remained stable while the traits or features that creoles acquired in the New World were only changeable *accidents*. In any case, according to Cárdenas, these accidents might represent improvements; creoles were more intelligent than Spaniards, if, perhaps, physically weaker. These formulations represented the first instance of an essentializing European "race" theory, unrelated to, and long preceding the well-known formulations of the nineteenth century (Cañizares-Esguerra 1999).

Creoles and creolization reappeared with very different implications in Franz Boas's influential critique of nineteenth-century racial determinism. In this study, commissioned by the United States immigration authority and submitted to Congress, Boas measured the cranial shape of children born to immigrants in America and contrasted these data with measurements of their European-born parents and siblings (Boas 1912; Gravlee et al. 2003). Earlier I posed the rhetorical question: "How could the one child, who shared the same parents, be different from its sibling?" Boas offered an anthropometric answer. Those born and raised in the United States exhibited noticeable physical departures in body weight, stature, and head shape from their European-born parents and older siblings, whose physical form remained close to one another. Round-headed East European Jews became more long-headed in the United States, whereas long-headed southern Italian crania became more rounded. Some observers interpreted this as showing that all immigrants were converging on a standard American type, but Boas modestly concluded only that "[h]ead forms may undergo certain changes in course of time, without change of descent" (cited in Herskovits 1943:48). By showing the flexibility of human physiology in new and different environments, this research undermined assumptions about the stability of "human types" found in nineteenth-century "race" theory (1982 [1916]). This antiracist message has been a significant part of the Boas legacy in anthropology, as can be seen in the idea of Luso-Tropicalism developed by his Brazilian student Gilberto Freyre (see Vale de Almeida, this volume).

At different historical periods, then, the phenomenon of New World creolization has orientated opposed formulations of "race." In defending creoles in a colonial situation Cárdenas stressed their participation in an enduring European Spanishness, thereby inventing a "racial" essentialism where none had previously existed. Three hundred years later, during a period of mass immigration in the United States, Boas documented the physical plasticity of immigrants, thereby emphasizing human adaptability to environmental influences as against "racial" determinism.

CREOLIZATION AND DIASPORA

As Benedict Anderson recognized, in a chapter of his book *Imagined Communities* entitled "Creole Pioneers," the process of creolization raised questions about the allegiance that fellow countrymen might have in diaspora. Their bodies changed, and so did their political consciousness.[14] Although labeling American colonials such as Benjamin Franklin "creoles" misrepresents Franklin's own self-definition (Palmié, this volume, a), Anderson did productively identify creolization as a motivating force behind nationalism. It worked by splintering a preexisting politicocultural unity; through creolization the self became other; one national body became two. This is a process still very much alive today in the postcolonial world, where so many people reside far from their original homelands. National identities and loyalties are constantly stretched, contradicted, reembraced, or rejected altogether.[15]

As an American who has resided outside the United States over the last twenty-five years, largely in Britain, homeland-diaspora recriminations about physical, cultural, moral, and political change—or suspicions of change—have become an area of personal interest. After a few years away, my distinctive American accent had largely disappeared, and I realized that people in the States did not assume that I was American. On learning that I was, indeed, American but had somehow altered my accent, I had the sense—particularly in California—of being viewed as inauthentic and treated with suspicion if not derision. In an American publication of a work written in England I used the word "courgette," and, even though I varied it with the word "zucchini," an American reviewer criticized my introduction of confusing vocabulary. When passing United States Immigration I said as little as possible for fear that my accent would cause me to be detained for further identity checks. In general terms, I had reversed the direction of an earlier creolization by moving from the New to the Old World, thereby retracing the journey my great grandparents made when they departed from Eastern Europe a century ago. With respect to my country of origin, this was, nonetheless, significant creolization.

This is a small, personal story, but the same factors are negotiated in many places today, usually in conditions of much greater power disparity. How greatly, and in what ways, does someone who was once one of us become different from us? This question admits worthwhile ethnographic exploration inspired by the history of creolization in the early colonial period. To pursue such research, one must be prepared to consider situations as involving creolization even when the people concerned do not use the terms "creole" or "creolization." Joshua Roth's contribution to this volume presents precisely such a case. He studies how Japanese Brazilians negotiate homeland Japanese perceptions that they have degenerated and lost Japaneseness while abroad. The frameworks of the seventeenth century—homeland, diaspora, and discourse on physical and cultural deviation—are strikingly relevant for understanding the current transnational world. A history (of early colonization) suggests a general research agenda entailing the ethnographic study of what people in "homelands" say about their compatriots who live abroad, and what people in diaspora say and feel about the homeland, and how they might get along with their conationals after long periods away.

Postcolonial British residents of Africa and India find it hard to contemplate relocating to Britain for a whole list of reasons (space, climate, lack of "help"). West Indians who have spent thirty and forty years working in the United Kingdom return to the Caribbean but stand out on account of their accents, clothes, attitudes, the sorts of houses they build—with manicured lawns, grilled verandas, and visible burglar bars on the windows (Horst 2004:81). In Grenada they call them JCBs—Just Come Backs. The locals vandalize their property and ridicule them (Davies 1999). Similarly, many Turks raised in Germany are not versed in Turkish norms, sexual mores, or codes for expressing social respect. Their compatriots in Turkey do not accept them as wholly Turkish but rather as somewhat Germanized. Increasingly many of them are beginning to view Turkey as a vacation spot, and they approach their putative homeland with German notions of time, work, and leisure (Mandel 1990:162). This example suggests that creolization may occur through a falling out of synchrony with the homeland; creolization as temporal restructuring.

In the 1970s and 1980s large public debates in Japan surrounded the children of international executives who attended schools in foreign countries, even for as little as three months. They were considered to have absorbed dangerous foreign influences, to have lost Japaneseness and therefore to encounter difficulty reentering Japanese society. Their condition was medicalized and labeled "nonadaptation syndrome" (*futekio shojo*), and they were sent to special schools once back in Japan where the educational objective was variously described as "Japanization," "re-dyeing," or "the stripping of foreignness" (Goodman 1994). Similar schools or programs exist in many countries, not least in Germany, where ethnic Germans (*Aussiedler*) from eastern Europe, and the former Soviet Union, some of whom have lost German linguistic and cultural competence, are taught the acrolectal homeland forms (Senders 2002). Such schools furnish excellent opportunities for ethnographic research into what a society deems "normal" cultural competence to be. In tackling the problem from this angle, one does not need to formulate a list of what might be essential cultural attributes, or even be convinced that there is such a thing as "culture." One may simply study how people in the social field put their own idea of a nationality into practice and negotiate performative competence, or its lack.

CREOLIZATION AND THE BODY

Consider the following vignette from Paul Stoller's *Embodying Colonial Memories* (1995), which draws on research carried out among the Songhay in Niger. At one point during his fieldwork an eminent Songhay noble came to stay with him at the compound he was renting. This visitor lived in France where he had trained in medicine and currently held a highly qualified position in the field of nursing. One day a local man came to the door and asked to see the "foreigner." Stoller volunteered himself, but the man intended his visitor from France. If a Songhay learns a European language or lives in Europe then he is considered to be European. Being classed as a foreigner by his childhood friends dismayed this émigré, and he tried to prove to his erstwhile covillagers that he was perfectly local. Along with his friends he drank unpurified water from the Niger River rather than be seen not to drink along with the others, or to set himself apart by drinking bottled water. As a health care professional he knew the dangers of drinking this water, yet he did not wish to compromise his claim to be a real Songhay. "I'll drink the same water as my brothers," he snapped (Stoller 1995:153). The result was that he spent much of his time sick with dysentery. Stoller's visitor had physically creolized while abroad, and no amount of rhetorical denial, or appropriate cultural performance, could mask that.

This example illustrates that creolization also involves actual physical alterations, just as it did in the early period of colonization when so many settlers, slaves, soldiers, and Indians died of diseases for which their bodies had no preparation. The French, for example, lost 40,000 soldiers to yellow fever in Santo Domingo in 1802, leading to the independence of Haiti and the sale of Louisiana in the following two years (Arnold 1996:95). Creolizing entailed "seasoning"—acclimatizing, acquiring immunities against the diseases swirling around in the colonies, especially in the inhospitable torrid zone.

The American physician George Beard defined neurasthenia as a New World ailment in his 1881 book, *American Nervousness, Its Causes and Consequences*. Beard considered that Americans greyed prematurely and went bald in greater numbers than did Europeans. He attributed these conditions to a general state of nervousness, found particularly in the northeast, and produced by modern technology. Steam, the telegraph, and other such developments produced nervous exhaustion in the populace manifesting in hysteria, hay fever, and headaches. Dryness of the air, extremes of heat and cold, civil and religious liberty, and excessive mental activity all played a contributing role (1881:vi). After a long stay in Germany, the American G. Stanley Hall, then a Harvard professor, wrote:

> Whatever he may say of its quality, the German official or man of business is always appalled at the quantity of work his compeer [that is, American] can turn off in a given time. We may be born larger, carry less flesh, mature earlier, and decay younger than the German; but in despatch, executive ability, impromptu practical judgement, we can as far excel them, as they excel us in science and philosophy. (cited in Beard 1883:16)

Beard and the British sociologist Herbert Spencer concurred that American nervousness was both a disease of civilization and, paradoxically, a disease caused by having not yet attained civilization. Civilization would present a buffer against necessity, and allow people to relax in security (Beard 1883:3). Nervousness was bound to exist in the western hemisphere until it was fully tamed and settled.

Tropical medicine subsequently elaborated Beard's nervousness into "tropical neurasthenia," the symptoms of which were physical exhaustion, headaches, and incipient madness (Arnold 1996:153ff). Twentieth-century descriptions of tropical neurasthenia parallel the symptoms and conditions identified by Cárdenas in his 1591 inquiry into the creole body in Mexico. We are in the presence of a three-hundred-year-old stereotype about the American body and character.

The Hippocratic authors, Bodin, and Montesquieu mainly addressed themselves to the nature of people indigenous to various climatic zones in order to explain the distinctive effects of climate on character. Their observations are interesting for the study of creolization in so far as they informed assumptions about what would happen to people who moved from one climate zone to another for a significant period of time. The literature on colonial or tropical medicine offers ample materials for documenting ideas about physical creolization. In 1905, for example, the U.S. army surgeon Charles Woodruff published a volume entitled *The Effects of Tropical Light on White Men,* in which he observed that "it is quite likely that everyone who lives in the tropics for more than one year is more or less neurasthenic" (cited in Kennedy 1990:122). The pith helmet made its appearance around this time, taking its place alongside the veranda and the afternoon siesta as a defence against "nervous exhaustion" possibly brought on by the sun's rays. The symptoms of this exhaustion were those of tropical neurasthenia: insomnia, loss of memory, lethargy, irritability, insanity, and suicide (Kennedy 1990:123). The pith helmet symbolized the intention not to acclimatize to the tropics. To venture out in the midday sun unprotected—something that tourists nowadays do all the time—expressed practical abandonment of the white "race" since it was taken for granted that whites could not thrive in the tropics.

This example, and others cited in this section, point to the interest of ideas about the effects of climate and disease on the body in contexts of migration. The structural situation is that of individual migrants, or a whole diaspora, carefully monitored by a homeland. Departures from social or physiological norms were regarded as suspect and dangerous. The rubric of "creolization" might help to organize this topic for interdisciplinary study by the history of medicine, social/cultural history, medical anthropology and comparative ethnography.

CREOLIZATION AS THEORY

Ultimately history, ethnography, and theory are not eternally discrete categories. Ethnographic studies become historical documents almost immediately, and yesterday's theory belongs to the domain of history. The linkages among history, ethnography, and theory emerge clearly in the last two chapters of this volume. At the center of Mary Gallagher's study (this volume) lies a text—the manifesto entitled *Éloge de la créolité/ In Praise of Creoleness,* first published in France in 1989 by three Martinican authors. Although their formulation of *créolité* seems primarily aimed at creating a literary/artistic movement, it also sketches a scenario of pancreole and pan-Caribbean political alliance. The text identifies a certain social history and uses this to promote a contemporary social role for followers to embrace and cultivate:

> We declare that Creoleness is the cement of our culture and that it ought to rule the foundations of our Caribbeanness. Creoleness is the inter-actional or transactional aggregate of Caribbean, European, African, Asian, and Levantine cultural elements united on the same soil by the yoke of history. (Bernabé et al. 1993 [1989]:87)

In Praise of Creoleness is quintessentially a social document, one in which literature, history, and social and aesthetic theory all come into play. As Gallagher points out, the *créolistes* may have excluded more groups (for example, women, maroons, East Indians, and so on) than was in their interest, and certainly more than the creole banner would imply. This has not prevented them from attaining major success in France.

The Martinican *créolité* movement presents a situation in which self-denominating creoles stand back and theorize their own social history and social position. Whether their formulations will come to shape every-day creole practice and self-understanding on Martinique is an open ques-tion. Drawing on ethnographic research in Trinidad, Aisha Khan (this volume) addresses this general question of the relationship between de-scriptive/analytical "models of" society and self-consciously program-matic "models for" how a society should become.[16] It could be said that history and ethnography typically furnish descriptive "models of" soci-eties, whereas theory provides "models for." In the case of the Martinican *créolistes* these two models have been elided. The *créolistes* have presented a description of creole society that misrepresents as present and vital numerous cultural elements that have largely slipped away as Martinique gets absorbed into France (Price & Price 1997:15). Their "model of" is thus already a "model for" an idealized *créolité* ready to be recommended to the world.

Unless they are members of the society in question, historians and anthropologists usually only attempt to present "models of" a society. The task of converting these descriptions into models for aspiration gen-erally falls to members of the particular society who can claim, and be conceded, the authority to do this. Once creolization is academically or aesthetically identified as a "model of" and then politicized into a "model for," however, it ceases to represent the complexity, contradictoriness, and power of lived creolization. In Trinidad and Mauritius (see Eriksen, this volume) governments attempt to fit creole communities into the framework of multiculturalism, but the result is friction and inconsistency. You can't have a rainbow of discrete colours/communities and creolize it too.

CONCLUSION

"Creolization" is probably the last word that anyone should try to pin down with a monolithic definition. It carries multiple meanings and is constantly applied in novel ways. This volume does, nonetheless, offer suggestions that can move us beyond the current fixation on mixture as the prime characteristic of creolization. The general idea of "restructuring" (that is, not borrowed from linguistics or any other particular discipline) might present a useful change of perspective on how creolization operates.

Restructuring can involve mixture, and in some instances any distinction between the two is arbitrary. But restructuring can also occur through the internal reorganization of elements or through a simplification of features without the addition of any exogenous elements. The idea of restructuring comes to the fore in the early history of creolization that foregrounded adaptation and acclimatization. This accords with the sociologist Orlando Patterson's distinction between segmentary creolization (localizing) and synthetic creolization (mixing), which he posed as successive moments in the historical creolization process (1975:317). There is perhaps no better description of creolization as restructuring than that provided in Frederick Jackson Turner's classic essay on the significance of the American frontier:

> Our early history is the study of European germs developing in an American environment. Too exclusive attention has been paid by institutional students to the Germanic origins, too little to the American factors. The frontier is the line of most rapid and effective Americanization. The wilderness masters the colonist. It finds him a European in dress, industries, tools, modes of travel, and thought. It takes him from the railroad car and puts him in the birch canoe. It strips off the garments of civilization and arrays him in the hunting shirt and the moccasin. It puts him in the log cabin of the Cherokee and Iroquois and runs an Indian palisade around him. Before long he has gone to planting Indian corn and plowing with a sharp stick, he shouts the war cry and takes the scalp in Indian fashion. In short, at the frontier the environment is at first too strong for the man. He must accept the conditions which it furnishes, or perish, and so he fits himself into the Indian clearings and follows the Indian trails. Little by little he transforms the wilderness, but the outcome is not the old Europe. . . . The fact is, that here is a new product that is American. (Turner 1893:2)

The experiences of disease, deprivation and general adaptation to a new environment in the context of migration all exemplify creolization as restructuring. Physical appearance, consciousness, and the immune system emerge rearranged, having acquired new properties, features, and abilities. The historical studies in this volume prompt contemporary investigations, such as Roth has presented here, into homeland—diaspora debates about physical denaturing, cultural competence, and the anxiety provoked in those striving to retain or regain the status of ethnic authenticity.

Perhaps it is too optimistic to think that "creolization" will be embraced much longer as a category for organizing anything. Linguists concede that there are no agreed criteria according to which a written sample of language can, without any contextual information, be identified as a creole as opposed to a pidgin. Many linguists now reject the very idea that creoles develop out of intermediate pidgins, whereas others maintain that the whole field of "creole linguistics" is moribund, asserting that language contact is better tackled via sociolinguistics rather than the decontextualized grammatical analysis of speech samples (Harris & Rampton 2002:46). Peter Mühlhäusler has suggested that the field of creole linguistics could be substantially recast in the terms of linguistic ecology (1995).

Ideas sometimes stick around on account of the problems they create rather than solve. Looking at creolization through the lens of restructuring shows this to be the case. How much restructuring can an entity undergo before it loses any substantive relationship to its former self? Linguists address this in their disagreements over whether creole languages should be viewed as dialects of European languages, or as new languages. Theorists such as Glissant, as quoted by Vergès (this volume), claim that, "Creolization always contains a part of the unexpected, whereas *métissage* can be calculated." Here the creolization idea converges on the idea of hybridity as expressed by Bhabha:

> The importance of hybridity is not to be able to trace the two original moments from which the third emerges, rather hybridity to me is the "third space" which enables other positions to emerge. This third space displaces the histories that constitute it, and sets up new structures of authority, new political initiatives which are inadequately understood through received wisdom. (1990:211)

Although it offers a vision of the creative potential accruing to people in diaspora, this sort of formulation is problematic for some groups. For many African Americans—and certainly for exponents of Afrocentrism—the creative project is to connect with the African past, not displace it. In the debate over the continuity of African features in African-American society, as Palmié explains (this volume, a; Price 2001; Yelvington 2001), anthropologists and historians have lined up on either side. The ideal of having a cultural tradition that substantially connects to Africa is currently directing the minute analysis and reanalysis of African-American ways of life as they are. A "model for" is governing the (re-)interpretation of the "model of." Much hinges on how one understands the process of creolization. Was the restructuring wrought by slavery so thorough that the African past was discontinued? Or did some elements and/or organizing structures filter through? The stress placed by Glissant and the *créolistes* on the opacity of the creole condition offers little common cause. Those seeking a more Africa-centered understanding of African American culture want, at least, a translucent creolization through which they may glimpse the African past. The suggestion by Mintz and Price (cited in Palmié, this volume, b), that creolization may only have allowed "less concrete" elements of the African heritage, or "unconscious 'grammatical' principles," to slip through presents too dark a picture for some eyes. At the same time other historians use the term "creolization" to refer to the transposition of readily identifiable African features into the American context (Palmié, this volume, b). It seems inevitable, therefore, that debates over what exactly constitutes creolization will yet be with us for some time to come.

Notes

1. The word "creolization" is not attested until the nineteenth century (*OED*, s.v.), whereas "creole" appeared in the 1500s. Sixteenth- and seventeenth-century discussions of how creole people differed from their erstwhile compatriots in the Old World are, effectively, meditations on creolization as will be discussed below in this chapter.
2. "*Le monde va en état de créolité*" (Bernabé et al. 1993:112, 51).
3. Bhabha (1994) and Papastergiadis (1997) for hybridity; Shaw and Stewart (1994) for syncretism.
4. "*La créolité redéfinie comme tout espace de métissage ou de mixité . . . est, en ce sens, notre avenir.*"
5. José de Acosta's, *Historia natural y moral de las Indias* (1590) presents the word spelled *crollo* (*OED*, s.v. "creole," Stephens 1983:30). The Portuguese term *crioulo* derives from *cria*, meaning "infant, nursling, sapling" but also "a person without family, without material means"; cp. *criada*, "domestic servant" (Houaiss, s.v. *cria*; cp. *criadouro*, "nursery [for infants, plants]"). The word contains overtones of domesticating, nursing. Linguists generally account for the *–oulo* ending as a diminutive suffix so *crioulo* is taken to mean "a child of slaves brought up in the master's house" (Arrom 1951:175).
6. In his 1862 history of the United States, J. M. Ludlow wrote that 'there are Creole whites, creole negroes, creole horses, etc; and creole whites are of all persons the most anxious to be deemed of pure white blood' (*OED*, s.v. "creole").
7. According to Chaudenson (2001), *bozal* meant "muzzle," which he interprets as a reference to the inability of newly arrived slaves to speak the local language in the New World. Stephens (1983:29) glosses it as "fresh, green, inexperienced."
8. The ancient Greeks considered the Scythians to be Europeans, although placed on the extreme eastern edge of Europe. That the author of *Airs, Waters and Places* should contrast Europeans with Europeans in a treatise arguing for the continental differences between Europe and Asia is odd, as Thomas (2000:94) has noted.

9. "The cavities of their bodies are extremely moist, especially the belly, since, in a country of such a nature and under such climatic conditions, the bowels cannot be dry. All the men are fat and hairless and likewise all the women, and the two sexes resemble one another" (Chapter 19, see also Chapter 22; Pigeaud 1983:51).
10. Gen. 9.22ff. Upon awakening from his drunken slumber Noah cursed Ham's *son*, Canaan. This curse was popularly affixed to Ham in medieval Christianity in the context of rising prejudice against Jews, Muslims, and Africans, since Ham's progeny became the inhabitants of Palestine, North Africa, and Ethiopia.
11. Quotations drawn from works by Giovanni Botero and Juan de la Puente dating from 1596 and 1612, respectively (cited in Cañizares-Esguerra 1999:46).
12. Buenaventura de Salinas y Córdova, *Memorial de las historias del Nuevo Mundo Piru* (1630), cited in Cañizares-Esguerra 1999:34.
13. Cárdenas did not use the term *creole*. He referred to *españoles nacidos en las indias* (Spaniards born in the Indies) and also to *los hombres que nacen y se crían en las indias* (people born and raised in the Indies), whereby the verb "to be raised" is etymologically related to *criollo* (1980 [1591]:245). Cárdenas opposed the locals to "Spaniards born in Spain," whom he also referred to as *gachupínes* (1980 [1591]:250). According to Corominas (s.v. *cacho* I), "they were named thus by the creoles . . . on account of their slowness and their ignorance of things American." Derived from *cachopo*, "a hollow or dry log"; the term *gachupín* might be rendered very literally as "blockhead," "thick as two planks," or perhaps "a stuffed shirt" or a "hollow man."
14. Ann Stoler (1992) studies these basic issues of "creolization" and allegiance in colonial Indonesia, where it was recommended that children of Dutch colonists be sent back to Holland for schooling to counteract creeping indigenization.
15. Anderson (1994) has himself recognized colonial creolization as a heuristic for thinking about contemporary transnationalism.
16. Clifford Geertz proposed this distinction in an essay on religion. "Models of" are descriptions/explanations of existing phenomena, formed by making deductions about the thing (structure, function, history). "Models for" are blueprints for the establishment of objects that do not yet exist; they proceed through a logic of induction—putting together ideas and images that appear to be realizable (Geertz 1973:93).

References

Alter, S. 1999. *Darwin and the linguistic image: Language, race and natural theology in the nineteenth century*. Baltimore, MD: Johns Hopkins University Press.

Anderson, B. 1991. *Imagined communities*, rev. ed. London: Verso.

——— 1994. Exodus, *Critical Inquiry* 20:314–327.

Arnold, D. 1996. *The problem of nature: Environment, culture and European expansion*. Oxford: Blackwell.

Arrom, J. J. 1951. Criollo: Definición y matices de un concepto, *Hispania* 34:172–176.

Beard, G. 1881. *American nervousness: Its causes and consequences*. New York: G. P. Putnam.

——— 1883. *Herbert Spencer and American nervousness: A scientific coincidence*. New York: G. P. Putnam.

Bernabé, J., et al. 1993 [1989]. *Éloge de la créolité/In praise of Creoleness*. Paris: Gallimard.

Bhabha, H. 1990. The third space: Interview with Homi Bhabha. In *Identity: Community, culture, difference*. J. Rutherford, ed. London: Lawrence and Wishart, pp. 207–221.

——— 1994. *The location of culture*. London: Routledge.

Boas, F. 1912. Changes in the bodily form of descendants of immigrants, *American Anthropologist* 14:530–562.

—— 1982 [1916]. New evidence in regard to the instability of human types. In *Race, Language and Culture*. F. Boas, ed. Chicago: University of Chicago Press, pp. 76–81.

Bodin, J. 1945 [1566]. *Method for the easy comprehension of history*. B. Reynolds, trans. New York: Columbia University Press.

Brathwaite, E. K. 1971. *The development of Creole society in Jamaica, 1770–1820*. Oxford: Clarendon Press.

Cañizares-Esguerra, J. 1999. New world, new stars: Patriotic astrology and the invention of Indian and Creole bodies in Colonial Spanish America, 1600–1650, *American Historical Review* 104:33–68.

Cárdenas, J. de. 1980 [1591]. *Primera parte de los problemas y secretos maravillosos de la Indias*. Mexico City: Academia Nacional de Medicina.

Chaplin, J. 1997. Natural philosophy and an early racial idiom in North America: Comparing English and Indian bodies, *William and Mary Quarterly* 54:229–252.

—— 2002. Race. In *The British Atlantic world, 1500–1800*. M. Braddick and D. Armitage, eds. London: Palgrave, pp. 154–172.

Chaudenson, R. 2001. *Creolization of language and culture*. Revised with S. Mufwene. London: Routledge.

Clifford, J. 1988. *The predicament of culture*. Cambridge, MA: Harvard University Press.

Corominas, J., and J. Pascual, eds. 1980. *Diccionario crítico etimológico Castellano e Hispánico*. Madrid: Editorial Gredos.

Cottenet-Hage, M. 1995. Introduction. In *Penser la créolité*. M. Condé and M. Cottenet-Hage, eds. Paris: Karthala.

Dash, J. M. 1998. *The other America: Caribbean literature in a New World context*. Charlottesville, VA: University of Virginia Press.

Davies, H. 1999. Back to the future, *The Guardian*, 27 February.

Drummond, L. 1980. The cultural continuum: A theory of intersystems, *Man* 15:30–43.

Earle, R. 2001. Creole patriotism and the myth of the loyal Indian, *Past & Present* 172:125–145.

Fought, J. 1982. The reinvention of Hugo Schuchardt, *Language in Society* 11:419–436.

Geertz, C. 1973. Religion as a cultural system. In *The interpretation of cultures*. C. Geertz, ed. New York: Basic Books, pp. 87–125.

Gerbi, A. 1973. *The dispute of the New World: The history of a polemic, 1750–1900*, revised ed. J. Moyle, trans. Pittsburgh, PA: University of Pittsburgh Press.

Glacken, C. 1967. *Traces on the Rhodian shore: Nature and culture in Western thought from ancient times to the end of the eighteenth century*. Berkeley and Los Angeles, CA: University of California Press.

Glissant, É. 1989 [1981]. *Caribbean discourse: Selected essays*. Charlottesville, VA: University of Virginia Press.

—— 1995. Creolization in the making of the Americas. In *Race, discourse and the origin of the Americas*. V. Hyatt and R. Nettleford, eds. Washington, DC: Smithsonian Press, pp. 268–275.

Goodman, R. 1994. Kikokushijo no Kenkyū: Shakai Kagakuteki na Kenkyū no Hensen to Mondaiten (*Kikokushijo* research: Shifting paradigms and the problem of social scientific research). In *Jidō Shinrigaku no Shinpo (Annual Review of Japanese Child Psychology)* 33: 325–352.

Gravlee, C., et al. 2003. Boas's *Changes in bodily form*: The immigrant study, cranial plasticity, and Boas's physical anthropology, *American Anthropologist* 105:326–332.

Hall, S. 1990. Cultural identity and diaspora. In *Identity: Community, culture and difference*. J. Rutherford, ed. London: Lawrence and Wishart, pp. 222–237.

Hall, S. 2003. Creolization, diaspora and hybridity in the context of globalization. In *Créolité and Creolization*. O. Enwezor et al., eds. Ostfildern-Ruit, Germany: Hatje Cantzpp, pp. 185–198.

Hannaford, I. 1996. *Race: The history of an idea in the West*. Baltimore, MD: Johns Hopkins University Press.

Hannerz, U. 1987. The world in creolisation, *Africa* 57:546–559.

———— 1992. *Cultural complexity: Studies in the social organization of meaning*. New York: Columbia University Press.

———— 1996a. Stockholm: Doubly creolizing. In *Transnational connections*. U. Hannerz, ed. New York: Routledge, pp. 150–159.

———— 1996b. Kokoschka's revenge: Or, the social organization of creolization. In *Transnational connections*. U. Hannerz, ed. New York: Routledge, pp. 65–78.

Harris, R., and B. Rampton. 2002. Creole metaphors in cultural analysis: On the limits and possibilities of (socio-)linguistics, *Critique of anthropology* 22:31–51.

Herskovits, M. 1943. Franz Boas as physical anthropologist, *American Anthropologist* 45:39–51.

Hippocrates. 1983 [400 B.C.E.]. *Airs, waters and places*. In *Hippocratic writings*. G. E. R. Lloyd, ed. J. Chadwick and W. N. Mann, English trans. London: Penguin, pp. 148–169.

———— 1996. *Airs, eaux, lieux*. J. Jouanna. Greek text, French trans. Paris: Les Belles Lettres.

Horst, H. 2004. "Back a yaad": Constructions of home among Jamaica's returned migrant community. Ph.D. dissertation, University College London.

Houaiss. 2001. *Dicionário Houaiss da língua portuguesa*, 1st ed. Rio de Janeiro: Editora Objectiva.

Jouanna, J. 1996. Notice. In *Airs, eaux, lieux*. J. Jouanna, ed. Paris: Les Belles Lettres (Budé), pp. 7–184.

Kennedy, D. 1990. The perils of the midday sun: Climatic anxieties in the colonial tropics. In *Imperialism and the natural world*. J. McKenzie, ed. Manchester, UK: Manchester University Press, pp. 118–140.

Khan, A. 2001. Journey to the center of the Earth: The Caribbean as master symbol, *Cultural Anthropology* 16:271–302.

———— 2004. *Callaloo nation: Metaphors of race and religious identity among south Asians in Trinidad*. Durham, NC: Duke University Press.

Mandel, R. 1990. Shifting centers and emergent identities: Turkey and Germany in the lives of Turkish *Gastarbeiter*. In *Muslim travellers: Pilgrimage, migration and the religious imagination*. D. Eickelman and J. Piscatori, eds. New York: Routledge, pp. 153–171.

Mercer, K. 1988. Diaspora culture and the dialogic imagination. In *Blackframes: Critical perspectives on black independent cinema*. M. Cham and C. Andrade-Watkins, eds. Cambridge, MA: The MIT Press, pp. 50–61.

Mintz, Sidney. 1971. The socio-historical background to pidginization and creolization. In *Pidginization and creolization of languages*. D. Hymes, ed. Cambridge: Cambridge University Press, pp. 481–496.

———— 1996. Enduring substances, trying theories, *Journal of the Royal Anthropological Institute*, 2:289–311.

———— 1998. The localisation of anthropological practice, *Critique of Anthropology*, 18:117–33.

Munasinghe, V. 2001. *Callaloo or tossed salad? East Indians and the cultural politics of identity in Trinidad*. Ithaca, NY: Cornell University Press.

Mühlhäusler, P. 1995. Pidgins, creoles and linguistic ecologies. In *From contact to Creole and beyond*. P. Baker, ed. London: University of Westminster Press, pp. 235–250.

Neumann-Holzschuh, I., and E. Schneider. 2000. *Degrees of restructuring in creole languages*. Amsterdam: John Benjamins.

Oxford English Dictionary (OED) Online. Oxford University Press, 2004.

Palmié, S. 2006. Creolization and its discontents, *Annual Reviews in Anthropology* 35: 433–456.

Papastergiadis, N. 1997. Tracing hybridity in theory. In *Debating cultural hybridity: Multicultural identities and the politics of anti-racism.* P. Werbner and T. Modood, eds. London: Zed Books, pp. 257–281.

———— 2000. *The turbulence of migration: Globalization, deterritorialization, hybridity.* Cambridge: Polity.

Patterson, O. 1975. Context and choice in ethnic allegiances: A theoretical framework and Caribbean case study. In *Ethnicity: Theory and experience.* N. Glazer and D. Moynihan. Cambridge, MA: Harvard University Press, pp. 305–349.

Pigeaud, J. 1983. Remarques sur l'inné et l'acquis dans le *Corpus Hippocratique.* In *Formes de pensée dans la collection Hippocratique.* F. Lasserre and P. Mudry, eds. Geneva: Droz, pp. 41–55.

Price, R. 2001. The miracle of creolization: A retrospective, *New West Indian Guide* 75:35–64.

Price, R., and S. Price. 1997. Shadowboxing in the mangrove, *Cultural Anthropology* 12:3–36.

Puri, S. 1999. Canonized hybridities, resistant hybridities: Chutney soca, carnival, and the politics of carnival. In *Caribbean romances.* B. Edmondson, ed. Charlottesville, VA: University of Virginia Press, pp. 12–38.

Sassi, M. M. 2001. *The science of man in ancient Greece.* Chicago: University of Chicago Press.

Schuchardt, H. 1972 [1885]. On sound laws: Against the neogrammarians, B. Edmondson, ed. In *Schuchardt, the neogrammarians, and the transformational theory of phonological change: Four essays.* T. Vennemann and H. Wilbur, eds. Frankfort: Athenäum.

Senders, S. 2002. *Ius sanguinis* or *ius mimesis*? Rethinking "ethnic German" repatriation. In *Coming home to Germany? The integration of ethnic Germans from central and eastern Europe in the Federal Republic.* D. Rock and S. Wolff, eds. Oxford: Berghahn, pp. 87–101.

Shaw, R., and C. Stewart. 1994. Introduction: Problematizing syncretism. In *Syncretism/Anti-syncretism: The politics of religious synthesis.* C. Stewart and R. Shaw, eds. London: Routledge, pp. 1–26.

Stephens, T. M. 1983. Creole, créole, criollo, crioulo: The shadings of a term, *SECOL* (Southeastern Conference on Linguistics) *Review* 7:28–39.

———— 1999. *Dictionary of Latin American racial and ethnic terminology*, 2nd ed. Gainesville, FL: University of Florida Press.

Stewart, C. 1999. Syncretism and its synonyms: Reflections on cultural mixture, *Diacritics* 29:40–62.

Stoddard, E., and G. Cornwell. 1999. Cosmopolitan or mongrel? Créolité, hybridity and "douglarisation" in Trinidad, *European Journal of Cultural Studies*, 2:331–353.

Stoler, A. L. 1992. Sexual affronts and racial frontiers: European identity and the cultural politics of exclusion in colonial southeast Asia, *Comparative Studies in Society and History* 34:514–551.

Stoller, P. 1995. *Embodying colonial memories: Spirit possession, power and the Hauka in West Africa.* New York: Routledge.

Thomas, R. 2000. *Herodotus in context: Ethnography, science and the art of persuasion.* Cambridge: Cambridge University Press.

Turner, F. J. 1893. The significance of the frontier in American history. http://xroads.virginia.edu/~HYPER/TURNER.

Trouillot, M. R. 1998. Culture on the edges: Creolization in the plantation context, *Plantation Society in the Americas* 5:8–28.

Vaughan, M. 2005. *Creating the creole island: Slavery in eighteenth-century Mauritius*. Durham, NC: Duke University Press.

Wilbur, T. 1972. Hugo Schuchardt and the neogrammarians. In *Schuchardt, the neogrammarians, and the transformational theory of phonological change: Four essays*. T. Vennemann and H. Wilbur, eds. Frankfort: Athenäum, pp. 73–113.

Woodruff, C. 1905. *The effects of tropical light on white men*. New York: Rebman.

Yelvington, K. 2001. The anthropology of Afro-Latin America and the Caribbean: Diasporic dimensions, *Annual Reviews in Anthropology* 30:227–260.

Young, Robert. 1995. *Hybridity and colonial desire*. London: Routledge.

2 Creole Colonial Spanish America

Jorge Cañizares-Esguerra

Patrocinio de la Virgen de Guadalupe sobre el Reino de Nueva España ("Auspices of Our Lady of Guadalupe over the Kingdom of New Spain") (Figure 1) is an eighteenth-century canvas by an anonymous Mexican painter that rather vividly captures creole discourses in colonial Mexico. A garlanded Our Lady of Guadalupe stands on top of a fountain from which four kneeling nobles, two indigenous, two Hispanic, drink.

Fountains had long been associated with salvation and purity in Christian discourse (Miller 1983; Schama 1995, part 2). For example, in their 1596 Ghent altarpiece, *Fountain of Life and Mercy*, Gerard Horenbout (1467–1540) and his son Lucas Horenbout (d. 1544) have the community of the pious drink of a fountain whose source is the body of Christ (Figure 2).[1] Believers eucharistically partake of the blood of Christ, whose wounds refill the well. Some princes and clerics, including a turbaned potentate and a tonsured friar, who stand for the Turks and Luther, respectively, turn their backs on the fountain as they gather to worship Dame World. To reinforce his Counter-Reformation message, the Flemish Horenbouts have angels hovering over the pious and demons over the infidels and heretics.

The same theological and compositional principles organize the Mexican painting, but the fountain's spring is Our Lady of Guadalupe, and both

This chapter is a slightly modified version of my "Racial, Religious, and Civic Creole Identity in Colonial Spanish America," *American Literary History* 2005 (17):420–37.

Figure 1   Anonymous (eighteenth-century) *María de Guadalupe como fuente de gracia sobre el imperio español*

natives and Hispanics kneel to drink from the well. Using this virgin as the source of the "fountain of life and mercy" came naturally to those who thought of Our Lady of Guadalupe as an Immaculate Conception, for some of the imagery underlying the belief in the immaculate conception came from the Song of Songs, one of the strangest books of the Old Testament. According to Christian theology, the Song of Songs prefigures the mystery of St. Mary's conception by describing a woman, the

Figure 2   Gerard Horenbout and Lucas Horenbout, *Fountain of Life and Mercy*, 1596, Altarpiece. Ghent, Belgium

lover of God, as a walled garden (*hortus conclusus*) and a fountain ("A garden inclosed is my sister, my spouse; a spring shut up, a fountain sealed" [Song of Solomon 4.12]).[2] The most striking difference between the Mexican painting and the Horenbouts's is that in the former no party turns its back on the fountain: both Amerindians and Europeans belong in the same community of the pious.

To further make his point, the anonymous Mexican painter places a bouquet on top of each pair of Amerindian and Hispanic royalty. This symmetrical distribution of flowers is fraught with meaning. As with the trope of two communities gathered around a fountain, one partaking of the body of Christ and the other refusing to do so, it was a common visual metaphor to have the tree of life and knowledge separate the community of the elected from the damned (Schama 1995:221–26). Take, for example, the case of *Fall and Grace* by Lucas Cranach (1472–1553) (Figure 3). In this engraving, two radically different narratives unfold on opposite sides of a tree: to the denuded side belongs the story of the fall, hell, and the apocalypse; to the verdant one the story of deliverance and salvation brought about by Christ's passion and resurrection. In Cranach's composition, the Jews led by Moses fall in the barren, postlapsarian world of sin and demons, whereas the Christian community (one made of sheep and shepherds) belong in a world of bounty and plenty. The Mexican painting under review, once again, does not exclude anyone from the Christian community; both the Amerindian and Hispanic nobles kneel in equally verdant sides of the canvas.

I have chosen the painting *Patrocinio de la Virgen de Guadalupe sobre el Reino de Nueva España* to introduce this essay because it summarizes much of what I believe to be distinct about Creole discourse in colonial Spanish America: Creoles saw their lands to be equally rooted in the indigenous and Hispanic pasts. In their imagination, colonial Spanish American societies were kingdoms, ancien régime societies made up of social estates and corporate privileges, with deep, ancient dynastic roots in both the New World and Spain. For heuristic purposes, I have divided this essay to coincide with the compositional elements of the painting: creoles and Amerindians; creoles and religion, particularly Our Lady of Guadalupe; and creoles and Spain. But before turning to my tripartite analysis, we need first to clarify who the creoles were.

CRIOLLOS

The self-styled *criollos*, or creoles, were local elites who presided over racially mixed colonial societies of Amerindians, blacks, Spaniards, and *castas* (mixed bloods) (Katzew 2004). Creoles felt entitled to rule over these racially and culturally heterogeneous societies, as part of a loosely held Catholic composite monarchy whose center was back in Madrid. By and large they succeeded in their efforts to obtain autonomy vis-à-vis Spain, but their rule over these local "kingdoms" was always precarious and negotiated. Although peninsular newcomers, including representatives of the sprawling lay and religious bureaucracies that the crown created in Spanish America, were usually marshaled into serving creole interests either through bribes or marriage, creoles felt voiceless and discriminated against. To be sure, they were right to complain. Back in Spain, the Indies were seen as corrupting, degenerating environments:

Figure 3 Lucas Cranach the elder, *Fall and Grace*, engraving ca. 1530

frontier societies where one could get rich but sorely lacking in sophistication and culture. On arrival in the Indies, *peninsulares* felt naturally entitled to hold political, religious, and economic power, and creoles resented such pretensions (Brading 1991).

Creole patriotism originated in the late sixteenth and early seventeenth centuries as the American-born descendants of Spanish conquistadors complained that the crown was turning its back on its original commitment to foster a class of grandees in the New World. As the monarchy phased out the grants of Amerindian tribute and labor given to the conquistadors (*encomiendas*) in the most economically dynamic areas of Mexico and Peru, creoles lost the right to become a privileged landed nobility surrounded by communities of Amerindian retainers. All over Spanish America, creoles articulated a somewhat misleading view of themselves as dispossessed nobles outcompeted by ravenous, transient, peninsular upstarts. Creoles then turned to the Catholic church, whose branches (the ecclesiastical establishment or "secular" church, as well as some of the religious orders) they gradually came to dominate. During the seventeenth and eighteenth centuries, ensconced in universities, cathedral chapters, nunneries, and parishes, creoles in greater Peru and Mexico produced countless patriotic sermons and treatises that praised the wealth of their ecclesiastical establishments as well as their own learning and piety, including that of the many saints the church canonized—or failed to—in the Indies (Brading 1991; Lafaye 1974; Lavallé 1993; Rubial García 1990).

The creole project was aimed at establishing an orderly polity composed of hierarchical social orders in nested subordination. Spanish America was indeed a society built on corporate privileges and social estates that overlapped with additional racial hierarchies. Although *castas* grew in the interstices of the original three-tier system of Spaniards, Amerindians, and Africans and, therefore, blurred the colonial boundaries of class and race, Spanish America was a society obsessed with identifying and enforcing racial hierarchies (Cahill 1994; Israel 1975; Katzew 2004; Mörner 1967; Seed 1982).

A case could well be made that creole patriotism took on different aspects in different periods and geographical regions according to historical contingencies and local political circumstances. Yet my own effort in this article is to identify aspects of the creole project that remained constant across time and regions. This, then, is a study of a discourse (in Foucault's terms) that first surfaced in the early seventeenth century and flourished well into the eighteenth century, particularly in viceroyalties such as Mexico and Peru with large Amerindian populations (an analysis of creole discourse in areas with large Afro-American populations is, to my knowledge, yet to be offered).

CREOLE AND AMERINDIANS

How could an ancien régime society in which social and racial estates overlapped produce a painting such as *Patrocinio de la Virgen de Guadalupe sobre el Reino de Nueva España,* in which both Amerindians and Hispanic nobilities are held to be equal participants in the ideal Christian commonwealth? The answer lies precisely in the very nature of the ancien régime the creole elites envisioned. Creoles saw themselves as the product of the biological, racial amalgamation of Amerindian and Spanish elites that took place during the first years of colonization.

Clerical writers considered the miscegenation of Spaniards and Amerindians appropriate only when it brought elites together. The initial colonial sexual embrace of Amerindian elites and Spanish conquerors was, therefore, welcomed and praised. The type of "vulgar" miscegenation that brought later commoners of different races together was another matter. The vulgar *mestizaje* was seen as a threat to the existence of idealized hierarchical polities. Mestizos were consistently portrayed as evil, out-of-control individuals responsible for bringing sinful lifestyles, including a culture of lies and deception, into Amerindian communities that the clergy sought to keep unsoiled (Cope 1994).

According to this discourse, there was not a clear demarcation between creoles and early colonial Amerindian elites. Creoles found inspiration in the ancient Amerindian rulers, sages in the art of statecraft, whom they saw as their "ancestors" (Brading 1991; Granados y Gálvez 1778: 229–30; Pagden 1990; Phelan 1960; Sigüenza y Góngora 1986 [1680]). This discourse had deep roots in the sixteenth century. Take, for example, the case of the epic *Historia de la Nueva México* ("History of New Mexico") (1610) by the captain-poet Gaspar Pérez de Villagrá (1555–1620). *Historia* was part of a spate of epics written in the late sixteenth and early seventeenth centuries in the Iberian empire to celebrate the deeds of modern Argonauts, the multinational bands of marauding soldiers who through sheer chivalric prowess brought the New World under the rule of the Spanish and Portuguese crowns. *Historia,* typical of the genre, lionizes Juan de Oñate (1549–1624), whose 1596 expedition finally allowed the Spanish empire to settle the lands of the Pueblo Indians. The crusading logic underlying early modern European colonial expansion is cast in this and other epics into Virgilian and Homeric idioms. Oñate appears engaged in a great struggle against Satan, a tyrannous lord who had enjoyed absolute sovereignty over the Amerindians of New Mexico. God, to be sure, sides with Oñate in his efforts to oust the devil. In the process Oñate slaughters hundreds of Amerindians, Lucifer's allies.[3]

In Pérez de Villagrá's eyes, Mexico was a society threatened not only by Satan's frontier Amerindians but also by the demonic envy of upstart peninsular authorities. Pérez de Villagrá describes in detail, for example, how the new viceroy Gaspar de Zúñiga y Acevedo (1560–1606), count of Monterey, sought to replace Oñate as the leader of the expedition with one of his own minions. The ancien régime logic of this creole discourse is reinforced in the poem when Pérez de Villagrá blames a century of failures in the colonization of New Mexico on the effeminate nature of the new peninsular arrivals. Unlike the original line of conquistadors who never allowed the harrowing trials of the frontier to intimidate them, the new arrivals were easily cowed, returning to the Spanish urban centers as soon as they encountered the first difficulty. These newcomers had polluted blood; they most likely were effeminate new Christians, *conversos*.[4] Oñate's old Christian blood and thus his willingness to countenance hardships were responsible for the recent Spanish triumphs in the northern frontiers. Yet what is remarkable about this epic is that Pérez de Villagrá presents Oñate as noble "mestizo," a proud relative of Moctezuma.[5] In Pérez de Villagrá's epic, the crusading knight Oñate appears as typical of the creole noble elites, rooted both in old Christian-hidalgo and Aztec blood.

Oñate's split identity continued unabated among creoles throughout the colonial period. Doris Ladd (1976) has shown that numerous Spanish and creole grandees in eighteenth-century Mexico boasted their mestizo heritage. The Counts of Moctezuma, Javier, and Guara, the Duke of Granada in Spain, and such titled grandees of New Spain as the Aguayo, Alamo, Jaral, Miravalle, Salinas, Salvatierra, Santa Rosa, Santiago, Valle Oploca, and Valle de Orizaba all claimed descent from precolonial Aztec rulers. The Count of Santiago decorated his mansion in Mexico City with Aztec motifs (21, 235n28). *Patrocinio de la Virgen de Guadalupe* reinforces this message; in this visual narrative Christian Mexico belongs both to "Indian" and "Spanish" nobles. Both populations are equally entitled to the liberating message embodied in the miraculous appearance of Our Lady of Guadalupe.

Creoles constantly called to task the colonial order for having allowed their ancestors, the indigenous elites Spaniards encountered everywhere, to "disappear." As the colonial order matured, the Amerindian communities looked socially undifferentiated. Although some indigenous elites adapted to the new colonial conditions, taking up Castilian names and becoming the new caretakers of Christian temples and saints, the rich tapestry of social hierarchies that had characterized past Amerindian polities underwent considerable simplification.[6] For most observers of

the mature colonial order, Amerindian communities looked like homo-
genous collectives of wretched commoners. From this perspective, the
creole clerical project appeared as one of restoration, a return to simpler
times in which virtuous Amerindian nobles had embraced the teachings
of the Church.

But at the same time that creoles claimed Amerindians as their biological ancestors, they (particularly the religious clergy) also derided
Amerindians as innately inferior children to protect or (particularly the
settlers) as brutes to exploit. Those seeking to understand representations
of the "Indian" in colonial Spanish America cannot help but be puzzled.
Creole representations are deeply ambivalent, often oscillating between
images of respect and outright racism (Taylor 1989; Walker 1998). Strict
hierarchical views of society allowed the creole clergy to represent the
Amerindian as both wretched and the creator of great ancient polities.

Many creole authors, for example, argued that forced labor systems
and forms of Baroque worship were the only institutions that drew
Amerindians out of their indolence to engage in market transactions,
and that great Aztec and Inca rulers such as Manco Capac had long realized this. Manco Capac, they argued, had, for example, devised institutions such as the *mita* and public floggings to make Amerindian commoners
work. Such practices, creoles claimed, had made the Incas prosperous
and civilized.[7] Authors such as José Hipólito Unanue (1755–1833), one
of the leading figures of the Enlightenment in the Viceroyalty of Peru,
argued that the natives were indolent and lazy by nature and recommended the use of "therapeutic" floggings. Unanue maintained that an
excess of "sensitivity" rendered the Amerindians melancholic and para-
lyzed them before the sublime landscapes of the Andean Mountains.
Not surprisingly, Unanue lionized the Inca. He claimed that the Inca
rulers had long known about the innate constitution of the Amerindians
and had created the appropriate institutions of forced labor and therapeutic floggings. Unanue recommended that the authorities follow Incan
insights to build a great, civilized society despite the melancholic and
lazy character of the Amerindians (Cañizares-Esguerra 1995).

As part of their effort to defend themselves from European-Peninsular
contempt, creoles were literally forced to devise a theory of the racialized
body. Creole colonists responded to disparaging European views of the
climate and constellations of Spanish America as threatening and degenerating by suggesting that there were racially innate body types which
changed only slightly under new environmental influences, thus rejecting
long-held theories of temperaments and constitutions (according to which
"European" bodies became "Indian" ones under the climate and stars of
the New World). Their new version of ancient astrological and medical

theories allowed some intellectuals to claim that the natives were racially different from them. These intellectuals, however, did not give up the notion of environmental influences altogether. They claimed that climate still had some effect on innate body types. Whereas the constellations of America caused the Amerindians to grow even weaker and more stupid, they argued, the same constellations had helped improve the European stock. Creoles in America were stronger and smarter than their Spanish forefathers (Cañizares-Esguerra 1999).

Racism toward Amerindian commoners notwithstanding, creoles lionized the accomplishments and grandeur of past Amerindian civilizations such as the Incas and the Aztecs. Spanish American creoles excluded the great Amerindian rulers of the past, their own ancestors, from the generalization of the Amerindians as degenerate or lazy. In this ancien régime colonial society, Amerindians came to inhabit the same niche that peasants had long occupied in the imagination of the European elites, that is, as an altogether different race. In European medieval discourse, the racialization of the bodies of commoners had helped justify the subordinate status of a variety of groups. The discourse of social estates, for example, contemplated immense bodily and mental differences between peasants and nobles (Freedman 1999). It was the operation of similar principles in colonial Spanish America that allowed authors to lionize Manco Capac while claiming most contemporary natives to be inferior. When creoles demeaned the Amerindians they had only commoners in mind (Cañizares-Esguerra 1999).[8]

Creole intellectuals claimed for themselves a monopoly over the interpretation of the Amerindian past, devising a form of patriotic epistemology that sought to call into question the reliability of foreign authors and travelers and of local mestizos and Amerindian commoners. The discourse of patriotic epistemology validated the historical knowledge produced only by learned clerical observers (most of whom were creoles, but not exclusively so) and by precolonial and sixteenth-century Amerindian nobles. Clerical creole writers sought to make careful distinctions between sources produced by reliable precolonial and early colonial indigenous elites and those produced later by unreliable commoners. The discourse of patriotic epistemology also privileged the knowledge and credibility of the representatives of the church. Since Amerindian nobles were considered to be almost an extinct species, the responsibility for all credible reporting on natural and ethnographic phenomena in the Indies fell now on the representatives of the church. Their alleged intimacy with the land and the indigenous communities supposedly rendered them impervious to deception and misrepresentation (Cañizares-Esguerra 2001).

In the discourse of patriotic epistemology, the foreign observer appeared as nemesis of the learned clerical witness. Foreign travelers were presented as helpless victims of time and Amerindian cunning. Travelers paid only short visits to the lands they studied and were, therefore, incapable of discovering natural and human behavior that escaped the norm. They also lacked the time and the inclination to develop lasting attachment to communities and were incapable of penetrating beneath the surface of local social phenomena. Travelers were at the mercy of communities that gulled foreigners and laughed at their expense. Moreover, since travelers did not know the Amerindian languages, they were forced to rely on translators and secondhand interpretations (Cañizares-Esguerra, 2001).

CREOLES, PREFIGURATIONS, AND SAINTS

As creoles used historiography and race to hold foreigners and Amerindian and mestizo commoners at bay, they turned to religion for signs of a providential destiny. Creoles in Mexico found in the miracle of Our Lady of Guadalupe precisely such a sign.

The story of the apparition of Our Lady of Guadalupe to Juan Diego, an Amerindian commoner, is well known. In 1531 at the small hill of Tepeyac, the Virgin appeared several times to a Nahua commoner, and every time she did so the Virgin asked Diego to go see the archbishop to build her a chapel. The prince of the church, to be sure, did not believe the blessed Amerindian, who, therefore, returned twice empty-handed to the Virgin. Finally, the Virgin ordered Diego to collect some flowers in his cape (*tilma*). When Diego visited the wary bishop for the third time, he unfolded his cape and, to everybody's surprise, the image of the Virgin appeared printed on it. According to tradition, after this miracle, the authorities built a chapel to house Diego's cape and sponsored the cult of Our Lady of Guadalupe. A small chapel was built near the base of the hill where an ancient Aztec goddess, Tonatzin, had long been worshipped. At first, Franciscan missionaries, influenced by iconoclastic, Erasmian tendencies, did not promote the cult, but after the Council of Trent (1545–1563) and the onset of the Catholic Reformation, the local ecclesiastical authorities enthusiastically integrated veneration of the Virgin into Mexican devotional practice. When the Virgin successfully controlled the waters during the flood of Mexico City in 1629, the cult began to spread rapidly among the creoles.

At first sight, it would appear that the creoles embraced the cult because the image was a narrative that successfully integrated the natives, the ancestors of the creoles, into Marian, Spanish rituals. This, of course, is misleading, because Diego was a commoner, not one of the many heirs of Moctezuma, whom the creoles most enjoyed claiming as their own. The question remains: why did the creoles choose this particular Marian image as their own, as the coat of arms, as it were, of their Mexican kingdom?

The ethnically "integrating" force of the story of the miracle had little to do with the newfound favor the image enjoyed among seventeenth-century creoles. As Francisco De la Maza (1984) and David Brading (2001) have clearly demonstrated, the key to understanding the creole devotion needs to be found in a tradition of biblical interpretation that identified the woman in St. John of Patmos's Book of Revelations to be a prefiguration of Our Lady of Guadalupe (see also Lafaye 1974; Poole 1995). Indeed, it was a well-established tradition within the church to claim that St. John's vision of a pregnant woman clad by the sun and stars and threatened by a multiheaded dragon was actually a reference to the Virgin Mary. In the Book of Revelation 12.3–5, God takes the newborn to his side, protects the woman by airlifting her into the desert, and sends the archangel Michael to oust the dragon and his Satanic armies from heaven. In Christian art and theology, it became common to claim that St. John had sought to capture in the figure of the woman both the mysteries of the Virgin's immaculate conception and the image of a persecuted yet nurturing and providential Christian church. It is not surprising, therefore, that the image of Our Lady of Guadalupe, a typical image of the Immaculate Conception, was read by creole theologians as a fulfillment of the woman of the apocalypse (Stratton 1994; Warner 1976: Chapters 16–17).

More significant for understanding creole sensibilities, however, was that the local theologians used the image to claim for Mexico a cosmic, central role in universal history. The cleric Miguel Sánchez (1594–1671), for example, wrote in 1648 an epochal treatise on creole consciousness. He claimed that St. John of Patmos's vision of a woman clad in stars battling the dragon prefigured the conquest and colonization of the New World, in general, and of Mexico, in particular. Every detail both in the woman of the Book of Revelations and in the image of Our Lady of Guadalupe supported this thesis, Sánchez maintained.

According to Sánchez, the angel holding the Virgin up in the image was the archangel Michael, who had ousted the dragon from heaven in the Book of Revelation. The dragon itself represented the sovereignty the devil had long enjoyed in the New World before the arrival of the Christian warriors. Partaking of a notion first made popular by the writings of the Jesuit José de Acosta (1540–1600) and the Franciscan Juan de Torquemada (1557–1664), Sánchez argued that the Aztecs had been

Satan's elect. Satan had sought to imitate in the New World not only the institutions and sacraments of the church but also the Bible's historical narrative. At the time Sánchez wrote his treatise, it was typical for Creole scholars to argue that the history of the Aztecs was the inverted mirror image of that of the Israelites. Satan, it was argued, had led the Aztecs in an exodus into a Promised Land. Like the Israelites, the Aztecs had endured hardship and persecution on arrival in Canaan. Also like the Israelites, the Aztecs had managed to come from under Canaanite rule to create a monarchy. And like the Israelites who were forewarned by the Prophets and witnessed the destruction of Jerusalem, the Aztecs had also seen signs warning them of the impending end of their kingdom and of the destruction of their city.

This satanic narrative of the history of Mexico allowed Sánchez to claim the image of Our Lady of Guadalupe as the most complete fulfillment of St. John of Patmos's vision of the woman of the apocalypse. Out of all the images of the Immaculate Conception in Christendom, that of Our Lady of Guadalupe was the most significant and important (Sánchez 1982 [1648]: 204–09). Sánchez offered interpretations of every detail of the painting. The moon underneath the Virgin represented the power of the Virgin over the waters (223–24); the Virgin eclipsing the sun stood for a New World whose torrid zone was temperate and inhabitable (219); the twelve sun rays surrounding her head signified Cortés and the conquistadors who had defeated the dragon (168); and the stars on the Virgin's shawl were the forty-six good angels who had fought Satan's army (Sánchez used cabala to calculate the number of good angels) (226–27).

More important, Sánchez deployed typology to argue that the encounter of Juan Diego with the Virgin at Mount Tepeyac was the antitype of that of Moses with God at Mount Sinai. This typological reading of the miracle meant simply that the image of Our Lady of Guadalupe corresponded to the tablets of the Ten Commandments, an object documenting the covenant that God made with the Mexican elect. Soon it was argued that the canvas was written in Mexican hieroglyphs, a script God had chosen to address the creole heirs of the Aztecs (Brading 2001). Typology, a reading technique first deployed by the gospel writers and the Church fathers (Goppelt 1984 [1939]; O'Keefe and Reno 2005), became a tool skillfully bandied about by creole theologians to claim for their viceroyalty-kingdoms a central role in the narrative of universal salvation. Sánchez's interpretation inaugurated a literature of exegesis that took on clear millenarian and messianic tones, a literature in which contemporary Mexicans appeared as God's new elect. In the imagination of creole scholars, Mexico became the place where the Pope and the crown would eventually retreat, ousted from Europe by the forces of evil

(Carranza 1749; De Elizalde Ita Parra 1744:18, 29–30). "Non fecit taliter omni nationi," drawn from Psalm 147:19–20 ("Qui adnuntiat verbum suum Iacob iustitias et iudicia sua Israhel/Non fecit taliter omni nationi et iudicia sua non manifestavit eis. [He sheweth his word unto Jacob, his statutes and his judgments unto Israel/He hath not dealt so with any nation: and as for his judgments, they have not known them]), was the motto that ever since the late seventeenth century accompanied most illustrations of the images of Our Lady of Guadalupe. The image and the motto documented the special relations of the Lord with his new Israelites.

The idea of "Manifest Destiny" has often been attributed to British American creoles, but Mexican creoles first coined the trope. Through prefigurative readings of the Bible, creoles gave their history and institutions cosmic significance. Prefiguration was a key historiographical resource in the intellectual toolkit of the creoles, allowing them to demonstrate that, far from being merely developments at the margins of the Catholic world, events in their homelands held extraordinary universal import. After all, crucial episodes of the confrontation between good and evil described by St. John of Patmos in the book of the apocalypse were taking place in Mexico. It is in this context that we need to understand other aspects of creole piety. As hagiographies of local pious men and women multiplied over the course of the colonial period, creoles lobbied hard in Rome to have many of their own canonized. Given the extraordinary amount of silver flowing from Mexico and Peru, creoles often succeeded (Flores Araoz et al. 1995; Myers 2003).[9]

CREOLES WITHIN THE SPANISH COMPOSITE MONARCHY

The composition in *Patrocinio de la Virgen de Guadalupe sobre el Reino de Nueva España* of Hispanic princes kneeling alongside Amerindian nobles, both partaking eucharistically of the image of Our Lady of Guadalupe, bears striking resemblance to earlier seventeenth-century images that sought to present "America" and "Spain" as equal members of a common Iberian commonwealth (Figure 4). As can be seen in the frontispiece to Juan de Solórzano y Pereira's 1629–1639 study of the laws of the Indies, *Disputationem Indiarum iure,* Philip IV (r. 1621–1665) comes across as a mighty ruler trampling over the very lord of the seas, Neptune, whose power extends to the very margins of the sky and the ocean (*subdivit Oceanu sceptris et margine coeali clausit opes*). Philip IV's empire, however, is equally made up of an armored, knightly "Hispania" and a scantily clad supine "America." This message of "equality" between America and

Figure 4 (Left) Title page of Juan de Solórzano y Pereira. *Disputationem Indiarum iure* (Madrid, 1629)
(Right) Title page of Antonio de Solis. *Historia de la conquista de México* (Madrid, 1684)

Hispania in the universal Spanish Catholic monarchy also comes across in the frontispiece to Antonio de Solis's *Historia de la conquista de Mexico* (1684). In the illustrated introduction to this early modern bestseller, Charles II (r. 1665–1700) appears presiding over a supine, naked, "reborn out of fire" (*renascetur*) Mexico and a fully clad, "renovated" (*renovabitur*) Hispania. The motto "*utraque unum*" (out of two, one) and the two spheres united by a single crown in the frontispiece reinforce the message of unity and partnership.

This symbolic message of "parity" within the empire was one fully embraced by the creoles. As we have already seen, creoles aspired for their local polities to the status of kingdoms within the larger Spanish composite monarchy. Despite the effort of the crown back in Madrid to curtail these autonomous impulses in the New World, the monarchy by and large failed. The chronic dependency of the crown on silver and resources from America gave creoles leverage, and all centralizing efforts from the metropolis floundered. Even after the Seven Years' War (1756–1763), when the relatively new Bourbon monarchy decided to launch an aggressive program of reform, including taking control of the colonies away from creole interests, these efforts proved futile. In fact, these efforts actually managed to exacerbate tensions, heighten patriotic consciousness, and unravel traditional mechanisms of imperial legitimation (by undermining the power of clerical bureaucracies, the glue that kept the sprawling and ramshackle empire together) (Taylor 1998).

Despite repeated statements to the contrary, from its inception the Spanish empire was highly decentralized, built from the bottom up, not the other way around (Kamen 2003). The unit on which the empire was built was the city council. Both the empire and creole consciousness were built on the back of *municipios* and *vecinos*.[10]

Vecinos were the "citizens" of the early modern Spanish world: bearers of rights (access to common land) but also burdened with duties (taxation and service in the militia and municipality). It fell ultimately on municipal local authorities, not the crown, to elucidate who was a *vecino*. *Vecinos* were those who had demonstrated through actions and religious compliance (Catholicism; homeownership; marrying into local families, living in town longer than ten years) that they wanted to belong in a community, usually a town or a city. "Foreigners" (outsiders to the original community) could become *vecinos* only if they demonstrated enough love and commitment to the new community where they now happened to reside.

Vecinos were the foundation of the larger national community and became *naturales* when they faced the authorities of the kingdom to which they belonged. At this level, the crown wielded more power, for *vecinos* as *naturales* had to wear the hat of vassals. The crown often sought to transform foreigners into *naturales* by fiat, thus favoring merchants and other powerful types, to the chagrin of most locals. Yet it was communal consensus and abidance by strict cultural norms that ultimately determined who could be *naturales*. Through this mechanism, municipal identities became enlarged when projected onto the larger canvas of the local kingdoms. Creoles saw themselves as *naturales* of their own local kingdoms and cast *peninsulares* as foreigners incapable of loving and caring for the local communities.

It was in the language of *vecindad* and *naturaleza* that the ideological struggles of the so-called Wars of Independence (1810–1824) were fought. Creoles sought to include Amerindians, mestizos and blacks as *naturales* of creolized Spanish American kingdoms, part of a larger Spanish commonwealth. Fearful of being outnumbered and of losing control of the commonwealth, *peninsulares* balked and sought to limit the franchise. After having struggled mightily to continue to be part of the empire for centuries, creoles finally realized that the only way to have their own kingdoms was by declaring independence (Rodríguez 1998). The new nations were born weak and fragmented, like the empire that came before, because they were also patchworks made up of cities and towns whose *vecinos* were competing over larger territorial spoils (Sabato 2001).

Notes

1. Schama (1995) identifies the author of this painting as Gerard Horenbout, whose years of life indicate that he could have only begun the piece (288). The altar might have been completed by Lucas. The triptych for the altar, it seems, was put together in 1596, for one can clearly see the date written on the frame. Yet the painting also has at the base of the fountain the inscription "LU. Horenbault fe" ("Luc Horenbault fecit"/ "Made by Luc Horenbault"). On these two painters, see Campbell and Foister (1986).
2. I use the King James Version of the Bible in English and the Vulgate in Latin. On the Virgin Mary and the Song of Solomon, see Warner (1976), Chapter 16. On Mary as garden and fountain, see Daley (1983).
3. See, for example, Pérez de Villagrá's dedication to Philip III, in which Pérez de Villagrá sees the king's role as providential, promoting the expansion of the Catholic faith against the kingdom of the devil: *"para ensalzamiento de Nuestra Fé catholica, y extirpación de los graves errores, y vil idolatria, que el demonio nuestro capital enemigo, siembra y derrama, por estas y otras Regiones"* (n. pag.).
4. See Pérez de Villagrá (1610) canto 4, verses 15–21. The following verse is typical of Villagrá's sensibilities:

   Sola una terrible falta hallo,
   Christianissimo Rey en vuestras Indias,
   Y es que están muy pobladas, y ocupadas,
   De gente vil, manchada, y sospechosa. (canto 4, verse 20)
   ("I only find one fault, oh most Christian of kings, about your Indies. And it is that they are populated and occupied by vile people: stained and suspect.")

5. See 3* recto and verso ("*canción pindárica*" by L. Trib. de Toledo). Toledo presents Oña as nephew of the governor of New Galicia, Christobal de Oña, relative of Moctezuma. See also 27 recto (canto sexto).
6. On continuity and change among indigenous elites in central Mexico and Yucatán, see Lockhart (1994) Chapter 4 and Farriss (1984):96–103, 164–68, 174–92, and 227–55.
7. See "*Caracter, usos y costumbres de los Indios, tributos que pagan al soberano, metodo de su cobranza y estado de ramo y reflexiones de los repartimientos antiguos y modernos*," MS 119, folios 180–89, Colección Malaspina, Archivo del Museo Naval, Madrid.
8. Compare these views of the racialized body in the New World with those explored by Joyce Chaplin in British America (2001).
9. Unlike creoles in Peru, Mexicans failed to persuade Rome to canonize any of their many outstanding athletes of the soul, with the exception of Felipe de Jesús, who was in fact suspected to have been born in Spain and who was part of a larger group of canonized Franciscans martyred in Japan in 1597 (Rubial García 1999).
10. The following two paragraphs are based entirely on the work of Tamar Herzog (2003).

References

Brading, D. 1991. *The first America: The Spanish monarchy, creole patriots, and the liberal state 1492–1867*. Cambridge: Cambridge University Press.

——— 2001. *Mexican phoenix: Our Lady of Guadalupe: Image and process*. Cambridge: Cambridge University Press.

Cahill, D. 1994. Colour by numbers: Racial and ethnic categories in the viceroyalty of Peru, 1532–1824, *Journal of Latin American Studies* 26:325–346.

Campbell, L., and S. Foister. 1986. Gerard, Lucas, and Susan Horenbout, *Burlington Magazine* 128:719–27.

Cañizares-Esguerra, J. 1995. La Utopía de Hipólito Unanue: Comercio, naturaleza y religión en el Perú. In *Saberes andinos. Ciencia y tecnología en Bolivia, Ecuador y Perú*. M. Cueto, ed. Lima: Instituto de Estudios Peruanos.

——— 1999. New world, new stars: Indian and Creole bodies in colonial Spanish America, 1600–1650, *American Historical Review* 104:33–68.

——— 2001. *How to write the history of the New World: Histories, epistemologies, and identities in the eighteenth-century Atlantic world*. Stanford, CA: Stanford University Press.

Carranza, F. X. 1749. *La transmigración de la iglesia a Guadalupe*. México City: n.p.

Chaplin, J. 2001. *Subject matter: Technology, the body, and science on the Anglo-American frontier, 1500–1676*. Cambridge, MA: Harvard University Press.

Cope, R. D. 1994. *The limits of racial domination: Plebeian society in colonial Mexico City, 1660–1720*. Madison, WI: University of Wisconsin Press.

Daley, B. 1983. The "Closed Garden" and "Sealed Fountain": Song of Songs 4:12 in the late medieval iconography of Mary. In *Medieval gardens*. E. MacDougall, ed. Washington, DC: Dumbarton Oaks Research Library and Collection.

De Elizalde Ita Parra, J. M. G. 1744. *Gloria de Mexico en la mayor exaltación y manifestación de la mayor gloria de Maria Santissima Señora Nuestra en su triunphante assumpción a los cielos en cuyo mysterio se venera titular de la Sta. Iglesia Metropolitana de dicha ciudad.* Mexico City: Viuda de Don J. B. de Hogal.

De la Maza, F. 1984 [1953]. *El guadalupanismo mexicano*. México City: Fondo de Cultura Económica, Secretaría de Educación Pública.

Farriss, N. M. 1984. *Maya society under colonial rule: The collective enterprise of survival*. Princeton, NJ: Princeton University Press.

Flores Araoz, J., R. Mujica Pinilla, L. E. Wuffarden, and P. Guibovich Pérez.1995. *Santa Rosa de Lima y su tiempo*. Lima: Banco de Crédito del Perú.

Freedman, P. 1999. *Images of the medieval peasant*. Stanford, CA: Stanford University Press.

Goppelt, L. 1984 [1939]. *Typos: The typological interpretation of the Old Testament*. D. H. Madvig, trans. (German). Grand Rapids, MI: William B. Eerdmans Publishing Company.

Granados y Gálvez, J. J. 1778. *Tardes Americanas*. Mexico City: D. F. de Zúñiga y Ontiveros.

Herzog, T. 2003. *Defining nations: Immigrants and citizens in early modern Spain and Spanish America*. New Haven, CT: Yale University Press.

Israel, J. I. 1975. *Race, class, and politics in colonial Mexico, 1610–1670*. Oxford: Oxford University Press.

Kamen, H. 2003. *Empire: How Spain became a world power, 1492–1763*. New York: HarperCollins.

Katzew, I. 2004. *Casta painting: Images of race in eighteenth-century Mexico*. New Haven, CT: Yale University Press.

Ladd, D. M.1976. *The Mexican nobility at independence, 1780–1826*. Austin, TX: Institute of Latin American Studies, University of Texas.

Lafaye, J. 1974. *Quetzalcóatl et Guadalupe: La formation de la conscience nationale au Mexique*. Paris: Gallimard.

Lavallé, B. 1993. *Las promesas ambiguas: Criollismo colonial en los Andes*. Lima: Pontificia Universidad Católica del Péru, Instituto Riva-Agüero.

Lockhart, J. 1994. *The Nahuas after the Conquest*. Stanford, CA: Stanford University Press.

Miller, N. 1983. Paradise regained: Medieval garden fountains. In *Medieval gardens*, E. MacDougall, ed. Washington DC: Dumbarton Oaks Research Library and Collection.

Mörner, M. 1967. *Race mixture in the history of Latin America*. Boston: Little, Brown.

Myers, K. A. 2003. Redeemer of America: Rosa de Lima (1586–1617), the dynamics of identity, and canonization. In *Colonial saints: Discovering the holy in the Americas*. A. Greer and J. Bilinoff, eds. New York: Routledge.

O'Keefe, J., and R. R. Reno. 2005. *Sanctified vision: An introduction to early Christian interpretation of the Bible*. Baltimore, MD: Johns Hopkins University Press.

Pagden, A.1990. *Spanish imperialism and the political imagination*. New Haven, CT: Yale University Press.

Pérez de Villagrá, G. 1610. *Historia de la Nueva México*. Alcalá de Henares: Luis Martínez Grande.

Phelan, J. L. 1960. Neo-Aztecism in the eighteenth century and the genesis of Mexican nationalism. In *Culture in history: Essays in honor of Paul Radin*. S. Diamond, ed. New York: Published for Brandeis University by Columbia University Press.

Poole, S. 1995. *Our Lady of Guadalupe*. Tucson, AZ: University of Arizona Press.

Rodríguez O., J. E. 1998. *The independence of Spanish America*. Cambridge: Cambridge University Press. (Comp: This is correct as is.)

Rubial García, A. 1990. *Una monarquía criolla: La provincia augustiniana de Mexico en el siglo VII*. Mexico City: Consejo Nacional para la Cultura y las Artes, Dirección General de Publicaciones.

——— 1999. *La santidad controvertida: Hagiografía y conciencia criolla alrededor de los Venerables no canonizados de Nueva España*. México City: Universidad Nacional Autónoma de México, Facultad de Filosofía y Letras, Fondo de Cultura Económica.

Sabato, H. 2001. On political citizenship in nineteenth-century Latin America, *American Historical Review* 106:1290–1315.

Sánchez, M. 1982 [1648]. Imagen de la Virgen María Madre de Dios de Guadalupe. In *Testimonios históricos guadalupanos*. E. De la Torre Villar and R. Navarro de Anda, eds. Mexico City: Fondo de Cultura Económica.

Schama, S. 1995. *Landscape and memory*. New York: A. A. Knopf.

Seed, P. 1982. Social dimensions of race: Mexico City, 1753, *Hispanic American Historical Review* 62:569–606.

Sigüenza y Góngora, C. 1986 [1680]. *Theatro de virtudes políticas que constituyen a un príncipe advertidas en los monarchas antiguos del mexicano imperio*. Mexico City: Porrúa.

Solis, A. 1684. *Historia de la conquista de México*. Madrid: Bernardo de Villa-Diego.

Solórzano y Pereira, J. 1629–1639. *Disputationem indiarum iure*. Madrid: Francisco Martínez.

Stratton, S. L. 1994. *The immaculate conception in Spanish art*. Cambridge: Cambridge University Press.

Taylor, W. 1989. . . . de corazón pequeño y ánimo apocado: Conceptos de los curas párrocos sobre los indios en la Nueva España del siglo XVII, *Relaciones* 39:5–67.

——— 1998. *Magistrates of the sacred: Priests and parishioners in eighteenth-century Mexico*. Stanford, CA: Stanford University Press.

Walker, C. 1998. The patriotic society: Discussions and omissions about Indians in the Peruvian War of Independence, *The Americas* 55:275–98.

Warner, M.1976. *Alone of all her sex: The myth and the cult of the Virgin Mary*. New York: Knopf.

3 Creoles in British America: From Denial to Acceptance

Joyce E. Chaplin

It's a puzzle: the first surge of creole patriotism that challenged European empires in the Americas was propelled by people who emphatically rejected the name "creole." The North American patriots who fought the American War of Independence were descendants of several generations of English-speaking colonists who thought of themselves first as English and then as British, but never as creoles. At most, they accepted the hyphenated name of British-Americans. Even during and after the war, the American-born patriots refused to call themselves "creoles," instead preferring the term "Americans." "Creole" and "creole patriotism" may be useful analytic categories for historians, but they were never actors' categories for the colonists in British North America.

That North America's English-speaking colonists achieved independence from Great Britain without utilizing the Iberian-American language of creolian heritage has made discussion of creole patriotism rather selective, focusing mostly on the revolts in Spanish America that followed that of 1776, with perfunctory inclusion of the earlier event in British America. For their part, historians of Anglophone America have simply assumed that "American" was destined to be the name for citizens

For their advice on drafts of this essay, I am very grateful to Charles Stewart, David Armitage, John Pocock, John Russell-Wood, and the other participants in the conference that generated this volume. Angeliki Laiou and Roy Mottahedah generously lent their expertise on the history of the term "Frank."

of the United States, never considering that this decision rejected available alternatives, especially that of "creole" (Anderson 1991:47–65, 191–95; Brading 1991).

Why did the first creole patriots deny that they were creoles? And what does their denial tell us about the historical formation of creole identities in the western hemisphere? To answer these questions, it is necessary first to understand that during the salient period, the sixteenth through eighteenth centuries, there was no "creolization," there were only "creoles" and persons or things that were "creolian." That is, the term "creole" referred primarily to individuals, to persons and their bodies, and only later and secondarily to other things, from languages to cookery. Creole was not yet an abstraction that described cultural processes; the words "creolization," "creolize," and "creolized" date from the nineteenth century. To be labeled "creole" was a very direct, personal, and experiential thing, not a remote and abstract designation (*Oxford English Dictionary* 2000).

But what was so bad about being creole? It was an Iberian designation that described how Europeans (and Africans) became native to America, adapting to the physical environment and adopting selected parts of Native-American culture. Spanish settlers at first resented the term "creole." Their descendants began to accept it, by the late eighteenth century, only when their desire to become independent of Spain supported a new sense of difference from the Spanish. To be considered creole was even more distressing to British colonists: they wanted to remain English in every possible way and had no wish to resemble either Iberians or Native Americans.

New world settlers' anxiety over the designation "creole" revealed their fear that human differences were unstable. If racism insists that human physical differences are essential, the term "creole" identified human differences that were in flux, that changed as people changed their customs and climate. Indeed, the usual assumption among early modern Europeans was that physical place created individual and national differences—France made humans into French people, and America made them into Indians. But the perceived malleability of humans was precisely what troubled English colonists. That their customs and very bodies might metamorphose in the new world was deeply revolting to them. They did not want to be like the original peoples of the Americas, the pagan Indians whose bodies were native to the Americas, those bizarre places where the gospel had never been heard. Nor did they want to be like the Spaniards and the Portuguese, those people originally called creoles, whose Catholic religion, Mediterranean culture, and warm climate represented what the English thought they should not be. They needed to maintain English language, law, and material forms in order to prevent their becoming estranged from the peoples of the mother country.

Suspicion over creole status in British America finally abated during and after the American Revolution because the former colonists swiftly declared their preference for the name "American." Having denied having any creole nature for a century and a half, the white denizens of the new United States finally accepted the possibility by relabeling it. The timing of this shift—the last quarter of the eighteenth century—was not accidental. It was then that theories of race had become more frequent and publicly intelligible. White people in the United States could reassure themselves that human differences were fixed; they could become a new people through new political institutions and customs yet remain racially distinct from the Indians (and Africans) who also lived in the western hemisphere. They could also distinguish themselves from the creoles of New Spain and Brazil by reiterating the cultural differences between themselves and these other populations, by stating new ideas about racial difference, and by exulting that they had removed the colonial yoke under which these other populations still groaned (Anderson 1991:63–64; Chaplin 2002:164–67; Hannaford 1996: 205–13).

This denial-then-acceptance of a native-born status was, above all, an outcome of British colonizers' distinctive relations with Amerindians. English colonists had frequently prophesied that the native population would almost entirely disappear, leaving the invaders to occupy the land in their stead. British colonists' denial that they were creoles, then United States citizens' rush to accept the name of Americans, showed that the fantasy of complete displacement of (rather than amalgamation with or resemblance to) an indigenous population was a peculiar feature of Anglo-America and of the United States. There, the anticreole patriots fought an *American* Revolution that simultaneously marked out English-speaking settlers' independence from North America's natives and from British authority. Colonists on the continent stood in contrast to those in the West Indies, for instance, both by their long resistance to the label "creole" and to their war against the British Empire. To deny creole status, and then to embrace American identity, was to maintain a distinctiveness that was itself quite different from developments elsewhere in the post-Columbian new world.

* * *

At two important historic moments of European expansion, Europeans acquired new corporate names for themselves. The first moment occurred during the era of the Crusades, when Western Europeans became known as "Franks." Ancient German-speaking peoples had called themselves

Franks, as did those, later, within Charlemagne's Frankish realm. Then, outsiders began to describe most Christians from western Europe as Franks. Byzantines were probably the innovators, substituting "Frank" for the older name of "Latin." Muslims followed suit, calling Catholic Europeans *al Ifrandj*. The name spread especially with the First Crusade of the eleventh century and began to describe Europeans outside Europe, which implied that group associations were portable. Proliferation of the term showed that the old names of Christian or Latin no longer seemed adequate to differentiate Catholic Europeans from the other populations contesting for the near east. Still, some Europeans were never Franks, as with the Vikings, Slavs (and others in the Orthodox Church), and Spanish Catholics (Bartlett 1993:101–05; Kazhdan 2000:89–91; Lewis 1971:1044–46).

The second new term emerged shortly after Spanish colonization of Central and South America, when the *peninsulares* (who, perhaps significantly, had never been Franks) began in the 1590s to designate as *criollos* those people of Spanish ancestry who were born in Spanish America. (The Portuguese would also call their American-born colonists *criuolos*; people of African-ancestry born in America would likewise be *criollos* or *criuolos*.) Later, anything distinctive to the Iberian colonies gained the name "creole," as with forms of food and language. If "Frank" had sharply differentiated between Catholic Europeans and non-Catholic populations in the near and far east, "creole" placed those residents of New Spain who had Spanish ancestry at a position somewhere between native Americans and *peninsulares*. Creole patriots would indeed graft themselves onto native history, as if they were heirs to the great empires of central America and the Andes. But if creole status indicated some acceptance of Indians, it also represented a desire to displace those populations and appropriate their lands and history (Brading 1991:Chapters 14, 24–27; Cañizares-Esguerra 2001:204–65; Pagden 1987:51–94, 1990:91–104).

The first thing to note about these two terms, "Frank" and "creole," is that they pull in opposite directions: the first emphasized continuity; the second, novelty. The origins of the terms partly explain the different valences—"Frank" was a self-description that outsiders adapted, whereas "creole" was applied from outside and then adopted as a self-description.

A stress on continuity had in fact long been the norm, which was probably why settlers in Spanish America did not welcome the name *criollo*. The Romans who had spread over Europe and the near east had kept calling themselves Romans, and indeed extended this designation (in the form of citizenship) to those they conquered. Likewise, medieval Europeans seemed not to think that Franks abroad were different from Franks at home—the neologism did not imply novel identity. Yet New Spain elicited qualitatively new claims about Spanish colonization and conquest, quite possibly because the scale of European invasion and resettlement were so much greater than had been the case during the Crusades. These American experiences generated new identities and were, by implication, historically unique. This was implied by Spanish *criollo* and Portuguese *crioulo*; the words meant someone created, formed, or nurtured (from the Latin *creo*, to create) rather than someone transplanted.

Creole status thus indicated the distribution of power in the Americas. The distribution began with military conquest of Indians, proceeded through the emergence of hybrid cultures dominated by people of European descent, and reached its highest stage in the creole overthrow of imperial governments. Along the way, "creole" had designated people who were outsiders both to indigenous and to European culture. As David Brading has defined (and as Jorge Cañizares-Esguerra has elaborated) for Spanish America, the apotheosis of creole patriotism represented a growing desire to differentiate between hemispheres, western versus eastern. Rather than emphasize how they only resembled *peninsulares*, creoles at last explained themselves as an amalgam—they enjoyed the cultural heritage of Christian Europe while benefiting from the marvels and advantages of life in a new landscape (Brading 1991; Cañizares-Esguerra 2001).

English colonists and even American-born settlers in British America were highly suspicious of the term "creole" and preferred to emphasize national continuity, as those who had accepted the term "Frank" had once done. If their decision resembled that of their Spanish-American contemporaries, it also reflected the vigorously anti-Spanish spirit of early English colonization. English raids on Spanish fleets and colonies, then settlement in North America and the Caribbean, represented attempts to profit from the spoils and margins of the Spanish empire. These goals appeared clearly in Richard Hakluyt's 1584 "Particuler discourse," better known under its much-later published title *A Discourse of Western Planting*. Hakluyt urged Queen Elizabeth and her councilors to back the colonial enterprise. His sixth reason for doing so was to "staye the spanish kinge from flowinge over all the face of . . . America"; the eighteenth, to challenge the "pride and tyranie" with which King Philip governed the Indies and to encourage the native people there to "revolte cleane from the Spaniarde" (Hakluyt 1979 [1584]:118, 120). It is hardly surprising that English colonists shied from Spanish terms such as *criollo* or *encomienda* (an award of land and Indian labor) to describe their efforts in the Americas (Maltby 1971.)

English settlers shunned the term "creole" even in the eighteenth century, when the American-born population of British America was growing apace and the colonies had a social and economic stability that might have inspired greater cultural confidence among colonists. Instead, the mother country remained their most important cultural reference. In this, they proved that they were what they wished to be: English. The English themselves had long been devoted to custom and tradition. These, rather than innovation or importation, were the foundations of common law and much of English public culture, and were touchstones for Anglo-colonial experience and identity. The almost hysterical colonial defense of custom was evident during the conflict that led into the American Revolution, but it had been strongly emphasized in the legalities of colonization from the late 1500s onward (Allen 1981; Bailyn 1967; Pocock 1967).

Further, the early modern English tended to regard changes in custom, religion, and language as evidence of degeneration. Continuity was greatly preferred, whether in pedigree, text, ceremony, or law. Degeneration could take two forms: a fall from an original and pure type or the accretion of elements from religious or cultural inferiors through the acquisition of pagan rites or barbarian customs. Even before they were deeply engaged in colonization of the Americas, the English had shown themselves, in Ireland, profoundly revolted by cultural transformation and hybridity; thus the denigration of the Anglo-Irish, whom the Elizabethan invaders of Ireland stigmatized as having gone native. Even as subsequent English colonizers of Ireland buttressed their claims to the island through selective appropriation of "Irish" customs and history, they were careful not to become Irish in any meaningful sense. They remained, fundamentally, creatures of English custom, and this omnipresent conservatism would be evident in the ways that the English colonized America (Canny 1973, 1981:195–96; Kidd 1999).

Again and again, English-speaking migrants to America steadfastly maintained that they were English and that their children, while born in the colonies, were likewise part of this corporate, national identity. The word "English" pervades the seventeenth-century accounts of initial colonization, even as a creole generation emerged in New England and the Chesapeake. Thus in the 1630s, William Wood maintained that New England was suitable for "our *English* bodies" (Wood 1977 [1634]: 31–32); at the end of the seventeenth century, Thomas Ashe claimed that Carolina's climate similarly benefited the "English" and the "English Children born there" (Ashe 1911 [1682]:141). And George Gardyner said of New England that its "English people are well-colour'd, and have many children which thrive well in that Countrey," a denial of the idea that an American climate might make settlers and creoles of a different complexion (Gardyner 1651:92). Rebuttal of this opinion recurs endlessly in colonial records, evidence of a lasting debate over which factors affected the malleable human body (Chaplin 2001).

Nature might need help, however—the colonists feared collapse into a non-English condition. Cotton Mather famously warned against the dangers of "criolian degeneracy" in Massachusetts Bay. The phrase occurred in a sermon of 1689, a year when a majority of New England's population had become, like Mather himself, American born. His sermon came after two generations of terrible warfare between New England's settlers and its original population, culminating in the bloody and debilitating Metacom's War of 1675 to 1676. Within this context of frontier antagonism, Mather warned that colonists might become barbarized, religiously dissolute. Unlike later Spanish *criollos*, Mather saw creole status as a specific and avoidable fate. English colonists might or might not be degenerate, depending on their vigilance against dissipation. Indeed, Mather later described "criolian" puritans as "vertuous objects of emulation," a strategic rebuke of the irreligious English who lagged behind their supposedly backward American counterparts (Canup 1989: 20–34, 1990).

In part, this antipathy toward the words "creole" and "creolian" continued to reflect an English sense that the terminology described Spanish America and therefore carried unpleasant connotations of national and religious differences. The first English printing of the word "creole," spelled "Crollo," occurred in Edward Grimstone's 1604 translation of Jose de Acosta's natural history of Spanish America, and indeed specified that "creole" was what "they call the Spaniards borne at the Indies"; Thomas Thorowgood's *Jewes in America* (1650) likewise used "Criolians" to describe colonists native to Spanish America. Not until William Dampier's 1698 narrative of his oceanic voyages was the word "creole" printed as a description of English settlers of the Americas, specifically those of the West Indian island of St. Christophers (*Oxford English Dictionary* 2000; Canup 1989:27–28).

Both "creole" and "creolian" would continue to designate certain kinds of persons from the western hemisphere, though, in English, the terms stuck most closely to Spanish America, to enslaved African populations, and to the West Indies. Only rarely, and for dramatic effect, did they describe the English continental colonies, as in Mather's jeremiad. Association of creoles with Iberians and with African-Americans continued, showing again an English chauvinism and conservatism.

These attitudes did not, however, extend to the West Indies, where colonists accepted the name of "creole" much more readily. Perhaps their hot climate, or proximity to Spanish colonies, resigned settlers to the term. Interestingly, both Britons and West Indians began to use the term in the same way, a convergence that might have been earlier apparent in William Dampier's description of St. Christopher's. Englishman John Oldmixon's *The British Empire in America*, first published in 1708, used the word *Creolean* frequently to describe the white people of Barbados; Oldmixon's 1741 edition defined Creoleans as "Such *Englishmen* as are born in Barbados." (Oldmixon 1741 II:126, 133). Jamaican Edward Long, in his *History of Jamaica* (1774), similarly described the inhabitants of his island as "Creoles, or natives; Whites, Blacks, Indians, and their varieties; European and other Whites; and imported or African Blacks." Long also specified a perceived sense of difference that *"Creolian* Negroes" felt between themselves and *"Salt-Water* Negroes" (Long 1774 II:260). Still, the West Indians sometimes preferred other names. By the early nineteenth century, for example, black and white Barbadians proclaimed themselves "neither Charib, nor Creole, but true Barbadian" (Greene 1981:265).

The Barbadians' touchy pride might have reflected a lingering suspicion that Britons looked down on West Indians as extraterritorial, outside the cultural and political bounds of English-speaking society. John Hill, in two novels of 1751, introduced to literature two creole characters from the West Indies, one of whom he described as "a true and genuine Creole, a Fellow, half-mad, half Fool, and thoroughly stocked with Absurdity and Impudence" (Hill 1751a, 1751b:177). Edward Thompson's *Sailor's Letters* of 1766 likewise referred to "that volatile spirit so peculiar to the Creole," including a characteristic "cruel tyranny" acquired from proximity to slaves (Thompson 1766:22).

Certainly, an English prejudice about West Indian inferiority appears in descriptions of the woman who is perhaps literature's most famous creole: the first Mrs. Rochester. She is *Jane Eyre*'s madwoman in the attic, Mr. Rochester's cast-off wife who rends Jane's bridal veil and burns her husband's house to the ground. In her novel of 1847, Charlotte Brontë described Mrs. Rochester as the daughter of an English-born West Indian merchant and a Jamaican "Creole . . . both a mad woman and a drunkard," characteristics the daughter has inherited in abundance. With lingering and lurid stereotypes such as these, no wonder West Indians only uneasily accepted the name of "creoles" (Brontë 1973 [1847]:293, 294).

Continental colonists resisted the name even more. A measure of their continuing antipathy can be gained from the *Pennsylvania Gazette*, the newspaper famously associated with Benjamin Franklin. A search for the word "creole" in the *Gazette* turns up eighteen instances spread over the period from 1728 to 1800. In these eighteen cases, none refers to white colonists. Ten of them, however, referred to "Negroes," mostly blacks from the West Indies (including the British islands); some of these were slaves designated as "creole born," implying nativity to the continent. Other uses of the term "creole" gestured south, toward the islands and Spanish colonies. Two "creoles" were natives of Spanish America, perhaps of European ancestry, since they were not also described as "negroes" or "mulattoes"; two other instances of the word referred to a West Indian brig, the *Amiable Creole* (*Pennsylvania Gazette* 1991– : terms that elicited no hits included *criollo, criolian, cirole, crollo, creol, creolean, creolian, creolism*).

The final four references from the *Pennsylvania Gazette* reveal much about Continental American anxieties and uncertainties. Two instances of creole described, in 1766, the "Creole Slavery" of West Indians who accepted British authority. These examples referred to documents, arriving in Philadelphia from the West Indies, that bore the hated stamp recently created by the Stamp Act of 1765. Continental colonists for the most part rejected the Stamp Act: they rioted, burnt stamp collectors in effigy, and refused to unload the stamps when they arrived in port cities. That West Indian colonists were more subservient was, therefore, evidence of the cringing acquiescence natural to a people who lived in hot climates among slave majorities and close to Catholics (Greene 1981; O'Shaughnessy 2000). The final two uses of "creole" named in a pair of advertisements "the beautiful elegant Horse CREOLE." The horse was rather confusingly described as "A FULL BLOOD, imported from Old England."

Perhaps Creole's owner (or sire or dam?) was West Indian, or perhaps the horse's temperament indicated to people in England something American or West Indian about the animal. If so, the horse measured the difference between the English and Anglo-Americans: the former tended to think that there *was* something distinctive about the western hemisphere that English birth and blood could not cover up. Certainly, Britons continued to believe that the Americas were source of all things exotic and unfamiliar. After a brief visit to London of four native American envoys during Queen Anne's War (1702–1713), some Londoners paid the Indian men the dubious compliment of naming a violent secret society after them; these "Mohocks" identified America as a place distant, different, and dangerous (Bond 1952:75–76).

It would have strained belief had colonists insisted they were identical to the English at home, but they were nonetheless extremely careful to describe themselves in ways that minimized cultural and bodily divergence. Everyone believed that the physical environment of the western hemisphere would be a trial for the English. Early reports warned, for example, that native corn or maize was unwholesome for humans, "though the barbarous Indians which know no better, are constrained to make a virtue of necessitie." Later commentators stressed, however, that the English had tested corn (perhaps because they were starving) and discovered that it would sustain them. By the 1550s, adaptation to American air, sustenance, and diseases had gained the name of "seasoning," a term originally applied to cut wood. The concept of seasoning was especially powerful among the first settlers in the seventeenth century, who worried that their and their children's bodies might not make an optimal adaptation to the western hemisphere, or, conversely, might degenerate into a non-English condition (Chaplin 2001:151–52).

Use of the term "seasoning" was thereafter most frequent in warmer, southern climates, places that seemed less English than the northern colonies. Even in the southern continental colonies, however, American-born settlers were not inclined to call themselves creoles, as West Indians did. In eighteenth-century South Carolina and Georgia, for example, native-born colonists described themselves as seasoned against yellow fever in contrast to "strangers," a term that designated cultural outsiders, whether from other British colonies, from Britain, from Europe, or from other parts of the Americas (Chaplin 1993:93–108). One Charlestonian reported in 1804 that some cases of yellow fever "afflict and destroy Strangers—But no Epidemic prevails among our citizens" (DeSaussure 1804). Absentees had to become reseasoned; another South Carolinian warned his native-born brother that, on his return to Charleston, the yellow fever "may treat you as a stranger" (Rutledge 1804). Yet seasoning could be meaningful on either side of the Atlantic. Severely ill on his second visit to London, in 1757, Benjamin Franklin referred to his ordeal as a kind of "seasoning" to the metropolis (Franklin 1961 [1757]).

Seasoning represented a balance between alteration in physical constitution and maintenance of English or European cultural forms. Custom was therefore tremendously important to British colonists, because it maintained continuity over the hemispheres and offered settlers a way to control their physical circumstances. Adoption of Indian customs, or Indian adoption of English manners, were both threatening unless colonists made clear that such practices were carefully controlled; cultural hybridity depended on an English material culture that protected colonists against outright degeneration. For example, it seemed safer to eat corn once it was grown with metal hoes or plows, and when it was cooked with small-grains, leavening, milk, and eggs. In one typical statement, from the 1640s, Roger Williams said that the English would eat samp (cracked corn) either "hot or cold with milke or butter, which are mercies beyond the natives plaine water, and which is a dish exceeding wholesome for the English bodies" (Chaplin 2001 201–42; Williams 1973 [1643]:101).

Likewise, English settlers insisted that it was custom, not climate, that created Indians' bodily type. Special oils and pigments created a darker Indian skin, and a punitive physical regime commenced in infancy created tough Indian bodies, resistant to extremes of climate, to scarcity of diet, and to torture and injury. To argue that custom, not climate, created Indians was to maintain that the English, whether born in the new world or not, would not become like Indians merely by living in America. If they adhered to English cultural forms, resisting any temptation to imitate Indians, they would be English in body and soul (Chaplin 2001: 138–39, 243–79).

Such practices were meant, as well, to maintain difference between colonists and enslaved Africans. A comparison between English and African only slowly joined the opposition between English and Indian. Slavery was surprisingly uncommon in the first half of the seventeenth century, when initial English colonial identity was being shaped. In the second half of the century, slavery would expand dramatically in the West Indies; only after about 1680 would the institution achieve comparable growth on the continent, yet never in the same proportions as on the islands (Berlin 1998). Still, it was particularly evident in plantation colonies that whites resisted any cultural convergence between themselves and enslaved Africans. One South Carolinian, for example, declared that he would never receive communion at the "Holy Table while slaves are received there" (Jordan 1968:183).

To emphasize their differences from Indian and African populations, English colonists began to ban intermarriage. Colonized Ireland was the model. As early as 1366, the Statutes of Kilkenny had prohibited unions between Irish and English. Anglo-American leaders did not initially ban intermarriage, though they tried to regulate sexual contact with Indians. Connecticut, for example, passed a 1642 law forbidding its settlers to "take up theire aboade with the Indians, in a prophane course of life." Then, from the 1640s onward, statutes discouraged marriage or extramarital sex between white settlers and Indians or Africans. At first, such laws simply placed legal burdens on children of composite ancestry. But with Virginia's 1691 law that flatly forbade marriage between English and "Negroes, mulattoes, and Indians," adults were directly prohibited from creating mixed-race relationships that would yield legitimate children and that would dignify non-Europeans with the status of Christian, legal spouse of an English person. Other colonies followed suit (Brown 1996; Brown & Schenck 2002:329; Chaplin 2001:186–93; Smits 1987a, 1987b).

Yet the law does not tell the whole story. As the recent debate over the paternity of Sally Hemings's children has shown, whites in the United States have tended to deny the existence of interracial sex and mixed-race children. In fact, several mixed populations had emerged by the early eighteenth century. First, there were the mestizo children of unions between Indians and white captives adopted into native societies, or between English traders and Indian women. Second, there were mixed-race children born from sexual coercion, usually English rape of Indian war captives or Indian or African slaves. Third, there were children of noncoercive alliances among whites, Indians, and Africans, whether these unions were recognized in law or not. Children from all these connections might either fade into a phenotypically dominant population or continue the overall pattern of mixture (Brown & Schenck 2002:321–38; Clinton & Gillespie 1997; Gordon-Reed 1997; Hodes 1997; Lewis & Onuf 1999; McCarney 1989; Smith 1998).

So, people of composite ancestry existed in British America (as in the other European colonies), but they were most often deemed illegitimate, subordinate, marginal, or invisible. Whereas the state in Spanish America and in New France was alert to the sexual behaviors of Christians, and to the engendering of people of part-Christian parentage, political and religious officials in the Anglophone colonies took no such interest. Such behaviors were private and illegitimate, and the children who resulted were likewise regarded as illegitimate and beneath public notice. The dominant white population tended to regard enslaved people of mixed ancestry as part and parcel of the slave population, and to insist that free people of mixed ancestry belonged outside the physical and cultural borders of the English colonies, especially within independent Indian populations (Berry 1972:194–97; Herndon & Sekatau 1997; Nash 1995).

Thus colonists' suspicion of hybridity reinforced their antipathy to creole status, and it paralleled their insistence that they were as English as those born at home. In his *History of Jamaica* (1774), Edward Long bundled together these fears and prejudices, especially in relation to questions of blood and lineage. Long provided charts for lines of descent from white and black ancestors and praised "the genuine English breed, untainted with these heterogeneous mixtures." He hoped that, in contrast to what he thought the mixed nature of Spanish Americans, British settlers would raise "in honourable wedlock a race of unadulterated beings." Note again the equation between legitimacy of birth and legitimacy of bloodlines as well as the negative assessment of Spanish America, fount of all American evils that the British sought to avoid (Long 1774:II, 260–61, 274, 276–77, 327).

The British in the metropolis, however, saw things differently. During the seventeenth century, the English called their colonial cousins "Indians," meaning residents of the West Indies, or lands beyond the Atlantic. A pregnant Lucy Downing, who considered following her Winthrop relatives to Massachusetts, said in 1637 that she preferred "to bring an Indyan then a coknye [cockney] into the world" (Forbes 1943– :367); none of the New England Winthrops contemplated giving birth to Indians. Cotton Mather did refer to his son, Increase, as "a *tame Indian*, for so the Europeans are pleased sometimes to denominate the children that are born in these regions" (Silverman 1971:178). But Mather was clearly quoting rather than accepting European practice. It was very rare for a settler to accept the name of "Indian," which is why all early Americanists know that Robert Beverley did. "I am an *Indian*," he claimed at the start of his 1705 *History and Present State of Virginia*. Beverley did so to win the reader's trust—"I hope the Plainness of my Dress, will give him the kinder Impressions of my Honesty" (Beverley 1947 [1705]: 9). More often, colonists insulted each other with the name of "Indian." Hence the disgust when captives of Indians adopted the customs of their captors (Axtell 1985:302–27).

Nor was the term "American" welcome. Many colonists first encountered it during the War of Jenkins's Ear, when British commanders referred to the "American" troops that assisted them. The name then spread to civilians (Harkness 1950). In his study of the *Symbols of American Community*, Richard L. Merritt discovered that, until the 1760s, it was far more common for residents of the colonies to be designated as British colonists or "His Majesty"s colonists." Then, in the period just after 1763 and the end of the Seven Years' War, British observers began routinely to call colonists "Americans," doing so ten to twelve years before colonists themselves would accept that name (Merritt 1966:130-33).

The colonists resented the label, fearing that Britons were lumping them with the Indian and African residents of the colonies, cultural inferiors who were subordinate to British authority and, by implication, culturally inferior (Breen 1997). A July 15, 1765, editorial in the *Boston Gazette* nervously asked "Are not the People of *America*, BRITISH subjects? Are they not *Englishmen*?" Not until after 1773 would colonists begin to call themselves Americans—only doing so once they believed that Britons would never accept them as equal citizens.

* * *

The American Revolution forced English-speaking creoles to embrace an American identity. This was two parts opportunism and one part desperation. To claim an independent and non-British status, white colonists were temporarily willing to compare themselves to Indians, much as the Londoners who had equated Mohawks with lawlessness had done. Thus the Boston Tea Party participants disguised themselves as "Indians." The movement for independence also needed recruits—any Indian or mestizo people willling to support the cause were welcome. Whites shed tears over the patriot martyr Crispus Attucks, the man of mixed Indian-African-European ancestry who was killed in the Boston Massacre. Whites created Tammany Societies, centered on an ersatz mythology of Tamenend, a

Delaware leader, and thereby appropriated Native-American history. And whites celebrated frontier life, as when the completely urbane Benjamin Franklin sported a fur cap rather than powdered wig in Paris (Deloria 1998:5–7, 10–70; Nash 1995).

The rage to be American continued even after the defeat of the British and achievement of independence. In his poem "The Hasty Pudding," Joel Barlow celebrated the dish also known as Indian pudding, a New England confection of ground maize boiled or baked with milk and molasses until its grains melt on the tongue. In 1793, Connecticut-born Barlow unexpectedly encountered a version of hasty pudding in a Savoyard farmhouse—"though distant from our native shore,/With mutual glee, we meet and laugh once more." Corn reminded him that he and his birthplace were as one:

> Thy constellation rul'd my natal morn,
> And all my bones were made of Indian corn.
> Delicious grain! whatever form it take
> To roast or boil, to smother or to bake,
> In every dish 'tis welcome still to me,
> But most, my Hasty Pudding, most in thee.

Barlow was to Indian pudding what Robert Burns was to haggis: each man defended, in verse and for nation, what outsiders thought was dietetically barbarous (Barlow 1796:Canto I, lines 75–76, 129–34).

The orgy of Americanization was temporary. Nostalgia for creole things and Indian persons would fade—whites preferred to ground civic identity in racial status and to insist that the continent's indigenous population was doomed to extinction. For the most part, comparison between white citizens and Indians remained sporadic and recreational, "playing Indian," as Philip Deloria has called it. In contrast to Spanish America, therefore, the United States has no deep-seated tradition, however opportunistic, of presenting Indian societies as foundational to the society, let alone the republic (Deloria 1998; Dippie 1982; Sheehan 1973).

Furthermore, it is notable that citizens of the new nation continued to refer to themselves as Americans but almost never as creoles, which, outside the lower Mississippi Valley, would never catch on as a term of art. White residents of the United States thus rejected any potential comparison between themselves and other creolized Europeans in the Americas; they may have been the first creole patriots to win independence from Europe, but they stood apart from the creole patriotism that flourished in what would later be called Latin America. Moreover, U.S. citizens, by using the unmodified and unhyphenated term "American," were claiming to be the preeminent new world population, a practice that persists, to the annoyance of Canadians, Mexicans, Argentines, and all others.

J. Hector St. John de Crèvecoeur, in his canonical *Letters from an American Farmer*, summarized this act of creation and appropriation by asking, "What then is the American"? and by answering that, whatever else he was, he was "this new man." Yet continuity with the old world still mattered; the American was, Crèvecoeur specified, "either an European, or the descendant of an European," not an Indian (Crèvecoeur 1957 [1782]:39). In other words, an American was the north American (and northern European) counterpart to the Spanish American (and Iberian) creole, even as the choice of the name American was final rejection of any similarity between English and Iberian populations in the Americas.

Thereafter, most U.S. whites did not use the term "creole" except to describe people from the Caribbean and Spanish America. Noah Webster stated clearly, in his *American Dictionary of the English Language* (first edition 1828) that a *creole* was, "in *the West Indies* and *Spanish America*, a native of those countries descended from European ancestors." In contrast, Webster defined an *American* as "A native of America; originally applied to the aboriginals, or copper-colored races, found here by the Europeans; but now applied to the descendants of Europeans born in America." Webster added to his definition of American a quotation from George Washington, one that firmly limited the term's scope to the United States: "The name *American* must always exalt the pride of patriotism" (Webster 1828). Thus creole patriotism without the name "creole."

It was a tricky balancing act. If "creole" smacked of Iberian culture and political dependency, "American" invited comparison with Indians, which was why Webster differentiated between the copper-colored aboriginals and their presumed successors, those Americans of European descent. Here, as elsewhere in the Americas, creolization masked or appropriated native history—that was its function. Whatever their differences, European colonists had all subjugated Native American populations. European-descended settlers had to define themselves against the peoples they had displaced. Yet in most of New Spain, as in New France, colonizers coexisted with large native populations; even as those populations shrank under the burdens of conquest, they often continued to outnumber the colonizers. In Spanish America, white creoles compared themselves to the Indians and to mestizos as well as Africans. In New France, settlers likewise had significant populations of native as well as métis peoples (of composite European and Indian ancestry) against whom to compare themselves.

English colonists had a fundamentally different experience with Indians, which explains a great deal about the negative cast that "creole" acquired in the English colonies. There, colonizers frequently stated their opinion that the native population would dramatically dwindle or even vanish.

This was not something that colonists in either Spanish America or New France thought likely, or even wanted. Nor was it what the English had expected would occur in Ireland. Yet as early as the mid-seventeenth century, English colonists in America and the Caribbean compared their birth and death rates to those of native Americans and argued that they seemed better suited, by nature, to the new world (Chaplin 2001: 125–25, 129–30). They exclaimed over "a facultie that God hath given the Brittish Ilanders to beget and bring forth more children than any other nation in the world" (Vincent 1637:[1], 21). Celebration of colonists' natural increase culminated with Benjamin Franklin's prediction, in the 1750s, that British America would soon become the population center of the empire and that people of a "Red and White" complexion, meaning those of European descent, would replace the "Blacks and Tawneys," meaning those of African or Indian descent (Franklin 1961 [1751]:234).

Indeed, long before Franklin's treatise on the rising colonial population, estimates of native populations emphasized decline, beginning with the dramatic epidemics of the seventeenth century and continuing with the triple impacts of disease, warfare, and dispossession throughout the colonial period. In the second quarter of the seventeenth century, Edward Johnson surveyed the early history of Massachusetts Bay colony and remarked that its original native population had fallen from 30,000 "able men" to fewer than 300; meanwhile, the English population had grown by leaps and bounds (Johnson 1654 [1910]:41, 48–49). By the end of the eighteenth century, the triumphant former colonists could blend their desire for Indian extinction with qualified predictions of the end of black slavery—they envisioned a racially pure United States, a vision that cloaked xenophobia with the positive goal of antislavery. Thus Ezra Stiles claimed that "we are increasing with great rapidity, and the Indians as well as the millions of *Africans* in America, are decreasing *as rapidly*." "In this way," both would "gradually vanish" along with slavery itself (Stiles 1783).

Political exclusion of Indians was apparent in the developing law of the new nation, even before Indian removal became stated U.S. policy. Article One, Section Two of the U.S. Constitution famously recognized, for instance, only three categories of persons within the nation: "free persons," unfree persons (meaning slaves), and taxable Indians. The vast majority of untaxed Indians, who still lived in independent nations, were not citizens in the way that creoles and even migrant Europeans were. Laws within the individual states also followed this logic, the better to undermine any indigenous claims to land. Unlike the case in Spanish America, where coexistence with or ongoing appropriation of native status underpinned key aspects of creole patriotism, it did no such official work in British America. Displacement of Indians, not appropriation of their culture, was the basis of "American" identity (Finkelman 1987:188–225; Thornton 1987:212–13, 216).

Not even marriage to Indians could transform whites. Several leaders in early national Virginia recommended intermarriage. Governor Patrick Henry wanted the state to pay bounties for such unions and to educate the children that would result (Johnston 1970:270). Thomas Jefferson weighed in on the question, with complicated motives. He publicly deplored sex between whites and blacks and wanted to force all white mothers of "mulatto" children and eventually the children themselves to emigrate. His promotion of white-Indian marriage may seem comparatively open-minded. But note his peremptory tone. In 1808, he told a group of Delaware and Mohican that "you will unite yourselves with us . . . you will mix with us by marriage, your blood will run in our veins, and will spread with us over this great island." Blood marked race, an indelible Indianness that Jefferson seemed to think would solidify white hegemony over the land; he did not contemplate that creoles' blood also ran in Indians' veins and that this might strengthen the true natives' claims to lands they had lost or were about to lose (Brown & Schenck 2002:329–30; Jefferson 1903:452).

* * *

That all or nothing attitude—colonists must be English, however seasoned to their environments, and white Americans must be the only true Americans—helps explain why it took so long for the Anglophone settlers of North America to admit that they were what we would call "creoles," a people different from, though descended from, Europeans. In the end, the redefinition of the term "American" was no less significant than the crafting of the earlier terms "Frank" and "creole" to describe invading European populations. British colonists' denial of creolization, then United States citizens' rush to accept the name "Americans" showed how the fantasy of complete displacement of an indigenous population was and remains a distinctive feature of U.S. politics and culture. Analytically, the framework of "creolization" helps explain many things about British America and the United States; historically, whites' refusal to accept the term "creole" may explain even more.

References

Allen, D. G. 1981. *In English ways: The movement of societies and the transferral of English local law and custom to Massachusetts Bay in the seventeenth century.* Chapel Hill, NC: University of North Carolina Press.

Anderson, B. 1991. *Imagined communities: Reflections on the origins and spread of nationalism*, rev. ed. New York: Verso.

Ashe, T. 1911. *Carolina* [1682] in *Narratives of early Carolina, 1650–1708*. A. S. Salley, ed. New York: Scribners.

Axtell, J. 1985. *The invasion within: The contest of cultures in colonial North America*. New York: Oxford University Press.

Bailyn, B. 1967. *The ideological origins of the American revolution*. Cambridge, MA: Harvard University Press.

Barlow, J. 1796. *The Hasty-Pudding: A poem in three cantos*. New York: n.p.

Bartlett, R. 1993. *The making of Europe: Conquest, colonization and cultural change, 950–1350*. Princeton, NJ: Princeton University Press.

Berlin, I. 1998. *Many thousands gone: The first two centuries of slavery in North America*. Cambridge, MA: Harvard University Press.

Berry, B. 1972. America's Mestizos. In *The blending of races: Marginality and identity in world perspective*. N. P. Gist and A. G. Dworkin, eds. New York: Wiley Interscience.

Beverley, R. 1947. *The history and present state of Virginia* [1705]. L. B. Wright, ed. Chapel Hill, NC: Institute of Early American History and Culture.

Bond, R. P. 1952. *Queen Anne's American kings*. Oxford: Clarendon Press.

Brading, D. A. 1991. *The first America: The Spanish monarchy, Creole patriots, and the liberal state, 1492–1867*. Cambridge: Cambridge University Press.

Breen, T. H. 1997. Ideology and nationalism on the eve of the American revolution: Revisions *once more* in need of revising, *Journal of American History* 84:13–39.

Brontë, C. 1973 [1847]. *Jane Eyre*. M. Smith, ed. London: Oxford University Press.

Brown, J., and T. Schenck. 2002. Métis, mestizo, and mixed-blood. In *A companion to American Indian history*. P. J. Deloria and N. Salisbury, eds. Oxford: Blackwell .

Brown, K. M. 1996. *Good wives, nasty wenches, and anxious patriarchs: Gender, race, and power in colonial Virginia*. Chapel Hill, NC: Institute of Early American History and Culture.

Cañizares-Esguerra, J. 2001. *How to write the history of the New World: Histories, epistemologies, and identities in the eighteenth-century Atlantic world*. Stanford, CA: Stanford University Press.

Canny, N., and A. Pagden, eds. 1981. *Colonial identity in the Atlantic world, 1500–1800*. Princeton, NJ: Princeton University Press.

Canny, N. 1973. The ideology of English colonization: From Ireland to America, 3d ser., *William and Mary Quarterly* 30:575–595.

——— 1981. Identity formation in Ireland: The emergence of the Anglo-Irish. In *Colonial identity in the Atlantic world, 1500–1800*. N. Canny and A. Pagden, eds. Princeton, NJ: Princeton University Press.

Canup, J. 1989. Cotton Mather and "Criolian degeneracy," *Early American Literature* 24:20–34.

——— 1990. *Out of the wilderness: The emergence of American identity in colonial New England*. Middletown, CT: Wesleyan University Press.

Chaplin, J. E. 1993. *An anxious pursuit: Agricultural innovation and modernity in the lower South, 1730–1815*.Chapel Hill, NC: Institute of Early American History and Culture.

——— 2001. *Subject matter: Technology, the body and science on the Anglo-American frontier, 1500–676*. Cambridge, MA: Harvard University Press.

——— 2002. Race. In *The British Atlantic world, 1500–1800*. D. Armitage and M. J. Braddick, eds. New York: Palgrave.

Clinton, C., and M. Gillespie, eds. 1997. *The devil's lane: Sex and race in the early South*. New York: Oxford University Press.

Crèvecoeur, J. Hector St. Jon de. 1957 [1782]. *Letters from an American farmer*, New York: E. P. Dutton.

Deloria, P. J. 1998. *Playing Indian*. New Haven, CT: Yale University Press.

DeSaussure, H. W. 1804. Letter to Ezekiel Pickens, Aug. 22, 1804, Henry William DeSaussure Papers, South Caroliniana Library, Columbia, South Carolina.

Dippie, B. W. 1982. *The vanishing American: White attitudes and United States Indian policy*. Middletown, CT: Wesleyan University Press.

Finkelman, P. 1987. Slavery and the Constitutional Convention: Making a covenant with death. In *Beyond confederation: Origins of the Constitution and American national identity*. R. Beeman, S. Botein, E. C. Carter II, eds. Chapel Hill, NC: Institute of Early American History and Culture.

Forbes, A. B., et al., eds. 1943. *The Winthrop Papers, 1498–1654,* vol. 3. Boston, MA: Historical Society.

Franklin, B. 1961 [1751]. Observations on the increase of mankind. In *The papers of Benjamin Franklin,* vol. 4. L. W. Labaree et al., eds. New Haven, CT: Yale University Press.

——— 1963. Letter to Deborah Franklin, Nov. 22, 1757, *Papers of Benjamin Franklin,* vol. 7.

Gardyner G. 1651. *A description of the New World*. London: n.p.

Gordon-Reed, A. 1997. *Thomas Jefferson and Sally Hemings: An American controversy*. Charlottesville, VA: University of Virginia.

Greene, J. P. 1981. Identity in the British Caribbean. In *Colonial identity in the Atlantic world, 1500–1800*. N. Canny and A. Pagden, eds. Princeton, NJ: Princeton University Press.

Hakluyt, R. 1979 [1584]. A particuler discourse . . . . In *New American world: A documentary history of North America to 1612*. D. B. Quinn et al., eds., vol. 3. New York: Arno Press.

Hannaford, I. 1996. *Race: The history of an idea in the West*. Baltimore, MD: Johns Hopkins University Press.

Harkness, A., Jr. 1950. Americanism and Jenkins' ear, *Mississippi Valley Historical Review* 37:61–90.

Herndon, R. W., and E. W. Sekatau. 1997. The right to a name: The Naragansett people and Rhode Island officials in the Revolutionary era, *Ethnohistory* 44:433–462.

Hill, J. 1751a. *The adventures of Mr. George Edward. a Creole*. London, n.p.

——— 1751b. *The history of a woman of quality . . . .* London, n.p.

Hodes, M. 1997. *White women, black men: Illicit sex in the nineteenth-century south*. New Haven, CT: Yale University Press.

Jefferson, T. 1903. *The writings of Thomas Jefferson,* vol. 16. A. E. Bergh, ed. Washington, DC: Thomas Jefferson Memorial Association.

Johnson, E. 1910. *[Edward] Johnson's wonder-working providence, 1628–1651* [1654]. J. F. Jameson, ed. New York: Scribners.

Johnston, J. H. 1970. *Race relations in Virginia and miscegenation in the south, 1776–1860*. Amherst, MA: University of Massachusetts Press.

Jordan, W. D. 1968. *White over black: American attitudes toward the negro, 1550–1812,* Chapel Hill, NC: Institute of Early American History and Culture.

Kazhdan A. 2000. Latins and Franks in Byzantium: Perception and reality from the eleventh to the twelfth century. In *The crusades from the perspective of Byzantium and the Muslim world*. A. E. Laiou, E. Angeliki, and R. P. Mottahedah, eds. Washington, DC: Dumbarton Oaks.

Kidd, C. 1999. *British identities before nationalism: Ethnicity and nationhood in the Atlantic world, 1600–1800*. Cambridge: Cambridge University Press.

Lewis, B. 1971. Ifrandj. In *Encyclopedia of Islam*, new ed. B. Lewis et al., eds., vol. 3. Leiden: Brill.

Lewis, J., and P. S. Onuf, eds. 1999. *Sally Hemings and Thomas Jefferson: History, memory, and civic culture*. Charlottesville, VA: University of Virginia Press.

Long, E. 1774. *The history of Jamaica*, 3 vols. London.

Maltby, W. S. 1971. *The black legend in England: The development of anti-Spanish sentiment, 1558–1660*. Durham, NC: Duke University Press.

McCarney, M. W. 1989. Cockacoeske, Queen of Pamunkey: Diplomat and suzeraine. In *Powhatan's Mantle: Indians in the colonial southeast*. P. H. Wood, G. A. Waselkov, and M. T. Hatley, eds. Lincoln, NB: University of Nebraska Press.

Merritt, R. L. 1966. *Symbols of American community, 1735–1775*. New Haven, CT: Yale University Press.

Nash, G. B. 1995. The hidden history of mestizo America, *Journal of American History* 82:941–962.

Oldmixon, J. 1741. *The British empire in America*, 2 vols. London, n.p.

O'Shaughnessy, A. J. 2000. *An empire divided: The American revolution and the British Caribbean*. Philadelphia: University of Pennsylvania Press.

Oxford English Dictionary (OED). 2000. New ed. New York: Oxford University Press.

Pagden, A. 1987. Identity formation in Spanish America. In *Colonial identity in the Atlantic World*. N. Canny and A. Pagden, eds. Princeton, NJ: Princeton University Press.

———— 1990. *Spanish imperialism and the political imagination*. New Haven, CT: Yale University Press.

Pennsylvania Gazette, 1728–800. 1991– . Electronic edition, Accessible Archives. Provo, UT: Folio Corporation.

Pocock, J. G. A. 1967. *The ancient constitution and the feudal law: A study of English historical thought in the seventeenth century*. New York: W. W. Norton.

Rutledge, F. 1804. Letter to John Rutledge, Sept. 22, 1804. John Rutledge Papers, folder 18, Southern Historical Collection. Chapel Hill, North Carolina.

Sheehan, B. W. 1973. *Seeds of extinction: Jeffersonian philanthropy and the American Indian*. Chapel Hill, NC: Institute of Early American History and Culture.

Silverman, K., ed. 1971. *Selected letters of Cotton Mather*. Baton Rouge, LA: Louisiana State University Press.

Smith, M. D. 1998. *Sex and sexuality in early America*. New York: New York University Press.

Smits, D. D. 1987a. We are not to grow wild: Seventeenth-century New England's repudiation of Anglo-Indian intermarriage, *American Indian Culture and Research Journal* 11:1–32.

———— 1987b. Abominable mixture: Toward the repudiation of Anglo-Indian intermarriage in seventeenth-century Virginia, *Virginia Magazine of History and Biography* 95:157–192.

Stiles, E. 1783. *The United States elevated to glory and honor*. New Haven, CT: n.p.

Thompson, E. 1766. *Sailor's Letters*. London: n.p.

Thornton, R. 1987. *American Indian holocaust and survival: A population history since 1492*. Norman, OK: University of Oklahoma Press.

Vincent, P. 1637. *A true relation of the late Battell*. London: n.p.

Webster, N. W. 1828. *An American dictionary of the English language*. New York: n.p.

Williams, R. 1973 [1643]. *A key to the language of America*. J. J. Teunissen and E. J. Hinz, eds. Detroit, IL: Wayne State University.

Wood, W. 1977 [1634]. *New England's prospect*. A. T. Vaughan, ed. Amherst, MA: University of Massachusetts Press.

4 The "C-Word" Again: From Colonial to Postcolonial Semantics

Stephan Palmié

In her contribution to this volume, Joyce Chaplin astutely exposes the ironies attendant on the fact that the first properly Andersonian "creole nationalists," the rebellious British colonists of North America, vigorously—and, at times, vociferously—rejected the term "creole" as a possible designator of their individual and collective identities. Smacking of the dangers of indigenization and hence "Indianness," or alternatively of the "criolian degeneracy" of the popish Spaniard to the south, the semantics that the "c-word" early on seems to have acquired among notional Englishmen "freeborn" on the other side of the North Atlantic occasioned what we today might be apt to perceive as a syndrome of massive collective denial. Much like Benedict Anderson's (1991) original formulation, however, such a diagnosis rests on the assumption that the term "creole" (in both its nominal and adjective senses) can designate a historically specific identity (or even only state of being) acknowledged, embraced, or rejected by *anyone* in the colonial Americas. Yet whether this is really so, or whether we are dealing with a mere label superimposed on categories of people lumped together according to criteria whose salience originates in our, rather than their, worlds, is all but clear.[1] For, to marshal a rather preposterous analogy, unless we wanted to book off the term "creole" as a designator of a pan-Euro-American neurosis that Latin Americans, for some unclear reasons, were able to acknowledge (whereas North Americans could not), we are left with the question of whether the term *ever* functioned to more than evoke its own antithesis (the "un-creole" Indian or metropolitan European) before it got snatched up by the rhetoric of Latin-American liberators in search of postcolonial nations. In other words, and particularly in light of this volume's aim to probe the analytical (rather than merely descriptive) usefulness of concepts built from terms such as *criollo* or "creole," it may be worthwhile to weigh in as the devil's advocate on the question of the historical semantics of *lo criollo* (that is, "matters creole") in some of the regions against which not only Chaplin's carriers of portable "British" and latter-day "American" identities compared themselves, but against whose inhabitants *we* are apt to compare *them now*.

The following cursory remarks are, thus, not just a pedantic quibble about words and people. For if we want to cast our critiques of "modern" (and hence, at least implicitly, European or North American) essentialisms in a terminology that has its roots in concrete Latin American or Caribbean historical and ethnographic situations, we would do well to probe the historical contextual significance of terms such as "creole" before we prematurely elevate them to the status of comparative—or, in a more contemporary language, transculturally salient—analytical devices expected to deliver whole (late twentieth-century) "worlds in creolization" (for example, Clifford 1988; Hannerz 1987). Speaking in a language borrowed from historically situated local social usages, social scientists and historians—unlike chemists whose compounds have no bearing on their own designation—have no choice but to fight an uphill battle against nominalism. But they can decide what level of ambiguity in reference and degrees of heteroglossia they are willing to tolerate in formulating concepts designed to capture more than appearances based on phonological semblance and ad-hoc conclusions about the nature of the phenomena subsumed under them. Nor is this a purely academic issue to do with the question of how well theories extrapolated from specific times and places "travel" (Appadurai 1986). For as Hale (1997, 1999) insists, the potential that metropolitan (or cosmopolitan, if you will) conceptual apparatuses are appropriated into, resonate with, or simply lend international legitimacy to deeply troubling peripheral politics of culture and identity calls for a certain measure of accountability regarding our current enthusiasm for the fluidity, fragmentation, and fusion of the heterogeneous that many of us associate with terms such as "creole" and "creolization." With that in mind, let us now turn to the word in question.

Disregarding its contested etymology (Corominas & Pascual 1980), words such as *crioulo* and *criollo* made their first appearance in the second half of the sixteenth century. As Peter Boyd-Bowman (1971:208) has documented, the term begins to crop up in rapid succession first in Nueva España (1562), then Cuba (1578), the Río de la Plata region (1587), and Venezuela (1597) to eventually appear in the 1609 *Comentarios reales* of the Peruvian El Inca Garcilaso de la Vega (1960–1965, II:373) in what seems to be a first attempt to trace its origins—in his case to a usage allegedly developed by enslaved Africans.[2] As becomes clear from even only a superficial examination of its historical semantics, the term rather quickly comes to circumscribe the transformations wrought on Old World life forms (that is, people, animals, and plants—and probably in that order; Cf. Arrom 1951, Chaplin this volume) on becoming native to the post-Columbian Americas.[3] Entirely consistent with these earliest documentable Spanish usages of the term *criollo* to designate the results of processes of indigenization is the fact that in the Hispanic Caribbean the term *criollo*, to this day, indexes not notions of hybridity but markers of local identity (as in *comida criolla*—roughly translatable as home-style cooking[4]). In this sense, what the term indicates are changes due not to hybridization but to adaptation to new natural and social environments. As early as the 1540s, Spanish officials and friars, thus, described American-born Spaniards as indolent, vice-ridden, haughty, and ignorant (Bacigalupo 1981:53ff, Brading 1991). Yet while some ecclesiastical authors blamed the excessive cruelty of their conquistador-fathers, or the woeful inadequacy of religious instruction, by 1574, the royal cosmographer Juan López de Velasco (1971:19–20) had come up with a climatic theory to explain the difference of the *criollos* from their Spanish parents.

> Even the Spanish who go to these parts and reside there for extended periods of time do not fail to be affected by the mutations of the heavens and the temperaments of the regions, and change somewhat in color and quality of person; but those who are born to them, and whom they call *criollos*, and who are all considered and treated as Spaniards, are known to turn out even more differentiated in terms of color and height, for all of them are tall and of a poor color which declines in accordance with the nature of the country; from this one takes the argument that the Spanish, even if they had not mixed themselves with the natives, would, in many years, become just like them: and not only do they change in their bodily attributes, but the state of their souls tends to follow that of the body, and changing that they change themselves as well; or perhaps because so many disturbed and lost spirits have found their way to these provinces, manners and social intercourse have degenerated, and affect more quickly those with less powers of virtue; and therefore there has always been and still is much calumny and uneasiness among the people.

Anticipating both Buffon and Lamarck, López de Velasco in many ways laid the groundwork for a discourse on what, for lack of a better word,

I provisionally call a conception of racially unmarked "creoledom."[5] We find it expressed in such sixteenth- and seventeenth-century expressions as *hijos de españoles, hijos del país, naturales,* or such more obviously derogatory epithets as *atoleros*—that is, eaters of the emblematically "Indian" staple, maize.[6] Polemically charged from its inception (cf. Bacigalupo 1981; Brading 1991; Cañizares-Esguerra 1999), it is a discourse that in the second half of the eighteenth century would come to provide the terms within which those New World elites—whom Benedict Anderson (1991) in a hemispheric sweep characterized as creole nationalists— asserted their difference from their hyperprivileged metropolitan compatriots as a positively valorized New World identity.

And this is where things already go wrong, once we lift such usages out of their specific historical contexts. It is not just that Benjamin Franklin— whom Anderson, on the grounds of his profession, calls the quintessential creole nationalist—would not have dreamed of claiming the term "creole" to designate any aspect of his identity.[7] Rather, and contrary to all Latin-American history-textbook harping on deep-seated conflicts between "creoles" and *peninsulares* at the root of the Latin American independence movements, what we are facing is a teleologically inspired backward extrapolation from the aftermath of the Bourbon Reforms (at best) to the early colonial period. Take as popular an introductory survey of colonial Latin American history as Lockhart and Schwartz (1983:132), where these authors first introduce a distinction between "creoles" and *peninsulares* as emergent social categories and then qualify it with the statement that the

> important thing to keep in mind about this ethnic [sic] division within the Spanish sector [of early colonial Latin American societies] is how little was made of it at the time. In the seventeenth century no one was yet called a *peninsular* and "creole" was only a derogatory nickname.

How, one wonders, can we analytically presume an ethnic division when the actors in question did not seem to perceive it themselves? For Lockhart and Schwartz are, of course, right. There was no concept of *lo criollo* that could reasonably be claimed as a predicate descriptive of anyone's strategies of identity-management in the seventeenth century. What there was, was a polemic about political interests expressed in an idiom suggestive of, but certainly not vital to, the invariable rifts that grew between metropolitan and colonial populations connected through commercial and administrative policies that seemed to privilege the former. What there was not, was a name for it.[8] Flipping forward through the pages of Lockhart and Schwartz is instructive here. For by the time

they get to the period immediately preceding the first bids for independence, they frankly admit that they (like other historians) have set
up their *criollos/peninsulares* dichotomy more for reasons of argumenta-
tive convenience than for substantially defensible ones. To be sure, the
term certainly had come to specify a person's place of birth (as in *criollo
de Michoacán*, "born and raised in Michoacán"), may have been used
"on some rare occasion" to refer to "a humble individual from the provinces," and began to appear "in the context of political sloganeering."
Yet even by the late eighteenth century, "individuals still did not call
themselves 'creoles' in the course of their daily affairs, nor does the word
appear in legal documents, censuses, baptismal and marriage registers,
and the like." Lockhart and Schwartz's conclusion is hardly surprising:
"Still and all," they write, "we today need a word to designate the locally
born Spaniards, the *españoles* of that time, so we will continue to use
'creole,' hoping that the reader will remain conscious that this is a partial
anachronism" (ibid.:321, my emphasis).

Here we have one of the older "just-so stories" that characterize the
scholarly usages of the term to this very day. For irrespective of the (locally
varying but often dramatic) cultural changes newcomer populations
underwent in the course of their "Americanization," it is really only in
postcolonial contexts such as, for example, that of Bolivar's Address to
the Congress at Angostura in 1819 that notions of heterogeneity and
hybridity become immediately salient referents of the term *criollo*. "We
are not Europeans," the liberator (himself probably of Afrohispanic descent) pronounced then:

> we are not Indians; we are but a mixed species of aborigines and Spaniards.
> Americans by birth and Europeans by law, we find ourselves in a dual
> conflict: we are disputing with the natives for titles of ownership, and
> at the same time we are struggling to maintain ourselves in the country
> that gave us birth against the [Spanish] invaders. Thus our position is most
> extraordinary and complicated. (Bierck 1951:175f.)

Extraordinary and complicated, indeed—and not simply because independence had barely been regained by then. For not only did the term
"creole" now come to carry the weight of theoretically as of yet unimagin-
able nations composed of racially heterogeneous populations (a conun-
drum preempted in the United States by the categorical exclusion of
nonwhites from the national project).[9] Especially in situations involving
large Native American populations, the word "creole" now also had to
take on the discriminatory work of the old concept of *casta* while ostensibly representing "national unity in diversity."

For what ironically corresponds most closely to our current concerns with hybridity, and the social organization of difference is not the colonial Latin American term *criollo* but a profusion of terms indicating—in theory at least—an impossibly complicated taxonomy of degrees of racial mixture within a culturally rapidly homogenizing social sector administratively set off both from slaves and those Native American communities accorded corporate status for fiscal purposes. This terminology came to apply to people technically assigned membership in the *república de los españoles* but who were collectively designated as *castas* (literally "breeds"), a term strongly suggestive of deviation from the status categories *españoles*, *indios*, and *negros* that had been operative in the immediate aftermath of the conquest. For indeed, the vigorous mating between incumbents of these original socioracial statuses gave rise to a bewildering variety of phenotypes that soon became associated with a profusion of quasizoological designations (*mestizo, mulatto, zambo, lobo, morisco, cholo, loro, saltatras, tente en el aire*, and so forth). These labels varied to a considerable extent between different regions of the Spanish American empire, but they always carried the implication of legal and political debasement.[10]

Identified by the colonial state mainly by virtue of their inability to successfully assert *limpieza de sangre* and their nonparticipation in the life of corporate Indian groups, the emergence and rapid growth of *casta* populations thus not only bedeviled attempts at colonial social engineering. It has also given rise to a most egregious waste of intellectual energy on the part of latter day analysts. I do not need to repeat here the scathing critique Julian Pitt Rivers (1971) heaped on the scholarly misuse of the word "caste" at a time when Latin Americanist historians were busily debating whether colonial Latin American individuals of mixed descent collectively constituted estates, classes, or "castes." The entire issue nowadays seems the result of a bizarre confusion of tongues arising out of a naive transposition of the categories of an ill-conceived colonial South Asian sociology to North American "race relations" since the 1920s, from where the term re-diffused to its original context of origin.[11]

None of this, of course, is to say anything about the cultural repertoires or allegiances of either *españoles de limpia sangre*, *castas*, or *indios*. *All of them* were essentially, and often involuntarily, developing novel quotidian practices in the shadow of the Spanish colonial state—new ways of eating, mating, comporting themselves, and interacting with one another—that completely evaded the legal categories and ethnic labels attached to those who, as the terminology of a bygone anthropology would have phrased it, were the "bearers" of such "mixed" cultural "traits and patterns." That the Spanish developed a taste for tobacco or cocoa, that the Indian nobility turned into voracious consumers of wheat and the meat of European livestock, or that both discovered their sweet tooth once sugar planting took off did not go entirely unremarked. Nor did more spectacular cases such as the Maya-speaking españoles of Yucatán, or the Guarani-speaking polygynous households classificatory Spaniards set up in Paraguay (Farriss 1984; Service 1951). No doubt, what Gruzinski (2002) calls a "mestizo logic" *was* at work not just at the fringes but sometimes right at the heart of the centers of Spanish colonial power. Yet, however much Native-American elites quoted Ovid in fluent Latin a mere generation after the conquest, and regardless of the zeal with which their later colonial "naturalized Spanish" counterparts sponsored New World Marian apparitions, or cobbled together Aztec or Incaic genealogical claims while despising their *indio* contemporaries (Cañizares-Esguerra, this volume)—none of this had much effect on the formation of colonial identities.[12] And no one would have associated such developments with the term *criollo*. Throughout the colonial period they simply escaped the process of ethnic or cultural marking, thus confirming—rather than weakening—ideas about monolithic identities.[13]

What is important to note, thus, is that it if we wanted to anchor our theories about heterogeneity, indeterminacy, fluidity, or hybridity in any historical usage, it decidedly is the word *casta* rather than *criollo* that we should elaborate on. For contrary to all wishful biopolitical taxonomising on the part of colonial administrators and ideologues—à la Spaniard with Indian woman = *mestizo*; *mulata* with Spaniard = *morisco*; *morisco* with Spanish woman = *chino*; *chino* with Indian woman = *saltatrás*, and so forth (cf. Aguirre Beltrán 1972:175–79; Katzew 1997; León 1924; Mörner 1967:53–90; Pérez de Barradas 1948:171–94; Stephens 1999)—what evolved out of such attempts to peg uncertain descent to ambiguous phenotype, and allowing for both to be modified by individually assessed performative criteria (such as *calidad* or *clase*), or the occupation of certain economic niches (Seed 1982), was an administrative nightmare: a system highly conducive to what McCaa (1984) called "racial drift" (that is, a divorce between the natural and the social reproduction rates of populations assigned seemingly descent-based corporate identities) and productive of the latter-day conceptual scandal that, contrary to the expectations of North American sociologists, the "castes of Latin America," on closer inspection, turned out to be "socially mobile and non-endogamous, open and fluid rather than enclosed and rigid, devoid of the notion of pollution, and giving rise to no segregation" (Pitt Rivers 1971:249).[14]

It was this shifting quicksand underneath a seemingly solid classificatory system that Bolívar worried over in Angostura.[15] For once the legal disqualifications associated with Spanish overrule had to be broken up in order to mold colonial subjects into enfranchised nationals, it became clear that most Latin American states could ill afford the ease with which Hector St. Jean de Crèvecoeur, during his stint in prerevolutionary North America, marveled at the way heterogeneous Europeans mutated into "American"—creole, if you will—"New Men" safeguarded in their social preeminence by their numbers, successful endogamous reproduction rates, and a legal tradition stringently enforcing social exclusion based on hypodescent.[16] It is in this dilemma—exacerbated by the steady systematicization of pseudo-Darwinist racism in Europe and the United States, and its avid consumption by "creole" elites in postcolonial Latin America (Hale 1986; Stepan 1991)—that we find the origins of truly genocidal programs such as those thought out by the Argentinians Domingo Sarmiento and Juan Bautista Alberdi as early as the middle of the 19th century, and implemented in that country by statistical and military means beginning in the 1880s (cf. Andrews 1980:102–06; Helg 1990). It is here, too, that we should look for the roots of the transformation of the old Spanish fiscal category of *Indios*—that is, tributary populations—into the designator of collective identities defined by performative failure apposite of (locally extremely variable and changing) ideals of *criollismo*, and entailing severe restriction of resource access, civic status, and political empowerment. The crux of the matter here lies in the eventual development of "nationalized" ideologies of hybrid cultural homogeneity that, by pegging citizenship to conformity to a national standard of cultural (and presumably biological) *mestizaje*, exclude those who would assert their "ethnic" or "cultural" distinctiveness.[17]

Related conceptual maneuvers in the formation of ostensibly hybrid but factually highly exclusionary "creole" identities are documentable in regions of the Hispanic Caribbean, Colombia, Venezuela, and Brazil, where the "nationalization" of emancipated Africans and their descendants posed analogous ideological problems. The occasional nineteenth-century antiracist (or political pragmatist, depending on perspective), such as José Martí notwithstanding, what we find, by the early twentieth century, are not only highly ambivalent debates about the virtues and vices of (oftentimes extremely violent) eugenic schemes of *blanqueamiento* (for example, Baud 1996; Helg 1990; Palmié 2002; Stepan 1991; Torres-Saillant 1998; Trigo 2000; Wade 1993a, b; Wright 1990). Perhaps even more troubling is the tendency on the part of (often, but not always, light-skinned) political elites to incorporate the cultural forms of subordinate groups into a self-consciously "hybrid" or "creole" cultural project, while not only continuing to marginalize the originators of such forms but to exclude them from the nation's imagined community if and when they claim an identity of their own.[18] Such instances of Gramscian "transformism" are clearly evident in the utterly contrived Cuban *afronegrista* vogue that emerged less than twenty years after the first and last attempt at formal black political self-assertion in that country was brutally crushed in 1912 (Helg 1995; Moore 1997; Palmié 2002) and that was largely carried by socially "white" poets and musicians. But we also find such mechanism at work in the writings of the Brazilian sociologist Gilberto Freyre or (if in a different racial inflection) in the work of the Mexican philosopher José de Vasconcelos, and the later writings of the Cuban Fernando Ortiz (cf. Hanchard 1994; Knight 1990; Palmié 1998; Stepan 1991).

Permutations of such ideological maneuvers are visible today, not just in the Mexican state's persistent denial of the resurgence of Native-American ethnicities as a political factor it cannot effectively repress (think here of the Zapatistas' use of the Internet) but also in the Cuban state's considerable worries over the fact that phenotypically "black" male Cuban youths are shaking their dreadlocks in the face of a nominally classless, and therefore raceless society.[19] What such examples point us to are questions pertaining to the role of the state—colonial or national—in the making and reproduction of "creole" identities that have little, if anything, to do with the theoretical work some of us nowadays expect the term to perform.[20] For there is little, indeed, in Latin American and Hispanic Caribbean *criollismo* to underwrite a potential of the term "creole" to deliver the analytical and political cargo of what Homi Bhabha (1990) might call a "third space" in the formation of ostensibly "hybrid" identities: that people in the Hispanic Caribbean, to this day, refuse to be categorized according to a binary racial logic characteristic of the United States is not a sign of their having superseded forms of racial discrimination. It is a symptom of that peculiarly non-U.S. American logic of exclusion that Roger Lancaster (1992) aptly describes as racism in the absence of corporate races.[21]

One might, of course, bracket these Latin American permutations in operationalizing non-Hispanic usages of terms such as "creole" and "creolization." But this is not very helpful either. Entering English, Dutch, French, and German toward the end of the seventeenth century, both adjective uses of "creole" and nominalized forms (that is, "the Creoles," *les Créoles*, and so on) appear in all major eighteenth-century descriptions of the Caribbean region as designators of locally born populations (for example, Hartsink 1770 for Suriname; Long 1774 for Jamaica; Oldendorp 1777 for the Danish Virgin Islands; Moreau de St. Méry 1797 for St. Domingue).

Still, as the single sustained attempt to untangle the semantic history of these terms in even only one non-Hispanophone local scenario (Dominguez 1986 study of Louisiana; cf. Tregle 1952, 1982, 1992) shows, beyond their use as diacritical indicators of either effective indigenization or unmitigated foreignness, their connotations likewise were highly unstable and equally subject to retrospective realignment in the service of increasingly exclusionary racial ideologies and projects. Hence, by the early twentieth century, terms such as "white Creole" and "creole white" (incidentally like "white Jamaican" and "Jamaican white") had come to mark seemingly unbridgable racial boundaries between individuals capable of pressing claims to "pure" European descent and merely phenotypically "white" persons.[22] By the same token, "black creoles" were increasingly becoming a conceptual (though not demographic!) nonentity. Although the phenomenon itself remains understudied, this situation appears far from unique. As David Lowenthal (1972:32f.) observed long ago,

> In Jamaica "Creole" designates anyone of Jamaican parentage except East Indians, Chinese, and Maroons (back-country descendants of runaway slaves, who are considered "African"). In Trinidad and Guyana it excludes Amerindians and East Indians; in Suriname it denotes the "civilized" coloured population, as apart from tribes of rebel-slave descent called Bush Negroes. In the French Antilles "Creole" refers more to local-born whites than to coloured or black persons; in French Guiana, by contrast, it is used exclusively for non-whites.

Far from dissolving naturalized markers of identity and otherness into liberating indeterminacy, Lowenthal's examples clearly demonstrate that any analytical terminology appropriating and applying concepts such as "creole" or "creolization" will create nothing but an illusory contrast to seemingly more rigidly exclusionary folk-typologies of human kinds and communities—especially if and when it disregards the differential political institutionalization of locally specific markers of "creoledom" and its opposites as vehicles of domination. Whether notions of racial or cultural hybridity become associated with the term "creole" or not, and whether this is extolled or decried, is therefore not really the issue.[23] We need to ask: at whose cost (Hale 1999; Smith 1996)?

Take for a final example the somewhat different, but not unrelated problems that arise in the case of Sierra Leone. There Skinner and Harrell-Bond's (1977) suggestion that the modern Krio identity had crystallized only in the twentieth century, and around an essentially colonial category, prompted angry retorts by Sierra Leonean scholars aiming to authenticate the Africanness of what these authors had described as an Anglophone westernized elite undergoing an ethnogenetic process when their privileges began to erode.[24] In a movement that virtually inverts the semantic structure of Latin-American *criollismo*, we thus find Akintola Wyse (1989) straining to etymologize the term *krio* toward Yoruba—a language locally no less allogenic than English but of indisputably African origin.[25] Presumably harking back to the famous Virgin Islander expatriate Edward W. Blyden's (1887) characterization of Islam as a more appropriate religion for black people than Christianity, Wyse similarly emphasizes pervasive Islamization among the Aku and extolls the Africanity of male hunter societies, while simultaneously downplaying the fact that these, by the twentieth century, had largely become coextensive with masonic lodges (Cohen 1981:101f.). Contrariwise, cultural and political relations between the Krio and the locally majoritarian populations, such as the Temne and the Mende remain largely unexplored. As in the Latin American case, in other words, we find a national project based on the self-representations of an indigenized allogenic elite of heterogeneous origin. What we do not find—and this is all but irrelevant for our considerations—is a dissolution of social boundaries between them and populations with prior claims to indigeneity. Self-perceived, and self-declared, "creoledom" we might conclude is a decidedly "modern" project—in all senses of the word, including those pertaining to uniquely "modern" forms of exclusion.

In the end, it may be we—and not just Chaplin's New World Britons and Americans—who are in denial. Rushing to incorporate an ill-understood historical vocabulary into our diagnoses of the malcontents of Euro-American modernist social and political thought, we may not only be doing serious injustice to the complexities and contradictions of the places and times from which we cull our analytical tropes. We may also be burdening our analyses and the critical agendas toward which we pitch them, with a lexicon that carries deeply troubling ideological ballast. For consider this: what if "creolization" turned out to be a mere variant of the processes we have long come to denounce as "Americanization"?

Notes

1. Quite obviously, we would not expect Calvin or Ben Franklin to have agreed with Max Weber's subsumption of their thought into the category of a "Protestant ethic" of "innerworldy asceticism" that Weber could have devised only from an early twentieth-century vantage point. Nor would we entertain much doubt that the connotations, in English, of Evans Pritchard's translation of the term *mangu* as "witchcraft" would have made little sense to his Azande interlocutors in the 1930s. None of this invalidates analytical endeavors based on such procedures as long as we remain cognizant of the fact that we cannot retroject the meanings we assign to such typological or classificatory abstractions into the concrete languages of other times and places. As the French

mediaevalist Marc Bloch (1953:178–81) once pointed out, although thirteenth-century Christian heretics may have spoken of a *medium aevum*, the term "Middle Ages" was not only still unknown to Voltaire but becomes utterly meaningless when projected back into the highly diverse societal formations characteristic of Europe between the fall of the western Roman empire and, say, the Columbian voyages.

2. For further documentation of its diffusion see Oscar Azevedo (1999).

3. Or perhaps any site of transplantation: one of the Cuban sources cited by Boyd Bowman (1971:238) thus designates a enslaved woman as a *criolla de Cabo Verde* (that is, born on those islands), thus implying—it would seem—previous use of the term to designate the offspring of continental Africans dragged to the Cape Verdes, and perhaps other islands off the coast of the African continent that the Portuguese had begun to build up as plantation colonies and slave trading entrepots since the second half of the fifteenth century (cf. Vale de Almeida, this volume). However, the decisiveness of the New World context for the formation of notions of "creole" collectivities or iden-tities becomes clear from the fact that the Luso-African groups emerging in Senegambia since the late fifteenth century steadfastly clung to forms of explicitly "Portuguese" identification (cf. Mark 1999).

4. Hence the Cubanism "aplatanarse," which indicates the process of acquiring a taste for plantain-using "creole" cuisine (as opposed to "proper" European food) but which, dif-ferent from the colonial Mexicanism *achocolatarse* (Aguirre Beltrán 1972:175), carries no racial connotations. (Cf. the distinction, noted by Mintz and Price [1985:6], between home-raised—that is, creole—and store-bought chicken in the contemporary Hispanic Caribbean and the general Dominican ambivalence, elaborated on by Derby [1998], toward foods conceptualized as foreign.)

5. "Race" must be understood here in its "modern" post-Enlightenment sense. Nothing would have kept, for example, seventeenth-century Spanish authors from referring to local creole populations as *raza* in the sense of forming a noticeably peculiar, but otherwise only vaguely conceptualized, "breed" of people rather than a presumably distinct biological entity (cf. Hogden 1964; Hudson 1996). In fact, even though the term *mala raza* implied notions of a lack of "purity of blood" (*limpieza de sangre*), the latter concept long served to exclude not so much people of "racially" (in the modern sense) mixed descent but the descendants of culturally suspect populations, namely Christianized Jews and Moriscos (converted Muslims). For different perspectives on this issue see Lewis (2003), Schwartz and Salomon (1999), Silverblatt (2002), Stolcke (1991), and Sweet (1997).

6. The name derives from the Nahuatl term for maize gruel, *atolli* (cf. Alberro 1992).

7. Anderson of course strikes an ironic note here. Still, the point is worth making: like most of the American founding fathers Franklin thought of himself as a freeborn Englishman with grievances caused by iniquitous legislative and commercial arrange-ments unilaterally cooked up by his compatriots in the metropole.

8. The fact that invectives such as *gachupines* or *chapetones*, targeting Spanish "late-comers," apparently arose very early on (Oscar Azevedo 1999) does not provide evidence for the emergence of specifically "creole" identities. Contrariwise, as Schwartz has shown elsewhere (1995), in the absence of a *named* contrast population, the term *español* acquired not only remarkable flexibility but also the capacity to absorb popu-lations of visibly mixed descent. This was the case in much of the early Spanish Caribbean, where the vertiginous decline of corporate Native-American groups led to the classification as *españoles* of large numbers of people who, for example, in contem-porary central Mexico, would have occupied a *casta* status (see below).

9. This became clear as soon as definitions of citizenship and political franchise began to be adumbrated. See Schüller (1999) and the useful literature review by Sabato (2001).

10. Stephens's (1999) massive compilation of such terms gives a good sense of the sheer classificatory excess of this nomenclature.

11. For the history of the "caste" concept in India began when the Portuguese originally transferred Latin American usages of the term *casta* (which, to some degree, had come to correspond with emergent economic niches increasingly occupied by "detribalized" Native Americans and people of mixed descent) to the Indian subcontinent. Robert E. Parks and W. Lloyd Warner seem to have introduced the "caste"-metaphor into the sociology of "race relations" in the United States. For a glimpse of the confusion its reimport into Latin American history caused, see the literature discussed in Seed (1982:602–04) who calls the controversy a "nondebate." On the Indian case compare Dirks (1992).

12. This is not to say that such identities were not, to a considerable extent, performative in nature—more so, in fact, in the earlier rather than late colonial period when, as Schwartz and Salomon (1999:491) note, the decay of the old juridical order of estates gradually led to a reorientation in the ideology of hereditary inequality from "group-oriented criteria (genealogy, surnames, fictive kinship) to purportedly inborn attributes of the individual, and especially to body type." See Smith (1996) and Poole (1997) on gender-specific aspects of this process.

13. To this day, much of what is locally regarded as emblematically "nonwestern" (that is, Indian or African) is clearly the product of latter-day rationalizations. See for example Friedlander's (1975) discussion of Amerindian foodways, or Dantas Gois (1988) and Matory (1999) on the historical complexities of "Africanity" in Afro-Brazilian religion.

14. Perhaps the most absurdly elaborate of such taxonomies was devised by Moreau de St. Méry (1797–1798) in French St. Domingue on the eve of the Haitian Revolution, where this author sets up a system of racial quanta tabulating the procreative outcomes of sexual encounters between eleven racial types in quanta of mixture up to the 128th degree (such that, for instance, a Quarteronné could result from one of four distinct combinations of parents and would therefore have between 122 and 124 parts of white ancestry and between four and six parts of black ancestry). Arbitrary (as Moreau admits), and of little use in correlating physiology with descent (which he strains to deny), what such arithmetics of race reveal is perhaps not so much an enlightened concern with what Comte would later call a science of society. Rather, they bespeak what Joan Dayan (1995:228–37) calls a "radical irrationality" born from an anxiety-ridden, but also rather prurient, obsession with the way in which power locally expressed itself in hierarchies that established an order of sexual domination over racial others, the results of which complicated and threatened to subvert the "racial" markers of inequality on which it was supposedly based. This, precisely, is the way in which the late Spanish colonial growth of the genre of the so-called "*casta* paintings" (*cuadernos de mestizaje*) has been interpreted: as an imaginary salvage, by pictorial fixing, of a racialized and gendered order of domination whose stability was constantly being undermined by the very logic of its own operation (Katzew 1997; Lewis 2003:74). See also Stoler (1997) on the (necessary) dialectics between fluidity and fixity in racial discourse, which seems to underlie not just these scenarios but also, for example, the peculiarly North-American phenomenon of "passing."

15. See Mörner (1967:86–90) for a discussion of Bolívar's ambivalent and changing attitudes toward the "race issue."

16. Nor could they afford Jean Jacques Dessalines' gesture of declaring the Polish deserters from General Leclerc's French forces "legally black" to assure them rights to landholding under the first Haitian constitution. Haiti, of course, was to be plagued by a structure of domination in which, as Sidney Mintz (1974:271) once put it, the physical appearance of the elite became a historical expression of its power.

17. In the Mexican case see Knight (1990) for a succinct overview of the development of "Indian" identities. See below for the consequences of the seizure of all-inclusive conceptions of hybridity by states. For concrete examples of the postcolonial creation of spoiled (in Erving Goffman's sense) "Indian" identities by default compare, for instance, Friedlander (1975) for Mexico; Whitten (1976) and Stutzman (1981) for Ecuador; Smith (1995) and Hale (1996, 1999) for Guatemala; Gould (1998) for Nicaragua; and de la Cadena (2000) for Peru.

18. Brackette Williams's (1991:30) comments on the situation in Guyana are highly apposite here. "Where the national process aimed at homogenizing heterogeneity is fashioned around assimilating elements of that heterogeneity through appropriations that devalue them or deny the source of their contribution," she writes, "it establishes what Gramsci referred to as transformationist hegemony. Under these conditions, those groupings associated with objects, acts, and ideas treated in this manner are placed at both a pragmatic and an ideological disadvantage. If they continue to insist on the root identity of their selves and the objects, acts, and ideas associated with those selves, they are not 'true' members of the ideologically defined nation."

19. See Alexander (1977) and Carnegie (1999) for the Jamaican case, as well as Segal (1994) and Khan (2001) for similar issues in Trinidad.

20. It is on similar grounds that Klor de Alva (1995:270) polemicizes against the application of the term "postcolonial" to Latin America, where he finds a continuity, across the threshold of independence, of domination by the "progeny of the mixtures of former colonialists, Africans and indigenes, who no longer identified themselves as the latter two." The subsequent social and political exclusion of those whom the "creole" national project left no choice but to bear nonhybridized identities by default might, thus, be seen as constituting a continuation of colonialism by other, viz. "national," means—a conclusion that Lomnitz's (2001) rather more subtle critique of Anderson's thesis comes close to as well. Hale (1997) provides a good overview of the literature on emergent "identity politics" in contemporary Latin America.

21. What complicates matters further is that binary identity formations are all but unknown in parts of Latin America where large Indian populations were excluded from postindependence national projects unless they relinquished their corporate identities and "assimilated" into an unmarked "national" culture. The irony is that the recent resurgence of indigenous activism—no less than the emergence of "black movements" in, for example, Colombia or Brazil (Wade 1993 a,b; Hanchard 1994)—is viewed with considerable anguish not just by local elites with vested interests in scenarios of national hybridity but also by metropolitan theorists who suspect the "cunning of imperial reason" at work (Bourdieu & Wacquant 1999).

22. In the latter cases ('Jamaican white' and "creole white"), the implication is that persons so designated might locally "pass" for white but that their "local social whiteness" would not withstand close genealogical scrutiny, or hold up against more stringent definitions of "whiteness" in place elsewhere. In Cuba, a related way of casting doubt on the identity of a person socially regarded as white is the question, usually deployed jokingly "¿Y tu abuela? ¿Donde está?" ("And where is your grandmother?"). Cf. Chaudenson (2001:5–6) for Mauritian parallels.

23. Cf. Martínez Echazábal (1998:23, emphasis in the original) who, apposite of the conceptually closely related term *mestizaje* speaks of a "pendulum effect" that allows a fundamentally "racialised discourse to oscillate from cultural absolutism to cultural relativism, from the means to a *homo*geneous and naturalized national cultural identity to the site of a *hetero*geneous postcolonial one."

24. Cf. Sundiata (1976) whose description of the "creolized" black elite of Fernando Po in starkly unfavorable terms explicitly recurs to E. Franklin Frazier's scathing strictures against the U.S. "black bourgeoisie."

25. The irony here is that the etymon *akiriyo*, which Wyse (1979, 1989:6) glosses as "to walk about and be satisfied" (as when visiting after Church services on Sundays), could well be a derogatory term that Nigerian Yoruba-speakers reserve for Christians (see Abrahams 1958:374, entry for *Kiriyó*). More recently, Maureen Warner Lewis (1997:91f.) has proposed a similarly teleological, if not fanciful, Kikongo etymology for New World usages of the term "creole" that posits the nominalized form **nkuulolo* "person excluded, an outsider" as the etymon of the Portuguese (along the lines of the following phonlogical progression: **nkuulolo>kuulolo~kurolu>kruolu> kriolo~kriulu.*

References

Aguirre Beltrán, G. 1972. *La población negra de México*. México, D.F.: Fondo de Cultura Económica.

Alberro, S. 1992. *Del gachupín al criollo*. México City: Colegio de Mexico.

Alexander, J. 1977. The culture of race in middle-class Kingston, Jamaica, *American Ethnologist* 4:413–435.

Amselle, J. L. 1998. *Mestizo logics*. Stanford, CA: Stanford University Press.

Anderson, B. 1991. *Imagined communites*. London: Verso.

Andrews, G. R. 1980. *The Afro-Argentines of Buenos Aires*. Madison, WI: University Of Wisconsin Press.

Appadurai, A. 1986. Theory in anthropology: Center and periphery, *Comparative Studies in Society and History* 29:356–361.

Arrom, J. J. 1951. Criollo: Definición y matices de un concepto, *Hispania* 34:172–176.

Bacigalupo, M. H. 1981. *A changing perspective*. London: Tamesis Books.

Barth, F. 1969. Introduction. In *Ethnic groups and boundaries*. F. Barth, ed. Boston: Little, Brown and Co.

Baud, M. 1996. "Constitutionally White": The forging of a national identity in the Dominican Republic. In *Ethnicity in the Caribbean*. G. Oostindie, ed. London: Macmillan, pp. 121–151.

Bhabha, H. K. 1990. The third space. In *Identity: Community, culture, difference*. J. Rutherford, ed. London: Lawrence and Wishart, pp. 207–221.

Bierck, H. A., Jr. 1951. *Selected writings of Bolívar,* vol.1. New York: The Colonial Press.

Bloch, M. 1953. *The historian's Craft*. New York: Vintage Books.

Blyden, E. W. 1887. *Christianity, Islam and the negro race*. London: W. B. Whittingham.

Boyd-Bowman, Peter. 1971. *Lexico hispanoamericano del siglo XVI*. London: Tamesis Books.

Bourdieu, P., and L. Wacquant. 1999. The cunning of imperialist reason, *Theory, Culture and Society* 16:41–58.

Brading, D. A. 1991. *The first America*. Cambridge: Cambridge University Press.

Cañizares-Esguerra, J. 1999. New world, new stars: Patriotic astrology and the invention of Indian and Creole bodies in colonial Spanish America, 1600–1650, *American Historical Review* 104:33–68.

——— 2001. *How to write the history of the New World*. Stanford, CA: Stanford University Press.

Carnegie, C. V. 1999. Garvey and the black transnation, *Small Axe* 5:48–71.

Chaudenson, R. 2001. *Creolization of language and culture*. London: Routledge.

Clifford, J. 1988. *The predicament of culture*. Cambridge, MA: Harvard University Press.

Cohen, A. 1981. *The politics of elite culture*. Berkeley and Los Angeles, CA: University of California Press.

Corominas, J., J. A. Pascual. 1980. *Diccionario crítico etimológico castellano hispánico*. Madrid: Editorial Gredos.

Dantas Gois, B. 1988. *Vovo Nagô e Papai Branco*. Rio de Janeiro: Ediçoes Graal.

Dayan, J. 1995. *Haiti, history, and the gods*. Berkeley and Los Angeles, CA: University of California Press.

de Crèvecoeur, J. H. St. Jean. 1968 [1782]. *Letters from an American farmer*. Gloucester, MA: Peter Smith.

De la Cadena, M. 2000. *Indigenous mestizos*. Durham, NC: Duke University Press.

Derby, L. 1998. Gringo chickens with worms: Food and nationalism in the Dominican Republic. In *Close encounters of empire*. G. M. Joseph, C. C. Legrand, and R. D. Salvatore, eds. Durham, NC: Duke University Press, pp. 451–493.

Dirks, N. B. 1992. Castes of mind, *Representations* 37:56–78.

Domínguez, V. A. 1986. *White by definition*. New Brunswick, NJ: Rutgers University Press.

Farriss, N. M. 1984. *Maya society under colonial rule*. Princeton, NJ: Princeton University Press.

Friedlander, J. 1975. *Being Indian in Hueyapan*. New York: St. Martin´s Press.

Gould, J. L. 1998. *To die in this way*. Durham, NC: Duke University Press.

Gruzinski, S. 2002. *The mestizo mind*. London: Routledge.

Hanchard, M. 1994. *Orpheus and power*. Princeton, NJ: Princeton University Press.

Hannerz, U. 1987. The world in creolization, *Africa* 57:546–559.

Hale, C. A. 1986. Political and social ideas in Latin America, 1870–1930. In *The Cambridge history of Latin America*, vol. iv, c. 1870–1930. L. Bethell, ed. Cambridge: Cambridge University Press, pp. 367–441.

―――― 1996. Mestizaje, hybridity and the cultural politics of difference in postrevolutionary Central America, *Journal of Latin American Anthropology* 2:34–61.

―――― 1997. Cultural politics of identity in Latin America, *Annual Reviews of Anthropology* 26:567–590.

―――― 1999. Travel warning: Elite appropriations of hybridity, mestizaje, antiracism, equality, and other progressive-sounding discourses in highland Guatemala, *Journal of American Folklore* 112:297–315.

Hartsinck, J. J. 1770. *Beschrijving van Guyana of de wilde kust in Zud-Amerika*. Amsterdam: Gerrit Tielenburg.

Helg, A. 1990. Race in Argentina and Cuba, 1880–1930: Theories, policies, and popular reaction. In *The idea of race in Latin America*. R. Graham, ed. Austin, TX: University of Texas Press, pp. 37–69.

―――― 1995. *Our rightful share*. Chapel Hill, NC: University of North Carolina Press.

Hogden, M. 1964. *Early anthropology in the sixteenth and seventeenth centuries*. Philadelphia: University of Pennsylvania Press.

Hudson, N. 1996. From "nation" to "race": The origin of racial classification in eighteenth-century thought, *Eighteenth-Century Studies* 29:247–264.

Khan, A. 2001. Journey to the center of the Earth: The Caribbean as master symbol, *Cultural Anthropology* 16:271–302.

Katzew, I. 1997. Casta painting: Identity and social stratification in colonial Mexico. www.gc.maricopa.edu/laberinto/fall1977/casta/1997.htm.

Klor de Alva, J. J. 1995. The postcolonization of the (Latin) American experience: A reconsideration of "colonialism," "postcolonialism," and "mestizaje." In *After colonialism*. G. Prakash, ed. Princeton, NJ: Princeton University Press, pp. 241–278.

Knight, A. 1990. Racism, revolution, and *indigenismo*: Mexico, 1910–1940. In Richard Graham, ed. *The idea of race in Latin America*. Austin, TX: University of Texas Press, pp. 71–113.

Lancaster, R. 1992. *Life is hard*. Berkeley and Los Angeles, CA: University of California Press.

León, N. 1924. *Las castas del México colonial*. México, D.F.: Museo Nacional de Arqueología, História y Etnografía.

Lewis, L. A. 2003. *Hall of mirrors: Power, witchcraft, and caste in colonial Mexico*. Durham, NC: Duke University Press.

Lockhart, J., and S. B. Schwartz. 1983. *Early Latin America*. Cambridge: Cambridge University Press.

Lomnitz, C. 2001. *Deep Mexico, silent Mexico: An anthropology of nationalism*. Minneapolis: University of Minnesota Press.

Long, E. 1774. *The history of Jamaica*. London: T. Lowndes.

López de Velasco, J. 1971. *Geografía y descripción universal de las Indias*. Madrid: Ediciones Atlas.

Lowenthal, D. 1972. *West Indian societies*. Oxford: Oxford University Press.

Mark, P. 1999. The evolution of "Portuguese" identity: Luso-Africans on the upper Guinea coast from the sixteenth to the early nineteenth century, *Journal of African History* 40:173–191.

Martínez-Echazábal, L. 1998. Mestizaje and the discourse of national/cultural identity in Latin America, 1845–1959, *Latin American Research Review* 25:21–42.

Matory, J. L. 1999. The English professors of Brazil: On the diasporic roots of the Yorùbá nation, *Comparative Studies in Society and History* 41:72–103.

McCaa, R. 1984. *Calidad, Clase*, and marriage in colonial Mexico: The case of Parral, 1788–1790, *Hispanic American Historical Review* 64:477–501.

Mintz, S. W. 1974. *Caribbean transformations*. New York: Columbia University Press.

Mintz, S. W., and S. Price. 1985. Introduction. In *Caribbean contours*. S. W. Mintz and S. Price, eds. Baltimore, MD: Johns Hopkins University Press, pp. 3–11.

Moore, R. 1997. *Nationalizing blackness*. Pittsburgh, PA: University of Pittsburgh Press.

Moreau de St. Méry, M. L. E. M. 1797–1798. *Description topographique, physique, civile, politique et historique de la partie française de l'isle Saint-Domingue*. Philadelphia: chez l'auteur.

Mörner, M. 1967. *Race mixture in the history of Latin America*. Boston: Little, Brown.

Oldendorp, C. G. A. 1777. *Geschichte der Mission der evangelischen Brüdergemeine auf den caraibischen Inseln S. Thomas, S. Croix, und S. Jan*. Barby: Christian Friedrich Laux.

Oscar Azevedo, E. 1999. *Baroco y terminología en Hispanoamerica*. Buenos Aires: Ciudad Argentina.

Palmié, S. 1998. Fernando Ortiz and the cooking of history, *Iberamerikanisches Archiv* 24:353–373.

——— 2002. *Wizards and scientists*. Durham, NC: Duke University Press.

Pérez de Barradas, J. 1948. *Los mestizos de América*. Madrid: Cultura Clásica y Moderna.

Pitt Rivers, J. 1971. On the word "caste." In *The translation of culture*. T. O. Beidelman, ed. London: Tavistock, pp. 231–256

Poole, D. 1997. *Vision, race, and modernity*. Princeton, NJ: Princeton University Press.

Sabato, H. 2001. On political citizenship in nineteeth-century Latin America, *American Historical Review* 106:1290–1315.

Schüller, K. 1999. Konzeptionen für die Stellung verschiedener Rassen in den Unabhängigkeitsbewegungen Lateinamerikas. Ein Beitrag zur Gleichstellung von "Minderheiten" im Revolutionszeitalter. In *Interethnische Beziehungen in der Geschichte Lateinamerikas*. H.-J. Dominick and H.-J. Prien, eds. Frankfurt: Vervuert, pp. 131–147.

Schwartz, S. B. 1995. Spaniards, pardos, and the missing mestizos: Identities and racial categories in the early Hispanic Caribbean, *New West Indian Guide* 71:5–19.

Schwartz, S. B., and F. Salomon. 1999. New peoples and new kinds of people: Adaptation, readjustment, and ethnogenesis in South American Indigenous societies (colonial era). In *The Cambridge history of the native peoples of the Americas* (vol. III South America, part 2). F. Salomon and S. B. Schwartz, eds. Cambridge: Cambridge University Press, pp. 443–501.

Seed, P. 1982. Social dimensions of race: Mexico City, 1753, *Hispanic American Historical Review* 62:569–606.

Segal, D. A. 1994. Living ancestors: Nationalism and the past in postcolonial Trinidad and Tobago. In *Remapping memory*. J. Boyarin, ed. Minneapolis: University of Minnesota Press, pp. 221–239.

Service, E. R. 1951. The encomienda in Paraguay, *Hispanic American Historical Review* 31:230–252.

Silverblatt, I. 2002. New Christians and New World fears in seventeenth century Peru. In *From the margins: Historical anthropology and its futures*. B. K. Axel, ed. Durham, NC: Duke University Press, pp. 95–121.

Skinner, D., and B. Harrell-Bond. 1977. Misunderstandings arising from the use of the term "creole" in the literature on Sierra Leone, *Africa* 47:305–320.

Smith, C. A. 1995. Race-class-gender ideology in Guatemala: Modern and anti-modern forms, *Comparative Studies in Society and History* 37:723–749.

———— 1996. Myths, intellectuals, and race/class/gender distinctions in the formation of Latin American nations, *Journal of Latin American Anthropology* 2:148–169.

Stepan, N. L. 1991. *The hour of eugenics*. Ithaca, NY: Cornell University Press.

Stephens, T. M. 1999. *Dictionary of Latin American racial and ethnic terminology*. Gainesville, FL: University of Florida Press.

Stoler, A. L. 1997. Racial histories and their regimes of truth, *Political Power and Society* 11:183–206.

Stolcke, V. 1991. Conquered women, *NACLA Report on the Americas* 24:23–28, 39.

Stutzman, R. 1981. *El mestizaje*: An all-inclusive ideology of exclusion. In *Cultural transformations and ethnicity in modern Ecuador*. Urbana, IL: University of Illinois Press, pp. 445–494.

Sundiata, I. K. 1976. Creolization on Fernando Po: The nature of society. In *The African diaspora*. M. L. Kilson and R. I. Rotberg, eds. Cambridge, MA: Harvard University Press, pp. 391–413.

Sweet, J. H. 1997. The Iberian roots of American racist thought, *William and Mary Quarterly* 54:143–166.

Torres-Saillant, S. 1998. The tribulations of blackness: Stages in Dominican racial identity, *Latin American Perspectives* 100:126–146. ·

Tregle, J. G., Jr. 1952. Early New Orleans society: A reappraisal, *Journal of Southern History* 18:20–136.

———— 1982. On that word "creole" again: A note, *Louisiana History* 23:193–198.

———— 1992. Creoles and Americans. In *Creole New Orleans*. A. A. Hirsch and J. Logsdon, eds. Baton Rouge, LA: Louisiana State University Press, pp. 131–185.

Trigo, B. 2000. *Subjects of crisis*. Hannover, NH: Wesleyan University Press.

Vega, G. de la. 1960–1965. *Obras completas del Inca Garcilaso de la Vega*. Madrid: Ediciones Atlas.

Wade, P. 1993a. *Blackness and race mixture*. Baltimore, ND: Johns Hopkins University Press.

———— 1993b. Race, nature, and culture, *Man* 28:17–34.

Warner-Lewis, M. 1997. Posited Kikoongo origins of some Portuguese and Spanish words from the slave era, *América Negra* 13:83–97.

Whitten, N. E. 1976. *Sacha runa: Ethnicity and adaptation of Ecuadoiran Jungle Quichua*. Champaign, IL: University of Illinois Press.

Williams, B. 1991. *Stains on my name, war in my veins*. Durham, NC: Duke University Press.

Wright, W. R. 1990. Café con leche: *Race, class, and national image in Venezuela*. Austin, TX: University of Texas Press.

Wyse, A. J. G. 1989. On misunderstandings arising from the use of the term "creole" in the literature on Sierra Leone: A rejoinder, *Africa* 49:408–117.

———— 1991. *The Krio of Sierra Leone*. Washington, DC: Howard University Press.

5 Creole Linguistics from Its Beginnings, through Schuchardt to the Present Day

Philip Baker and Peter Mühlhäusler

This article surveys the history of the study of creole languages from the eighteenth century to the present day. It also examines the different ways in which the word "creole" has been interpreted by linguists, anthropologists, and others. Attention is given to the various, and often conflicting, theories with regard to how these languages originated and developed, and to their significance for linguistics as a whole. In the course of this, the importance of the work of the German linguist Hugo Schuchardt on a wide range of these languages, covering four decades and starting in the 1880s, stands out as unparalleled in more recent times. The article concludes with a summary of the principal controversies that remain unresolved today, several of which date from Schuchardt's time.

THE WORD "CREOLE"

The word "creole" derives from Spanish *criollo* (feminine: *criolla*). Woll (1997:532–33) lists a total of fifteen attestations of the Spanish word in the period 1562–1599, all of them from the New World. Of these, eight refer to blacks born locally, three to blacks born elsewhere but outside Africa, three appear to refer to whites of Spanish descent born locally, and the remaining one refers to locally born calves. What unites all these is the sense of "born in a location in which their parents did not originate."

The same range of uses is found for English "creole" and French *créole* from the seventeenth century.

The earliest use of "creole" to refer to a particular kind of language comes from West Africa:

> There are among them certain blacks and mulattoes who call themselves Portuguese because they are descendants of a few Portuguese who formerly lived there [Albreda on the north bank of the River Gambia]. These people, in addition to the language of the country, also speak a certain jargon which has only very little resemblance to the Portuguese language, and which one calls the Creole language, [just] as in the Mediterranean Sea [one has] the lingua franca. (La Courbe 1685, in Cultru 1913:192, our translation)[1]

The same text also includes a reference to *le latin creole* ("Creole Latin"), and this could well be the first overt use of the word as an adjective indicating a nonstandard variety of another language:

> When I first arrived at Cacheau not knowing the Portuguese language at all I usually spoke Latin; but beyond the Catholic clergy, I found that few people understood this; there were however a few officers of the garrison who spoke it a little; but very imperfectly, and Captain Mor [the governor] who also knew something of it said on this subject that I spoke Portuguese Latin whereas they spoke Creole Latin. (La Courbe 1685 in Cultru 1913:230)[2]

Examples of "creole" as a language name are found from the eighteenth century. Stein (1982:12) notes the use of *Carriolse* for "Virgin Islands Creole Dutch" in 1739; the earliest attestation from the Indian Ocean is found in an advertisement in the lost and found column of *Annonces, affiches et avis divers pour les colonies des isles de France et de Bourbon,* 13 février 1773:

> A young male slave from Mozambique called Favori, aged 13 and belonging to Pierre Maheas, a planter at Long Mountain, has disappeared since January 31st. As this young slave is probably lost and does not understand the Creole language, he will not be able to give the name of his owner nor find his way home. (. . .) (our translation)[3]

This example is of particular interest for theories of creolization because of the clear implication that creole rather than French was what foreign-born slaves were expected to acquire. However, by the time this was published in Mauritius, the serious study of creole languages had already begun in the New World.

EARLY STUDIES OF INDIVIDUAL
CREOLE LANGUAGES

Philology developed as a discipline concerned with the interpretation of ancient literary or historical documents. Given the absence of such documents in most creole languages until quite recently, we should not be surprised that philologists did not care to comment on creoles. As commentators there remained visitors and residents in territories where they were spoken who contributed brief, amateur sketches, as well as missionaries whose work depended on knowledge of the languages spoken by their target populations. Leaving aside the question whether the Lingua Geral of Brazil (derived from Tupi) truly qualifies as a creole (see Holm 1988–1989:605ff), descriptions of this language by Jesuit missionaries predate other descriptions by more than a century. The first grammars of the Lingua Geral as used in the missions were those of José de Anchieta (1595) and Luis Figueira (1621). In common with other creoles derived from non-Indo-European languages, the Lingua Geral rarely features in comparative or universalist studies in spite of being one of the better documented creoles. Like most missionary grammars, descriptions of the Lingua Geral involve a considerable amount of standardization and language creation.

Missionary activities also account for serious work on other individual creoles. The two earliest serious publications on creoles derived from Germanic languages are Van Dyk's work on Sranan (ca. 1765) and Magens's grammar of Negerhollands (1770). Sranan is spoken in Surinam, which was an English colony for just seventeen years before it became Dutch. Negerhollands was spoken until quite recently in what are now the U.S. Virgin Islands, but these islands formed the Danish West Indies in the eighteenth century. Failing to find willing settlers in Denmark, the Danes successfully encouraged the Dutch from neighboring islands in the Caribbean to settle there. It is highly significant that both these creoles draw the bulk of their lexicon from a language that was not that of the colonial power. The implication is that European missionaries were more disposed to treat creole languages seriously if they were clearly not derived from their own language.

No comparable studies of French creoles were to appear until about a century later,[4] the three most elaborate being Thomas (1869) for Trinidad, Saint-Quentin (1872) for French Guiana, and Baissac (1880) for Mauritius. None of these were missionaries; Thomas was anglophone, whereas the other two were francophones. Shorter grammatical sketches of several other French creoles were also published toward the end of the nineteenth century. By contrast, Russell's very short, amateurish *The Etymology of*

Jamaica Grammar is probably the only grammatical study of an English-based creole spoken in a territory under British control to have been published before the twentieth century.

COMPARATIVE STUDIES AND THEORIES
OF HOW SUCH LANGUAGES AROSE

The comparative-historical (philological) approach to the study of language dominates the nineteenth century. One of the key concepts of philologists at that time was that the relationships among languages could be portrayed by means of a family tree. New languages were seen as resulting from clean splits of older languages. Divergence and parthenogenesis received most of the attention, and the notion that there could not be mixed languages was widely subscribed to by the profession. The existence of creoles appears to have been more an irritant than a serious counterexample, and by emphasizing their aberrant nature (unlike the languages favored by philologists, creoles exhibit little inflexional morphology) or denying them the status of proper languages philologists succeeded in protecting their paradigm. The first serious comparative study of any creole is that by William Greenfield (1830), a private scholar specializing in biblical languages. His monograph was written to defend the Bible Society's publication, in 1829, of a New Testament in Sranan (an English creole spoken in Surinam). In order to demonstrate that creoles are as complex and systematic as other languages, he compared English, Dutch, Sranan, and Negerhollands. His conclusion that creoles were indeed qualitatively comparable to "civilized" European standard languages was far ahead of its time, and his work remained forgotten, until rediscovered by Reinecke (1986).

By the second half of the nineteenth century sufficient information had been published on a range of creole languages for a start to be made on comparative studies. The first such study of any significance was Addison Van Name's *Contributions to Creole Grammar* (1869–1870). Van Name consulted the available publications on eight creoles: Negerhollands, Papiamentu, Sranan, and the French creoles of Haiti, Louisiana, Martinique, St Thomas, and Trinidad. He discussed the relative European and African contributions to these but took the view that African influence on them was very limited. He also saw a parallel between the development of French from Latin and the development of creoles from European languages. He might thus be considered the first "superstratist"—a word that today characterizes someone who studies creole languages but who regards each of them as essentially the offspring of a single parent, that is, the European language from which they draw most of their vocabulary, rather than as a mixed language.

Another early comparative study was that of Coelho (1880–1886). He examined the same studies as Van Name as well as two later publications, Saint Quentin (1872) and Baissac (1880). In addition, he had access to a number of publications on Portuguese creoles ranging from the Cape Verde Islands off West Africa to Macau in the Far East. Coelho's complete text exists only in the original Portuguese, but two extracts translated by Holm (1988–1989) are relevant here:

> The Romance and Creole dialects, Indo-Portuguese and all similar formations represent the first stage or stages in the acquisition of a foreign language by a people that speaks or spoke another. (. . .) (Coelho 1880–1886:195; Holm 1988–1989:27)

This was perhaps the earliest overt expression of the view, held by many people today, that creole languages result from incomplete second-language acquisition.

> Creole languages owe their origin to the operation of psychological or physiological laws that are everywhere the same, and not to the influence of the former languages of the peoples among whom these dialects are found. (Coelho 1880–1886:195; Holm 1988–1989:27)

This opinion foreshadows the "universalist" position, which gained support in the 1970s.

If Coelho, like Van Name, saw little evidence of non-European influence in creole languages, Lucien Adam (1883) took very much the opposite view. Adam had lived in French Guiana for three years and, drawing on that experience and examining the published accounts of several of the studies of individual creole languages already mentioned, came to the view that the phonology and the grammar of creoles came from the languages of slaves, whereas the lexicon came from the language of the slave owners. Adam could thus have been the first person to adopt what is today known as the substratist position. (A substratist is someone who takes particular interest in, and emphasizes, the contribution of non-European languages to creoles.)

Thus, by the end of the nineteenth century, several ideas on the process of creolization had been aired (followed by their usual modern names in italics):

1. Creoles are reduced forms of European languages with little or no non-European influences. *Superstratist*

2. It may be possible to account for the way in which creoles developed by some kind of rules that have nothing to do with the original languages of the slaves. *Universalist*
3. Creoles are the result of imperfect language acquisition. *Imperfect second-language acquisition*
4. Creoles have non-European grammars and European vocabularies. *Substratist*

HUGO SCHUCHARDT'S CONTRIBUTION TO CREOLE LINGUISTICS

Note that the positions 1–4 (see above) were arrived at largely by means of logical argumentation rather than empirical research and that often they just follow from the ideologies fashionable at the time, including ideologies of the inferiority of non-Europeans and the importance of racial and linguistic purity. Just how pervasive the last two factors were is perhaps not widely appreciated today, but their influence can be found even in the famous *Cours de linguistique generale* (1916)[5] of the "father of modern linguistics," Ferdinand de Saussure (see Joseph 2000).[6] His lesser known brother Léopold expressed such views overtly:

> The language of a civilized nation implanted among indigenous people in the colonies rapidly becomes unrecognizable; it can undoubtedly be spoken correctly by a certain number of educated individuals but it would be wrong to draw a general conclusion from that (. . .). The native who speaks a European language does not reflect the mentality of his race, but rather that of the civilized *milieu* to which he is obliged to conform by an effort of attention and of memory, and that is necessarily a very limited, imitative phenomenon. (L. de Saussure 1899:165–66, our translation)[7]

Perhaps even more surprising is the fact that a highly respected publishing house could permit such views to be expressed in print in the second half of the twentieth century:

> We thus confine ourselves to showing what became of a highly civilized language, such as 17th century French, reduced to its most simple expression as it passed through black brains and throats. (Jourdain 1956:xxii, our translation)[8]

Shortsighted explanations such as the preceding ones are not found in the work of Hugo Schuchardt (1842–1927), whose agenda was to overcome the limitations of the family model of language relationships by investigating empirically three extreme instances of human languages: (1) isolates such as Basque that had no family; (2) invented artificial languages such as Volapük; and (3) mixed languages. Schuchardt had been educated in Indo-Germanic (Romance) philology at Leipzig and for a brief period held a chair at nearby Halle. His acceptance of a chair at a distant Austrian provincial university (Graz) would seem to be symbolic of Schuchardt's distancing himself from mainstream neogrammarian philology and its ideology of exceptionless laws of sound change. His 1885 paper on sound laws bears the subtitle *Gegen die Junggrammatiker*, that is, against the prevailing paradigm. Schuchardt emphasizes the numerous exceptions to sound laws, particularly those resulting from language contact and mixing. He further rejects the neogrammarian predilection for written Indogermanic philology. He refers to his studies as *Sprachwissenschaft* and to himself as *Linguist*, and he admonishes his colleagues *Spaziergänge um die Welt zu machen* ("to wander around the world") in order to discover both *das Besondere* ("singularities") and *das Allgemeine* ("generalities") (quoted from Spitzer 1928:96). Schuchardt's creole studies adhere to this recommendation, though critics have at times accused him of losing sight of the general principles of language development. Bickerton (1979:1) refers to him as:

> A man who never married, who lived most of his life in the same provincial city, who suffered from chronic hypochondria, who wrote innumerable journal articles but who never even tried to pull his ideas together in a single volume.

It would appear that Bickerton's judgment is based on a very limited reading of Schuchardt's work and that Muysken and Smith's (1994:8) recognition of Schuchardt's contribution to creole studies as a systematic field of inquiry is closer to the mark.

Schuchardt had carried out a great deal of detailed work on language contact and mixing in a range of languages when, at the age of about forty, he began to publish on pidgins and creoles. By the end of his career he had published more than seven hundred pages on a large number of these languages. Of these:

- 72 percent were concerned with Portuguese creoles;
- 10 percent with English creoles;
- 6 percent with Spanish creoles; and
- 12 percent with others (French and Dutch creoles, and the Lingua Franca).

As was the case with other writers at the time, indigenous creoles (that is, those lexically based on local rather than European languages) receive no attention in his work.

His publications dealing with creoles cover the period from 1881 to 1914, of which the nine articles that constitute *Kreolische Studien* (1882–1888) are the most important.

Schuchardt was an armchair linguist *par excellence*. In just a few years he is known to have written requests for information and linguistic data to more than three hundred people living in places where contact languages were spoken. He received replies from more than one third of these and thus obtained a far greater range of linguistic data on such languages than had anyone previously.

A hitherto neglected but particularly interesting aspect of Schuchardt's correspondence is that his principal source of information about creoles came from missionaries. As Mühlhäusler (2001:136) has pointed out, about 60 percent of the language samples in his work can be traced to missionary correspondents. Missionaries in the nineteenth century often had a solid background in philology and entertained an extensive correspondence with scholars in Europe—as Wendt (2001) has put it, a kind of Internet. In the case of their dealings with Schuchardt, they provided not only data and intelligent answers to his questions but also independent observations. A key notion in Schuchardt's creolistic writings is that "Creoles are shaped by the 'foreigner talk' of the native speakers of the lexical source language" (Holm 1988–1989:3). This idea was suggested to him by the missionary-philologist Codrington (known for his work on Melanesian languages) who in a letter on Melanesian Pidgin English dated 1884 suggests: "I have not . . . found a case in which a native way of speaking has been followed: it is the way in which ignorant English people suppose natives most easily understand. . . ."

It is interesting that Schuchardt, whose initial agenda had been to use evidence from language mixing to falsify claims about family-tree relationships, at the end of his studies of creoles gives factors other than mixing greater importance, among them foreigner talk and universal factors (*der volapüksche Zug*).[9] Importantly, he distinguishes the early formative phase of creoles, where foreigner talk and linguistic universals dominate, from their later development, which involves borrowing and mixing, and he poses a question whose importance remains:

> Under what conditions could the African languages exert a pace-setting influence here? Not after the creole had already become the native language of the majority; nor yet when it was created as an emergency language. For the master and the slave it was simply a matter of mutual comprehension. The master stripped off from the European language everything that was peculiar to it, the slave suppressed everything that was distinctive. (Gilbert 1980:91; translation of Schuchardt 1914)

By differentiating between formation and later development, and by explicitly drawing attention to the changes a creole can undergo under the continued influence of a lexically related superstrate language, Schuchardt implicitly admits the possibility of both decreolization and postcreole continua:

> Go-between languages, auxiliary languages, languages of exigency are created everywhere and at all times. Most of them disappear again along with the condition that spawned them. Others endure and are stabilized without further substantial development. Some do this by edging out and replacing the languages which were once also used alongside them. It is in this manner, chiefly, that the Negro creole dialects have come into being, promoted by the rather great variety of languages within the slave population. (Gilbert's 1980:91 translation of Schuchardt 1914)

The preceding quotation implies that "creolization" (a word not yet coined) means "nativization of a contact language which hitherto lacked native speakers." This is essentially the definition subsequently adopted by Bloomfield (1933) and Hall (1962).

> . . . The Negro English that is most widely known is spoken in the southern United States . . . those variants which still show creole-like character are increasingly falling into disuse by being accommodated to the English of the whites by means of an intermediate speech variety. (undated ms., published posthumously in translation by Gilbert 1985)

This quotation introduces the idea of decreolization, another term not yet coined.

Apart from having initiated explanations that are still with us and having drawn attention to phenomena (such as continua) that are acknowledged as still being in need of adequate description and explanation today, the very fact that a linguist in the nineteenth century studied creoles as serious languages was a fairly revolutionary thing—far ahead of what other linguists, concerned with purity of languages, were willing to do. Readers should not ignore the significance of the disdain and neglect that mainstream historical and comparative linguists had of creoles and pidgins. A few examples of such linguists are Codrington, who spent ten years on Norfolk Island, where one of the most important contact languages—Pitcairn-Norfolk—was spoken by the Bounty-descendants; Sapir, who must have had ample opportunity for recording Chinook Jargon in his work on American Indian languages (cf. Mandelbaum, ed. 1985:167–250) but failed to do so; and the linguists of the Thilenius expedition to the German South Seas, who, in recording the languages of German Micronesia, employed Pidgin English as the language of elicitation but omitted any reference to this in their printed proceedings.

This leads to a general consideration of missed opportunities: when there was a great deal of actual pidgin and creole formation and use, very few linguists bothered to document this. In fact, in spite of all the questions by those who focused on creoles about creole formation, none of them bothered to get empirical evidence on the first phases. Around 1880 creolization occurred in the Torres Straits islands, and Pidgin German emerged in various German colonies. Ray (1907), who visited the Torres Straits in 1888 with the Cambridge Anthropological Expedition, presents only a sketchy account of a rudimentary pidgin spoken there but does not comment on creolization, whereas the German linguist Dempwolff, who documented the indigenous languages of New Guinea in great detail, left only a Tok Pisin translation of the Geneva Convention (Mühlhäusler, Dutton, & Romaine 2003:52–53), one unpublished sketch of Tok Pisin (in Mühlhäusler's possession), and no information whatsoever on Pidgin German. It might be that the fixation on written documents among philologists had something to do with this. Schuchardt's data are interesting in that he seems to privilege the languages that used printed documents (Saramaccan, Negerhollands, and so on); during travels to North Africa he did not bother to collect samples of spoken lingua franca.

Schuchardt is at times criticized for not having produced a coherent theory of creoles, but such criticism misses the point. Schuchardt was very much aware of the large number of singularities that played a role in the formation and the development of individual creoles and, by refusing to adopt a single explanation, anticipates recent thinking, influenced by chaos theory, that even small differences in causes can have large differences in outcomes. Schuchardt's contribution to creole studies was largely overlooked by his contemporaries, and it is interesting that Leo Spitzer's (1928) collection of Schuchardt articles omits his creolistic studies altogether. Further advances in the field were made largely independently of Schuchardt—for example, by Bloomfield. The following quotation from Bloomfield's (1933) book for American students of linguistics is noteworthy because it includes the earliest known attestations of the verbs "creolize" and "decreolize."

> When the jargon has become the only language of the subject group, it is a *creolized language*. The creolized language has the status of an inferior dialect of the masters' speech. It is subject to constant leveling-out and improvement in the direction of the latter. (. . .) With an improvement of social conditions, this leveling is accelerated; (. . .) It is a question whether during this process the dialect being *de-creolized* may not influence the speech of the community. (p. 474)

Bloomfield (p. 472) deplores the fact that these jargons have not been well recorded, but again he misses the opportunities to make his own recordings among Indian and African-American speakers in North America.

MID-TWENTIETH-CENTURY DEVELOPMENTS

Haiti is the one major variety of Creole French for which no study had appeared in the nineteenth century but three were published in the 1930s, around the time that Bloomfield's writings appeared. Of these, Sylvain's (1936) study was arguably among the best for any creole that had appeared up to that time. For each divergence from French, she looked for possible sources in both regional and dialectal varieties of French and in a range of African languages.[10] Her concluding sentence, suggesting a far more extreme substratist position than is evident from the rest of her book, has been quoted many times:

> We are in the presence of French poured into the mould of African grammar or, since languages are generally classified according to their grammatical parentage, of a Ewe language with French vocabulary. (p. 178, our translation)[11]

This takes up the idea of Adam (1883) cited earlier.

Like Bloomfield, Robert A. Hall was an American structuralist and a representative of the descriptive approach. His first publications in the creole field dealt with Tok Pisin, the topic having been suggested by the American military, who needed a course in this for the war effort in the southwest Pacific. Hall also produced grammatical sketches of Australian Pidgin English (1943a, b), Chinese Pidgin English (1944), and Taki-Taki (Sranan; 1948), and, after WWII, he turned to his specialist area of Romance linguistics, for which he produced several papers and a major grammar on Haitian Creole (1953). Hall's work undoubtedly helped to arouse interest in English creole varieties in the Caribbean, and a creole conference organized by Le Page and others in Jamaica in 1959 led to a slow but steadily increasing number of studies that have continued ever since. English creole studies rapidly began to catch up with French creole studies.

Hall's most influential publication could well be one of his shortest, a six-page article entitled "The Life Cycle of Pidgin Languages" (1962). In this, Hall argued that pidgins differ from other languages in that they come into being in particular circumstances and are liable to disappear once those circumstances change.[12] Only in a minority of cases do pidgins become "creolized" [his precise word] by being adopted as the first language of a speech community. Once so adopted, a creole can "reach the status of a 'normal' language, both by expansion of its structure and vocabulary . . ." (pp. 155–56). Four points are worth noting:

1. He extended the use of "pidgin" to all contact languages that lacked native speakers.
2. He effectively claimed that all creoles derive from earlier pidgins.
3. He also proposed definitions of "pidgin" and "creole" that were interdependent: A pidgin is a contact language that has not so far acquired native speakers; a creole is a former pidgin that has acquired native speakers.
4. Hall's ideas were not new, as can be seen by comparing them with quotations from Schuchardt (undated ms) and Bloomfield (1933). Nevertheless, they are frequently attributed to Hall.

Among the publications that followed the 1959 Creole Conference in Jamaica were Cassidy's *Jamaica Talk* (1961), Bailey's (1966) *Jamaican Creole Syntax,* and Cassidy and Le Page's (1967) *Dictionary of Jamaican English.* The last work was probably the first at-tempt at tracing the origin of the entire vocabulary of a creole, and the fact that it treated African and non-African words with equal care gave it great impact locally. That its title referred to "Jamaican English" rather than "Jamaican Creole" was also significant, implying that English and Creole English were not discrete entities, a matter subsequently made explicit by, for example, DeCamp (1971).

An equally significant publication, but for French creoles, was Chaudenson's (1974) *Le lexique du parler créole de la Réunion.* This included discussion of some 3,500 Réunion Creole words with forms, meanings, or functions not found in standard French. Chaudenson found origins in popular and dialectal varieties of French for all but 150 or so of these. Only five of the 150 were acknowledged as being African, the others having been brought to the island from India or Madagascar.[13] In this and subsequent publications, Chaudenson emphasized the importance of the range of regional and nonstandard varieties of French spoken by settlers and insisted that French creoles derived directly from these without passing through a pidginization stage. This established Chaudenson as the leading superstratist, but his ideas had little immediate impact on anglophone creolists, who rarely read anything not in English.

Another very influential book was Bickerton's (1975) *Dynamics of a Creole System.* It had long been recognized that, whereas French and Creole French coexist in many places as quite separate systems, in territories where Creole English is spoken and where English has official status, there is generally today no clear dividing line between the two. Bickerton studied the situation in Guyana and found what he termed, following DeCamp (1971), a "post-creole continuum." Bickerton assumed that there had originally been a single "Guyana Creole English" and that, over a couple of centuries, the Guyanese people had variably decreolized their speech according to their level of education, place of work, location of their home, and so on and that this decreolization had led to the continuum. He used "decreolization" to refer to a spectrum of interconnected lects, ranging from the acrolect (varieties close to standard English) through the mesolect to the basilect (varieties farthest from standard), which could not realistically be divided into two or more independent linguistic systems. An important finding was that each individual controlled quite a wide span, or two or more parts, of the continuum. This inspired an interesting article by Lee Drummond (1980), which has been quite influential within anthropology. Bickerton appeared to assume that what he found in Guyana and subsequently Hawaii was true of all creolophone societies in which the related standard European language has continuously had official status. Although broadly similar situations are found in some other territories where English is the official language such as Jamaica, no one has yet demonstrated convincingly that a comparable situation exists in any society where a Romance language has official status.

The major developments and trends in Creole Studies since 1975 are covered within the following sections.

The Superstratist Approach

Since the study of creole languages began, some people have drawn attention to these languages' overwhelming European component, whereas others have emphasized their non-European and usually African contribution. From the middle of the twentieth century, linguists specializing in the study of these languages and associated with these two tendencies have frequently been termed "superstratist" and "substratist," respectively. The metaphor is taken from geology and best suits the substratist position in that the overwhelmingly European lexicon is seen as the superficial outer crust (the superstrate) of languages that possess underlying African grammar and semantics (the substrate).[14]

Throughout the twentieth century, superstratists have been mainly French and South African. The French alone have been concerned to establish that Creole French is "genetically" French and not the offspring of mixed parentage. Chaudenson has long been the leading superstratist. His 1992 book, *Des îles, des hommes, des langues,*[15] sets out his ideas with regard to Creole French broadly as follows: the French (in slave plantation societies) spoke mainly regional and/or low status varieties of French.

The first slaves who were introduced into these territories acquired a reasonably good approximation of such French, but, as more and more slaves arrived, the newcomers tended increasingly to acquire their knowledge of this from slaves who had arrived before them, rather than from Europeans, and thus to learn an approximation of an approximation of French. Nevertheless, the Creole French that progressively emerged from this process was almost entirely composed of elements and rules that can be derived from French, the only exceptions being a small number of words adopted from the languages of slaves.

A notable feature of this approach is that it denies the existence of a previous pidginization stage; instead French Creole is held to derive directly from varieties of French. This contrasts with all other approaches that assume that creoles derive from earlier pidgins. In this context it is important to note that Chaudenson applies the word "pidgin" only to trading jargons such as Russenorsk or Chinese Pidgin English rather than to all contact languages that lack native speakers, which is its usual acceptation among anglophone creolists (following Hall 1962).

Chaudenson's approach derives primarily from his work on Réunion Creole and is fairly consistent with the nature and history of that language. But it has long been recognized that Réunion Creole is much closer to metropolitan French than is any other French creole, and the extension of his approach to Antillean varieties is not without problems. One problem is that samples of Pidgin French are attested in those islands in the seventeenth century (Bouton 1640; Chevillard 1659; Rochefort 1658) and, while these are attributed to Caribs, some of their features are also found in the earliest data from African slaves in those islands (Baker 1996:97). It is difficult to imagine how francophones with experience of communicating with Caribs in Pidgin French would not have used it in subsequently attempting to communicate with slaves newly arrived from Africa. Another problem is that Chaudenson's scenario envisages creole languages emerging only some time after blacks outnumber the white population; but a text containing many creole features is now known that purports to represent evidence given by slaves in Martinique in 1671, at a time when whites had only recently ceased to form the majority.[16]

The debate about the linguistic nature of Afrikaans affords another example. Efforts to demonstrate that Afrikaans is essentially the result of a mixture of Dutch dialects and hence a purely "white" language in the days of apartheid received praise from white South African linguists such as De Villiers (1960) and Raidt (1983) but were dismissed by scholars from other countries (surveyed by Roberge 1990). Valkhoff (1966) coined the term "diachronic purism" to describe the attempts to minimize the impact of Hottentot and Malayo-Portuguese, and it is only in post-apartheid days that the characterization of Afrikaans as a mixed language or a creole has become acceptable in South African linguistics.

The Substratist Approach

The aim of substratists has always been to identify African (or other non-European) words and grammatical features in creole languages. Up to the middle of the twentieth century they faced a difficult task, because reliable information on the origins of slaves was hard to find and because there were few adequate dictionaries and grammars of the relevant languages. Both these difficulties have largely disappeared in recent decades. Another difficulty for substratists has been their lack of a coherent theory of how creoles evolved. Their general assumption has been that non-Europeans were trying to maintain their languages and cultures but were overwhelmed by the circumstances. This led them to gradually adopt European words, but they often reinterpreted these in the light of semantic features of their own languages and also retained a good deal of "African" (or other non-European) grammar. Since the mid-1980s, Lefebvre has attempted to formalize the ideas of Adam (1883) and Sylvain (1936) in her relexification theory,[17] according to which Haitian Creole is essentially Fon relexified with French vocabulary.[18] There are several problems with this, including the following two.

1. Historically the occupation of Haiti by the French postdates their settlements in the Lesser Antilles (St. Kitts, Martinique, Guadeloupe, and so on) by several decades. It is known that many of the early settlers and slaves in Haiti came from the Lesser Antilles and that Haitian Creole shares many features with Lesser Antillean French Creole. Thus the preexisting Lesser Antillean Creole must have been one major input to Haitian Creole in addition to French and Fon.
2. Although Africans from the Slave Coast (which includes the area where Fon and several related Gbe languages such as Ewe are spoken) may briefly have accounted for about half the slave population of Haiti in the early decades of the eighteenth century (Singler 1993), they were not numerically dominant for a significant span of years and were ultimately outnumbered by speakers of Bantu languages. The theory also fails to account for what the non-Fon-speaking slaves were doing linguistically while the Fon were relexifying their language. Without significant numerical dominance of Fon-speakers, recourse has to be made to the assumption that the latter were in some way socially or culturally dominant, but there is little evidence to support this.

The Universalist Approach

In the heyday of structuralism—the 1920s to the mid-1950s—mainstream linguistic thinking was heavily influenced by behaviorism. Regarding creoles, an important claim of behaviorism was that prior knowledge affected the learning of any new knowledge, including linguistic knowledge. This view was compatible with both substratum and imperfect learning theories, and unsurprisingly these two theories dominated creole studies at the time (see, for instance, the first textbook on creolistics, written by the structuralist Hall [1966]). Structuralism also held that each language was a system *sui generis* and that the elements that made up grammatical systems were in principle not comparable. In actual fact, most structuralist creole scholars had been trained in comparative philology, and many of them managed to reconcile the seemingly unreconcilable paradigms by downplaying those properties of creoles that made them difficult to compare, though it is difficult to see how one can propose conventional family trees for creoles or any mixed language. Emphasis on the uniqueness of languages precluded one approach, however: that of universals. The reemergence of the universalist position coincides with the end of structuralist mainstream linguistics and the spread of Chomsky's ideas.

In the 1970s, a growing number of creolists came to the view that the "surface structure" of creole languages was much closer to their "deep structure" (in the terminology of the times) than was the case with the European languages to which they were related. Some saw this as a linguistically more relevant matter than the relative contributions of superstrate and substrate languages to creoles and called themselves "universalists." However, it was not until Bickerton (1981, 1984) that a theory of creolization based on this was proposed. It is interesting to note that Bickerton focused on substantive universals rather than on Chomskyan formal ones. His speculations concerned specific innate constructions—along the lines of: if your input lacks a nonpunctual marker, use a preposition—rather than the properties of Chomsky's "language acquisition device," which enabled L1 learners to acquire a perfect knowledge of the grammar of any language.

After carrying out research in Guyana, Bickerton had moved to Hawaii, begun studying its English Creole, and found a number of features that resembled those in Caribbean English Creoles. Given the absence of Africans in Hawaii, this required an explanation. This led to what Bickerton later called the Language Bioprogram Hypothesis. Limiting himself to creoles that arose in plantation settings—Hawaii imported labor to work on plantations, but the laborers were not Africans and came mainly from

East Asia and Portugal—he came up with the following scenario (here highly oversimplified).

Slaves or other workers were brought from diverse places speaking a range of mutually unintelligible languages to work on plantations. Instructions were given to them in a European language; therefore they acquired some European vocabulary with which they attempted to construct utterances based on the grammar of their own first languages. Bickerton refers to this as a "process of pidginization" but refuses to acknowledge that "a pidgin" with shared rules would have resulted. On the contrary, he assumes a Tower of Babel situation. Into this situation children were soon born. Bickerton assumes, adapting Chomsky's ideas, that humans have the innate ability to acquire language, that is, whatever language they are exposed to. Given the linguistic chaos he envisages, he believes that they would not be interested in acquiring the languages spoken natively by their parents because these languages would provide a means of communication with very few people. Instead, they would acquire words from the "process of pidginization" to which they were exposed, but, not finding this to conform to the norms of language that they were innately disposed to acquire, they would adapt it to fit those norms. In other words, they would apply the rules of the bioprogram to the vocabulary of the linguistic chaos and make an adequate language out of it. He claimed that this would have taken place within one or two generations. These children of the first generations would therefore have had grammars that conformed to the innate human capacity for language. After that, these children, and subsequent generations, might adapt their creole gradually toward the European language (insofar as they had access to the latter)—that is, decreolize their speech. Over time this would lead to the continuum situation he had earlier described in Guyana.

ASSUMPTIONS

The preceding approaches contain several assumptions:

1. They all assume that creole languages are not what those who participated in their origin and development wanted to speak.
2. Superstratists assume that non-Europeans sought to acquire the European language—often referred to as "the target language"—but failed (or only partly succeeded). While attributing some of the more typical features of creoles to language universals, Bickerton and other universalists nevertheless assume that, where a creole remained in contact with its related European language, creole speakers would still want to acquire the European language and

would tend to progressively decreolize their speech. (There is plenty of historical evidence to support this view with regard to Caribbean English Creoles, but curiously none so far as French Creoles of the same region are concerned.)

3. Many superstratists further assume that Europeans wanted non-Europeans to acquire their language and addressed the latter in that language (rather than in a pidginized or creolized variety of it). The underlying assumption is that slaves who best acquired the European language would gain access to a more tolerable mode of existence.[19] Although this is possible, we are not currently aware of any historical evidence to support it. Some further evidence against this assumption is to be found in the "world-wide features" identified by Baker and Huber (2001). These are widely attested in both Atlantic and Pacific pidgins and creoles, and their existence implies that anglophone sailors gradually constructed a repertoire of words and structures that they used when attempting to communicate with non-anglophones (rather than addressing them in their own varieties of English).

4. Substratists tend to assume that non-Europeans tried to retain their traditional languages but failed, being effectively forced to acquire the vocabulary of the language spoken by the European colonists. This view is based on the fact that some of the most salient non-European grammatical features of creoles have parallels in relevant African languages.

Doubts about all these assumptions have been expressed by Baker (1990, 2000), who claims that, in multilingual slave plantation societies, the initial need and (probably unconscious) aim of everyone (including the Europeans) was the development of a medium for interethnic communication. This raises the possibility that creole languages "are in essence what those who constructed them wanted them to be, rather than being the result of imperfect second-language learning" (Baker 2000:48). An interesting consequence of this possibility is that the selection of non-European grammatical features that became established in the creole might not depend simply on what proportion of the early slave population were native speakers of particular languages but could instead relate to what these diverse languages had to offer the evolving creole language. Two examples from Mauritian Creole (MC) may illustrate this. First, all MC verbs may be reduplicated but with either an attenuative or an augmentative interpretation according to stress placement and form—for example (where the acute accent marks stress) *márse* ("walk"), *marsmárse* ("go for a stroll [with no particular destination in mind]"), *márse márse* ("walk a long way/for a long time"). This system is undoubtedly inspired by Malagasy (see Baker 2003 for details). Second, MC has a diminutive prefix *ti,* which may potentially be attached to any noun and which differs from the adjective *píti* ("small") in form, function, distribution, and stress placement. This can be attributed to influence from Bantu languages, all of which have a diminutive noun class prefix (Baker 1994). Both these features may have been selected because of their vocabulary-building possibilities, potentially tripling the number of verbs and doubling the number of nouns without the need to acquire any new words, which would have been very useful in a language contact situation.

CONCLUSIONS

Although great progress has been made since the eighteenth century in providing detailed descriptions of the many creole languages spoken around the world, still no consensus exists as to how these languages originated and developed. The fundamental differences of approach that emerged in the second half of the nineteenth century are still very much in evidence. The main hope for resolving these differences lies in historical research. Since the 1970s, far more information has become available on the origins of slaves taken to particular territories in the Caribbean and the Indian Ocean, and there have been some significant but still limited successes in the search for previously unknown written records of these languages. Creolists have only just begun to consider the resources of missionary archives with promising results (Mühlhäusler 1999). Although the paucity of available records still allows linguists considerable leeway in their interpretation of such data, there is at least the general recognition that all theories must be able to account for whatever data come to light.

Creolist theory has been bugged by the tension between mainstream linguistics, with its emphasis on *la langue,* ideal speaker–hearer, and internal language, and the realization that explanations for creole genesis, development, and structures require detailed attention to *la parole,* performance, or external language.

In spite of the different theoretical approaches, there is near unanimity on one point—that all creole languages result from major restructuring. In other words, they are new languages that differ from the languages of the colonists in phonology, morphology, and syntax. They also differ in vocabulary, but this fact is generally seen by linguists as somewhat peripheral rather than central. By contrast, the examples of creolization of some influential authors such as Bailey and Maroldt (1977) and Hannerz (1987, 1996) seem to the present creolization to be broadly equivalent to what linguists misleadingly term "borrowing," that is, adopting words from other languages and cultures without any concomitant restructuring of the language that adopts the new term.

Notes

1. Original wording and spelling: *"Il y a parmy eux de certains negres et mulastres que se disent Portugais, parcequ'ils sont issus de quelques Portugais qui y ont habité autrefois; ces gens la, outre la langue du pays, parlent encore un certain jargon qui n'a que tres peu de ressemblance a la langue portugaise, et qu'on nomme langue creole, comme dans la mer Mediterranée la langue franque; . . ."*
2. Original wording and spelling: *"Dans le commancement que j'arrivay a Cacheau comme je ne sçavois point la langue portugaise je parlois ordinairement latin; mais hors les religieux, je trouvois peu de gens qui l'entendissent; il y avoit pourtant quelques officiers de la garnison que le parloient un peu; mais fort imparfaitement et le capitan maure [= Capitão Mor, governor] qui en sçavoit aussy quelque chose dit a ce sujet que je parlois le latin portugais, mais qu'eux parloient le latin creole; . . ."*
3. Original wording: *"Un jeune Négrillon Mozambique, nommé Favori, âgé de 13 ans, appartenant au Sr. Pierre Maheas, habitant à la Montagne Longue, a disparu depuis le 31 Janvier. Comme ce jeune noir s'est probablement égaré & qu'il n'entend pas la langue créole, il n'aura pu dire le nom de son maître ni retrouver sa maison."*
4. The earliest known is the brief grammatical sketch of Martiniquais by Goux (1842).
5. Compiled after Saussure's death in 1913 by a group of his former students.
6. Joseph notes, among other things, that "the Saussure brothers had grown up in the company of one of the most virulent theorists of Aryan superiority of the time, the linguist and Celticist Alphonse Pictet (1799–1875), an old family friend" (2000:48).
7. Original wording: *"La langue d'une nation civilisée implantée chez les indigènes des colonies devient bientôt méconnaissable. Elle peût, sans doute, être parlée correctement par un certain nombre d'individus instruits, mais c'est là un fait dont on aurait tort de tirer une conclusion générale . . . l'indigène qui parle une langue européenne ne reflète pas la mentalité de sa race, mais bien celle du milieu civilisé auquel il est oblige de se conformer par un effort d'attention et de mémoire. c'est la un phénomène d'imitation forcément très limité."*
8. Original wording: *"Nous nous bornerons donc à montrer ce que devient une langue de grande civilisation, telle que le français du xviie siècle, réduite à sa plus simple expression, en passant par les cerveaux et des gosiers noirs."*
9. One of Schuchardt's areas of interest was artificial languages, in particular the popular Volapük (from English "world speak"). What he appears to imply is that there are certain universal principles of language simplification that operate in language change, pidginization and creolization, and in the construction of artificial a posteriori languages.
10. The range was largely limited to the relatively small number of West African languages of which studies had been published by that time. Curiously, she failed to mention any Bantu languages.
11. Original wording: *"Nous sommes en présence d'un français coulé dans le moule de la syntaxe africain ou, comme on classe généralement les langues d'après leur parenté syntaxique, d'une langue éwé à vocabulaire francais."*
12. A brief history of the terms "pidgin" and "Pidgin English" would seem appropriate here. The first attestations of "Pidgin English" as the name of a language come from

the 1850s: "A-Tye will row you out, because she can speak *pigeon English*" (Anon. 1859:26); and "The auctioneer talked *pigeon-English* to them" (Smith 1859:29; these examples come from Macau and Hong Kong, respectively). The language had earlier been known as Canton English (among other names). The word "pidgin" (in a variety of spellings including pijin, pidgeon, and pigeon) is abundantly recorded in that language in the sense of "business" (its etymon) from fifty years earlier—for example, "This Jos take care fire pidgeon" (Morrison 1807; "This god is responsible for the business of fire"). Thus "Pidgin English" in the 1850s meant "business English."

During the nineteenth century, many contact varieties of English emerged in Australia and the Pacific area. From the 1880s, these also came to be termed "Pidgin English." As these gradually attracted more attention than did the older variety spoken in the Canton area, the latter began to be termed *Chinese* Pidgin English. This led to the re-interpretation of *pidgin* as "imperfect variety of" (rather than "business")—and this in turn led to the modern situation with the word being applied to other "imperfect" languages (resulting from contact situations)—for instance, "on the northern frontiers [of China] there is also *pidgin Russia*" (Ready 1903) and "A big burly planter [in Fiji] speaks *pidgin Hindustani* with a broad Scotch accent" (Burton 1910: 91).

13. A considerably larger number of African (mainly Bantu) words in Réunionnais was identified by Baker (1982). The very low figure reported by Chaudenson is partly due to his having largely limited his search for such items to Swahili, the only East African Bantu language for which a dictionary giving glosses in French then existed. (Swahili is unlikely to have been the first language of many slaves in Reunion.) Another reason is that he failed to appreciate that a substantial proportion of the lexicon of Malagasy consists of words of Bantu origin; that is, some of his "Malagasy" words are likely to have become established in Réunionnais by speakers of Bantu languages.

14. As indicated earlier, there are creoles that draw the bulk of their lexicon from Arabic or other non-European languages and that have an Asian or Oceanic substrate, but, for the sake of brevity and because most readers will be unfamiliar with them, there will be no mention of these in the following paragraphs.

15. An English translation of this, edited by Mufwene, was published in 2001 under the title *Creolization of Language and Culture*.

16. Two points need to be made here: (1) The existence of this text was not generally known at the time of the publication of Chaudenson (1992); (2) the text itself is a copy made in 1719, and it is thus not impossible that it might have been partially "modernized," reflecting some changes that had taken place in the language since the events of 1671 were first recorded; see Baker (2000:44, note 5).

17. Not to be confused with an earlier relexification theory according to which all pidgins and creoles stem from an original Pidgin Portuguese, which was relexified by the language of the colonial power (Dutch, English, French, and so on); cf. Thompson 1961.

18. Sylvain (1936) considered the grammatical source of Haitian Creole to be Ewe, a language related to Fon.

19. A seemingly equally plausible alternative possibility is that slave owners may not have wanted their slaves to acquire the white language as such; that is, they may have found it very useful to be able to converse with other whites in the European language without being (fully) understood by field slaves. In this connection, it is worth noting that the use of Dutch was not permitted among the indigenous inhabitants of the Dutch East Indies (Indonesia) until the 1860s. Somewhat similarly the use of *Herrensprache* ("master language") German was discouraged among the local population in German New Guinea and in other German colonies, especially where the use of a lingua franca was adopted by the colonial administration.

References

Adam, L. 1883. *Les Idiomes négro-aryen et maléo-aryen: Essai d'hybridologie linguistique.* Paris.

Anchieta, J. de. 1595. *Arte de gramatica de lingoa mais usada na costa do Brazil.*

Anon. 1859. A piece of China, *All the Year Round* 1:16–20, 37–40.

Bailey, B. L. 1966. *Jamaican creole syntax.* Cambridge: Cambridge University Press.

Bailey, C.-J. N., and K. Maroldt. 1977. The French lineage of English. In *Languages en contac–Pidgins—Creoles.* J. Meisel, ed. Tübingen: Gunter Narr, pp. 21–53.

Baissac, C. 1880. *Etude sur le patois créole mauricien.* Nancy.

Baker, P. 1982. The contribution of non-Francophone immigrants to the lexicon of Mauritian Creole. Ph.D. dissertation, SOAS, University of London.

———— 1990. Off target? *Journal of Pidgin and Creole Languages* 5:107–119.

———— 1994. Creativity in creole genesis. In *Creolization and language change.* D. Adone and I. Plag, eds. Tübingen: Niemeyer, pp. 65–84.

———— 1996. Pidginization, creolization, and français approximatif, *Journal of Pidgin and Creole Languages* 11:95–120.

———— 2000. Theories of creolization and the degree and nature of restructuring. In *Degrees of restructuring in creole languages.* I. Neumann-Holzschuh and E. W. Schneider, eds. Amsterdam: Benjamins, pp. 41–63.

———— 2003. Reduplication in Mauritian Creole with notes on reduplication in Reunion Creole. In *Twice as meaningful.* S. Kouwenberg, ed. London: Battlebridge, pp. 211–218.

Baker, P., and M. Huber. 2001. Atlantic, Pacific and world-wide features in English-lexicon contact languages, *English World-Wide* 22:157–208.

Bickerton, D. 1975. *Dynamics of a creole system.* Cambridge: Cambridge University Press.

———— 1979. Introduction. In *Hugo Schuchardt: The ethnography of variation. Selected writings on Pidgins and Creoles.* T. L. Markey. Ann Arbor, MI: Karoma.

———— 1981. *Roots of language.* Ann Arbor, MI: Karoma.

———— 1984. The language bioprogram hypothesis, *Behavioral and Brain Sciences* 7:173–221.

Bloomfield, L. 1933. *Language.* London: George Allen & Unwin.

Bouton, J. 1640. *Relation de l'establissement des françois depuis l'an de 1635 en l'isle de Martinique.* Paris: Cramoisy.

Burton, J. W. 1910. *Fiji of today.* London: Charles H. Kelly.

Cassidy, F. 1961. *Jamaica Talk.* London: Macmillan.

Cassidy, F., and R. B. Le Page. 1967. *Dictionary of Jamaican English.* Oxford: Oxford University Press.

Chaudenson, R. 1974. *Le lexique du parler créole de la Réunion.* Paris: Champion.

———— 1992. *Des îles, des hommes, des langues.* Paris: L'Harmattan.

Chevillard, A. 1659. *Les desseins de son Excellence de Richelieu dans l'Amérique.* Rennes.

Codrington, R. H. 1884. Letter written in Oxford and dated 10 January 1884. Item 01651, Schuchardt Archives, Graz, Austria.

Coelho, F. A. 1880–1886. Os dialectos ou neo-latinos na Africa, Asia e America, *Boletim da Sociedade de Geographia de Lisboa* 2:129–96, 3:451–78, 6:705–755.

Cultru, P., ed. 1913. *Premier voyage du Sieur de la Courbe fait a la coste d'afrique en 1685.* Paris: Société de l'histoire des colonies françaises.

DeCamp, D. 1971. Towards a generative analysis of a post-creole speech continuum. In *Pidginization and creolization of languages.* D. Hymes, ed. Cambridge: Cambridge University Press, pp. 349–370.

De Villiers, M. 1960. *Nederlands en Afrikaans.* Cape Town: Nasou.

Drummond, L. 1980. The cultural continuum: A theory of intersystems, *Man* 15:352–374.

Figueira, L. 1621. *Arte da lingua brasilica.* Lisbon: Manoel da Silva.

Gilbert, G., ed./trans. 1980. *Pidgin and creole languages: Selected essays by Hugo Schuchardt.* London: Cambridge University Press.

—— 1985. Hugo Schuchardt and the Atlantic creoles: A newly discovered manuscript "On the Negro English of West Africa," *American Speech* 60:31–63.

Goux, M. 1842. *Catéchisme en langue créole, précédé d'un essai de grammaire sur l'idiome usité dans les colonies françaises.* Paris: Vrayet de Surcy et Cie.

Greenfield, W. 1830. *A defence of the Surinam Negro-English version of the New Testament.* London.

Hall, R. A. 1943a. *Melanesian Pidgin English: Grammar, texts, vocabulary.* Baltimore, MD: Ams.

—— 1943b. Notes on Australian Pidgin English, *Language* 19:203–207.

—— 1944. Chinese Pidgin English grammar and texts, *Journal of the American Oriental Society* 64:95–113.

—— 1948. The linguistic structure of Taki Taki, *Language* 24:92–116.

—— 1953. *Haitian Creole: grammar, texts, vocabulary.* Philadelphia: American Folklore Society.

—— 1962. The life cycle of pidgin languages, *Lingua* 11:151–156.

—— 1966. *Pidgin and creole linguistics.* Ithaca, NY: Cornell University Press.

Hannerz, U. 1987. The world in creolisation, *Africa* 57:5460–59.

—— 1996. *Transnational connections.* London: Routledge.

Holm, J. 1988–1989. *Pidgins and creoles. Vol. 1: Theory and structure. Vol. 2: Reference survey.* Cambridge: Cambridge University Press.

Jespersen, O. 1922. *Language, its nature, development and origin.* London: George Allen & Unwin.

Joseph, J. E. 2000. Language and "psychological race": Leopold de Saussure on French in Indochina, *Language and Communication* 20:29–53.

Jourdain, E. 1956. *Du Français au parlers creoles.* Paris: Klincksieck.

Lefebvre, C. 1999. *Creole genesis and the acquisition of grammar: The case of Haitian Creole.* Cambridge: Cambridge University Press.

Le Page, R. B., ed. 1961. *Proceedings of the conference in Creole language studies.* London: Macmillan.

Magens. 1770. *Grammatica over det Creolske sprog.* Copenhagen: Gerhard Giese Salikath.

Mandelbaum, D. G. 1985. *Edward Sapir: Selected writings in language, culture, personality.* Berkeley and Los Angles, CA: University of California Press.

Morrison, R. 1807. Journal. Unpublished journal in Council for World Mission Archives, South China—Journals, Box 1.

Mufwene, S. S. 2001. *Creolization of language and culture.* New York: Routledge. (revision and translation of Chaudenson 1992).

Mühlhäusler, P. 1999. Exploring the missionary position, *Journal of Pidgin and Creole Languages* 14:339–346.

—— 2001. Die Rolle der Missionare in Hugo Schuchardts kreolischen Studien. In *Sammeln, Vernetzen, Auswerten. Missionare und ihr Beitrag zum Wandel europäischer Weltsicht.* R. Wendt, ed. Tübingen: Narr, pp. 131–144.

Mühlhäusler, P., T. E. Dutton, and S. Romaine. 2003. *Tok Pisin texts.* Amsterdam: Benjamins.

Muysken, P., & N. Smith. 1994. The study of pidgin and creole languages. In *Pidgins and creole. An introduction.* J. Arends, P. Muysken, and N. Smith, eds. Amsterdam: Benjamins, pp. 3–14.

Raidt, E. H. 1983. *Einführung in die Geschichte und Struktur des Afrikaans.* Darmstadt: Wisssenschaftliche Buchgesellschaft.

Ray, S. H. 1907. The jargon English of the Torres Straits, *Reports of the Cambridge Anthropological Expedition to Torres Straits*. Cambridge: Cambridge University Press, pp. 251–254.

Ready, O. G. 1903. *Life and sport in China*. London: Chapman & Hall.

Reinecke, J. 1986. A defence of the Surinam Negro–English version of the New Testament by W. Greenfield, *Journal of Pidgin and Creole Languages* 1:255–266.

Roberge, P. T. 1990. The ideological profile of Afrikaans historical linguistics. *Ideologies of language*. J. Joseph and T. Taylor, eds. London: Routledge, pp. 131–149.

Rochefort, C. de. 1658. *Histoire naturelle et morale des isles Antilles de l'Amérique*. Rotterdam: Arnould Leers.

Russell, T. 1868. *The etymology of Jamaica grammar, by a young gentleman*. Kingston.

Saint-Quentin, A. de. 1872. Etude sur la grammaire créole. In *Introduction à l'histoire de Cayenne (. . .)*. Antibes: pp. 101–169.

Saussure, F. de. 1916. *Cours de linguistique générale*. Paris: Payot.

Saussure, L. de. 1899. *Psychologie de la colonisation française*. Paris: Felix Alcan.

Schuchardt, H. 1882–1888. Kreolische Studien I–VIII, *Sitzungsberichte der kaiserlichen Akademie der Wissenschaften zu Wien*.

—— 1914. *Die Sprache der Saramakkaneger in Surinam*. Amsterdam: Johannes Müller.

—— [no date]. Über das Negerenglische von Westafrika. Unpublished ms, Schuchardt collection, Graz.

Singler, J. V. 1993. African influence upon Afro-American language varieties: A consideration of sociohistorical factors. In *Africanisms in Afro-American language varieties*. S. S. Mufwene, ed. Athens, GA: University of Georgia Press, pp. 235–253.

Smith, A. 1859. *To China and back*. London: the Author.

Spitzer, L., ed. 1928. *Hugo Schuchardt-Brevier*. 2nd ed. Halle: Max Niemeyer.

Stein, P. 1982. *Connaissance et emploi des langues à l'Ile Maurice*. Hamburg: Buske.

Sylvain, S. 1936. *Le créole haïtien: Morphologie et syntaxe*. Wetteren: de Meester.

Thomas, J. J. 1869. *The theory and practice of Creole grammar*. Port-of-Spain.

Thompson, R. W. 1961. A note on some possible affinities between the Creole dialects of the Old World and those of the New. In *Proceedings of the conference in Creole language studies*. R. B. Le Page, ed. London: Macmillan, pp. 107–113.

Valkoff, M. F. 1966. *Studies in Portuguese and Creole*. Johannesburg: Witwatersrand University Press.

Van Dyk, P. ca. 1765. *Nieuwe en nooit bevoorens geziene onderwyzinge in het Bastert Engels, of Neeger Engels*. Amsterdam.

Van Name, A. 1869–1870. Contributions to creole grammar, *Transactions of the American Philological Association* 1:123–167.

Wendt, R., ed. 2001. *Sammeln, Vernetzen, Auswerten. Missionare und ihr Beitrag zum Wandel europäischer Weltsicht*. Tübingen: Gunter Narr.

Woll, D. 1997. Esp. *criollo* y port. *crioulo*: volviendo a la cuestión del origen y la historia de las dos palabras. *Latinas et Romanitas. Festschrift für Hans Dieter Bork zum 65. Geburtstag*. A. Bollée and J. Kramer, eds. Bonn: Romanistischer Verlag, pp. 517–535.

6 From Miscegenation to Creole Identity: Portuguese Colonialism, Brazil, Cape Verde

Miguel Vale de Almeida

PORTUGUESE COLONIALISM AND CREOLIZATION

The term "creole" has three main usages in contemporary Portuguese-speaking contexts.[1] In Portugal it refers to the Cape Verdean language spoken by the large immigrant community from that country, whereas in Cape Verde itself it has come to mean also Cape Verdean identity and culture. In Brazil it carries the negative connotation of lower-class "black" identification and does not have the Spanish-American meaning of either *mestizo* or that of people of European ancestry born in the Americas. In several African contexts it refers to the historical roots of urban coastal social groups that mediated between Portuguese administrators or merchants and the hinterland populations.

The semiperipheral and subaltern nature of Portuguese colonialism allowed for the creation of many creolized communities, languages, and cultural expressions. The concept itself, however, has never become central in ideological definitions of Portuguese colonialism. Rather, *miscigenação* and *mestiçagem* were used and have been incorporated in discourses of national identity both in Brazil and Cape Verde although not in continental African excolonies. This was particularly true during the late colonial period in the twentieth century, when the dictatorial regime used Brazilian sociologist Gilberto Freyre's interpretation of Brazilian identity and Portuguese expansion as having been a hybridizing humanist endeavor, in order to justify the occupation of African territories at the same time that national liberation movements were starting their struggle in mainland African colonies.

Portuguese expansion started in the fifteenth century in the Atlantic, both with the discovery of the North-Atlantic archipelagos of Madeira and the Azores, and with the establishment of trading posts along the western coast of Africa. The first instances of "creolization" date from this period, mainly with the case of *lançados*—people who were left among indigenous populations in order to learn their languages and customs. Trading posts were, of course, ideal social settings for the emergence of pidgin linguistic forms of communication for trade.

The history of Portuguese expansion and colonialism can be roughly divided into three distinct periods, marked by the importance of different geographical settings, trade routes, and raw materials: India, Brazil, and Africa, roughly corresponding to the fifteenth and sixteenth, seventeenth and eighteenth, and nineteenth and twentieth centuries. Initially, expansion was based on the search for the control of the commercial routes of "Oriental" spices. Along the coast of Africa trading and slaving posts were established in fortresses that were cut out from the local populations but still allowed for a degree of pidginization and creolization between the Portuguese and local intermediaries between the coast and the hinterland.

When the maritime route to India was discovered in the late fifteenth century, the Portuguese crown's purpose was not to occupy territory but rather to achieve dominance over sea routes. The experience of coastal trading posts or *feitorias* in Africa was replicated in India; nevertheless a territorial base was established in Goa as of the early sixteenth century. Instances of miscegenation occurred mainly in the Atlantic islands of Cape Verde and São Tomé, off the Atlantic coast of Africa, settled by African slaves and a minority of Portuguese settlers. In India, there are indications that a policy of mixed marriages between Portuguese males and local females was promoted, but this may be largely the result of myth making by both Portuguese colonial ideology and the small group of Goa's "Luso-descendants."

Portuguese expansion and early colonialism were mainly a state enterprise. Without a trading middle class (as opposed to Venice, Holland, or Genoa), the Portuguese crown rented out privileges in trade, and there was a need for considerable foreign capital investment; the Portuguese can be said to have been, initially, transporters on behalf of others. A subaltern form of colonialism was to be the outcome of this situation later in history, as both capital and demographic scarceness continued to characterize the Portuguese social and economic landscape. Also, and from an ideological point of view, early Portuguese "colonialism" or, more accurately, expansion, was strongly based on the notion of a crusade for "Christianization" (and, in the nineteenth and twentieth centuries, for "Civilization").

The "First Portuguese Empire," in Asia (mainly in Goa, India, but also in Malacca and Macau in southeast Asia and China) was stable from the sixteenth century until 1630, when Dutch and English encroachment increased. In 1665 the eastern empire was reduced to Goa, Macau, and Timor (in Indonesia). Concerns with social classification based on ancestry, geography, and what was to become "race" were already present as in the case of Portuguese India, where the local population was divided into several categories along a scale of blood purity, such as "white Portuguese born in India," *castiços* (those born from a European father and an Indian "white" mother), *mestiços* (who were more mulatto in appearance), and "pure" Indians.

The settlement of Brazil (officially "discovered" in 1500) also followed the model of settlement on the coast, with feudal rights granted to captain-generals. Jesuit resistance to enslavement of the local indigenous population contributed to the economically motivated importation of African slaves—which increased in the second half of the sixteenth century—as labor for the sugar plantations. This economic activity was paramount in the sixteenth and seventeenth centuries and compensated for the decline of Oriental commerce. Brazil became the first real colony of settlement and that trend increased with the discovery of gold in 1700. Brazil was the core of Portuguese empire from the eighteenth century until independence in 1822. The whites and those with white ancestry made up for the dominant class, mainly as large estate owners and, later, as merchants and traders. A distinction was made, however, between those born in Brazil and those born in Portugal, called *reinóis* (from the Realm) or *marinheiros* (sailors). As for the slave population, it came from diverse ethnic backgrounds in Africa, but the relevant distinction was established between those born or raised in Brazil and in the plantations (*crioulos*, from the Portuguese verb *criar*, to raise or to create, and the noun *cria*, human infant or animal cub) and those recently arrived (*boçais*). Another category, that of *ladinos* (roughly meaning "smart" or "astute") were those with some linguistic proficiency in Portuguese. With the increase in manumission, slavery in the domestic and household sphere and in the number of *mulatos* (mulattoes) born of white male-black female intercourse, social and "racial" classifications became more intricate, eventually leading to the Brazilian system of classification based more on phenotype/color than on ancestry.

As a result of Napoleon's invasion of Portugal in the early nineteenth century, the Portuguese royal family fled to Brazil and established the Portuguese capital in Rio de Janeiro. Brazil was raised to the status of a realm and was to become independent owing to the pressure of the local merchant and slave-owning classes and with the support of England as a major trade partner. The heir to the Portuguese throne stayed behind in Brazil when the king returned to Portugal, and Brazil became independent in 1822 as a monarchy, with Prince Pedro as emperor. In 1888 slavery was abolished, and in 1889 Brazil became a Republic.

The total abolition of slavery in what remained of the Portuguese empire took place in the 1880s (abolition in Portugal had been declared in 1869). Until the decade of 1850 colonial economy was based on slavery, with the transit of slaves from Guinea to Cape Verde and from Angola to São Tomé and Príncipe, and Brazil. Cape Verde was a main point of sojourn for the "adaptation" of slaves before further exportation. Angola, the main colony in Africa, had become specialized in supplying slaves for Brazil between the seventeenth and eighteenth centuries and was actually more of a colony of Brazil than of Portugal. Local white settlement was scarce, although some forms of intermediary creolized groups did emerge in the coastal towns.

The turn to Africa—and the start of the "Third Portuguese Empire"—was a consequence of the independence of Brazil. Portuguese expeditions in the 1840–1850s tried to map the African hinterland in order to claim sovereignty over large tracts of Southern Africa between Angola on the Atlantic coast and Mozambique on the Indian Ocean coast. In the aftermath of the Berlin Conference (started in 1884) that carved up Africa for European colonialism, England issued an ultimatum to Portugal in 1890, stating that Portuguese claims had to be based on effective occupation of the claimed territories. The last years of Monarchy in Portugal and those of the First Republic (1910–1926) were marked by the effort to obtain actual control over the claimed African possessions. But only with the dictatorial regime that started in 1926 (and which was to last in different shapes until 1974) did Portuguese colonialism in its modern sense start. In 1930, when the totalitarian regime was being established, the Colonial Act was issued, proclaiming the need to bring indigenous peoples into western civilization and the Portuguese nation. Assimilation was proclaimed as the main objective, except for the colonies of Cape Verde, India, and Macau. Cape Verde was seen as an extension of Portugal, and India and Macau as having their own forms of "civilized" peoples, whereas in mainland Africa a real—if not always legal—distinction was made between white settlers, *assimilado* in-betweens and the indigenous, "uncivilized" population. In 1953 a new law renamed the Colonies as

Provinces, and in 1961 the laws that defined the status of indigenous peoples as non-Portuguese were abolished. This was the result of international pressure for decolonization in the post-WWII period.

The system of coastal fortresses and *feitorias* based on agreements with local African polities had been altered by the increasing economic importance of the slave trade, mainly to Brazil. Besides this country, Portuguese settlement as such occurred only in the islands of Madeira and the Azores (with Portuguese settlers), and in Cape Verde and São Tomé e Príncipe with both Portuguese settlers and African slaves. These two African archipelagos witnessed the emergence of populations of mixed origins, and Creole languages developed fully. Efforts to keep an empire in Africa had a strong ideological motivation, based on Portuguese self-representations of national identity as the pioneering country in the "discovery" and Christianization of the heathen world. This trend was to be accentuated by the fact that Portuguese modern colonialism in Africa was actually the enterprise of a dictatorial and ultraconservative regime. Until the late 1950s, miscegenation was seen as a negative occurrence, but after Gilberto Freyre's influence, the regime radically changed its rhetoric to one of appraisal of miscegenation and assimilation within a "pluri-continental and pluri-racial nation."

But miscegenation and the emergence of forms of mixed culture occurred mostly as side effects, not as the result of a policy. Portugal had a small population throughout its imperial and colonial history; it lacked an entrepreneurial class; the crown rented out trade routes, lands, and labor to foreign interests, when it did not promote semifeudal forms of occupation. But the religious motivations (conversion of the heathen), the tradition of coastal *feitorias*, miscegenation between unequal gender and racial categories (between white men and African women), forms of manumission of the children of these unions, and the emergence of a color continuum of phenotypical scaling rather than what was to be the USA one-drop rule certainly were factors that allowed for the emergence of intermediary groups in phenotype, language, and culture.

In the Asian locations, commercial activities and religious conversion allowed for the formation of a small group of Eurasians in Macau and Malacca, as well as for a small elite of Christianized Portuguese descendants in India. In both Malacca and Macau, creole languages emerged. In the cases of Angola and Mozambique, creole languages did not emerge, and a policy of coastal shipping of slaves—in the Angolan case largely by Portuguese Brazilians—did not create economic and social conditions for the emergence of significant intermediary groups. Some coastal towns in Angola, however, did see the emergence of something of the sort.

Dias (1984) uses the term *crioulo* to refer to descendants of Europeans born locally (both whites and *mestiço*) or detribalized Africans (*civilizado* or *assimilado*). Although her nomenclature is tentative she claims that their behavior was similar to that of other African elites as identified by Curtin (1972) and Cohen (1981) for Sierra Leone, Ghana, and Senegal. The word, however, was seldom used in nineteenth-century Angola and referred mostly to slaves born in the colony. In another paper, Dias (2002) expands on the population of Mbaka as descendants of mixed marriages between Portuguese men and African women, who had become traders between the coast and the hinterland and who had adopted diacritic signs of Portugueseness in dress and language.

What happened in the African colonies of Angola and Mozambique can, then, hardly be described as creolization. As we shall see later, twentieth-century attempts at promoting assimilation were rhetorical. In Guinea Bissau a creole language did emerge, but as an interethnic communication language side by side with indigenous ones and related to the Cape Verdeans' role as surrogate administrators of Portuguese interests in Guinea Bissau. On the other side of the globe, creole languages and mixed identities were limited to the Christians of Goa, the Kristang (that is, "Christians") of Malacca, and the Eurasians of Macau, all populations that have dwindled considerably to this day.

From a linguistic point of view, forms of Portuguese-based creoles expanded with the slave trade. D. Pereira (2002) provides us with a list of creole languages of Portuguese extraction: in Africa, the Upper Guinea creoles include languages spoken in Cape Verde, Guinea-Bissau, and Casamanse (in Senegal), and those of the Gulf of Guinea include São Tomé and Príncipe, and Anobon. Indo-Portuguese creoles are those of India proper (Diu, Daman, Bombay, Chaul, Korlai, Mangalor, Cananor, Tellicherry, Mahé, Cochin, Vaipin, Qilom, and the Coasts of Coromandel and Bengal), as well as the creoles of Sri Lanka (Trincomalee and Batticaloa, Mannar, and the Puttallam area). As for the specific case of Goa—the location of a longer and more intense Portuguese settlement in Asia—she says that it is not clear whether a creole was formed. In Asia, Portuguese-based creoles appeared in Malaysia (Malacca, Kuala Lumpur and Singapore) and in some islands of Indonesia (Java, Flores, Ternate, Ambon, Macassar, and Timor), known as Malayo-Portuguese. Sino-Portuguese creoles could be found in Macau and Hong Kong. In the Americas, Papiamento—the Iberian-based creole of Curaçao, Aruba, and Bonaire—can be included in the list, as well as Saramacan (Surinam), because of strong Portuguese lexical bases, although they are sometimes classified as respectively Spanish and English-based. Some authors talk of a semi-creole in Brazil and of some Afro-Brazilian forms that could correspond to an advanced phase of decreolization. Note that the colony of settlement *par excellence*, Brazil, did not develop a creole form but rather what is (linguistically but certainly also politically) considered as a "variation" of Portuguese. Access to the Portuguese language model and the role of the elites in building the nation-state may be explanatory factors here.

This leaves us with the two instances of, simultaneously, the development of creole languages as mother tongues, the emergence of creole social landscapes, and "racial" miscegenation: the archipelagos of São Tomé and Príncipe, and Cape Verde. The latter case is what comes to the mind of any Portuguese when the word *crioulo* is pronounced. It refers foremost to the language. For Cape Verdeans themselves it has increasingly become a metaphor for their own self-description as a group and national culture, a case that will be analyzed further on.

To assess the importance of creolization today, one needs, therefore, to contextualize creoles and creolization within the historical, cultural and political-economic history of expansion, colonialism and postcolonialism. Of particular importance is the period of late colonialism in the twentieth century. That is because the period corresponds to one of mutual constitution of postcolonial identities in the ex-colonies and the reinforcement of conservative discourses of national identity in Portugal. The ways in which elite anthropological, colonial, and emancipatory discourses were intertwined, first in Brazil, then in late-colonial Portugal and in Cape Verde, around the concepts of miscegenation, Luso-Tropicalism, and, marginally, creoleness are a case of the colonial production of hybrids that challenges naïve assumptions about creolization.

MISCEGENATION AND LUSO-TROPICALISM FROM BRAZIL TO THE PORTUGUESE EMPIRE

One of the classical locations for discussions of hybridism and *miscigenação* or *mestiçagem* (and its relation with the idea of nation) is Latin America, especially the national contexts with a strong presence of descendants of Africans. Peter Wade (1993) has conducted one of the best analyses of the interaction between discrimination and *mestiçagem* (*mestizaje* in the Hispanic case). This interaction between patterns of discrimination and tolerance happens within the identity project of the national elites, who set forth the notion of an essentially mixed—*mestiza*—nation. Although it is generally accepted that "races" are social constructions or categorical identifications based on a discourse on the physical aspect and ancestry, Wade notes, however, that that which passes for physical difference and ancestry is not at all obvious. Apparently there is a "natural fact" of phenotypic variation on the basis of which culture constructs categorical identifications. But the act of defining a nature/culture relation mediated by this productionistic logic (Haraway 1989:13) obscures the fact that there is no such thing as a prediscursive and universal encounter with "nature" and, therefore, with phenotypic variation (Wade 1993:3). Therefore, racial categories are doubly processual: first as a result of the variable perceptions of the nature/culture division that they mediate; second, as a result of the play between claims and attributions of identity in the context of relations of power (1993:4).

The emergence of nationalism in Latin America did not involve the national incorporation of the lower classes in the European fashion. It was mediated by creole elites (in the Hispanic sense: Europeans born in the Americas) who had been excluded from political control during the colonial period (Anderson 1983:50). One central problem was the contradiction between the mixed nature of the population and the "white" connotations of progress and modernity. The problem was "solved" with a compromise: to celebrate *mestizaje* as the core of Latin American originality. However, blacks and Indians were romanticized as part of a glorious past, and it was foreseen that they would be integrated in the future—in a process that would involve further racial mixing, preferably with whitening consequences (Wade 1993:10). This compromise is obvious in the way racial theories of the time were received. They tended to classify blacks and Indians as inferior, and hybrids were thought to be negatively influenced by these "races." But the elites tended to downplay the negative implications by downplaying biological determinism, emphasizing instead environmental and educational factors (as Gilberto Freyre was to do in Brazil, for instance, with the use of neo-Lamarckianism). However, underneath the democratic discourse on *mestiçagem* and *mestizaje*, lay a hierarchical discourse on whitening.

In Brazil, according to Seyferth (1991), both those who supported whitening and those who were against African or Asian immigration (as well as those who privileged European immigration in the post-abolition of slavery period) believed that the Brazilian people or "race" needed yet to be formed through a melting pot process that would result in homogeneity. But they all imagined European immigrants as representatives of superior "races" destined to whiten a *mestiço* and black population. The belief that Brazil has no racial question because there is no prejudice—a common feature in both everyday and social science theories—has paradoxically served to legitimize the emphasis in the miscegenation of "races" seen as unequal—thus presupposing the "triumph" (genetic but also civilizational) of the white "race."

"AN UNFORTUNATE EXPERIMENT
OF THE PORTUGUESE"

I would like to focus on the Portuguese case, while keeping in mind the Brazilian one, since Brazil has been an object of transfer and projection in the construction of Portuguese national representations. Once Brazil became independent, the focus of Portuguese governments shifted direction toward the African colonies. The new colonization of Africa was slow and did not amount to much in the way of practical results (see Alexandre & Dias 1998). But the notion of Empire and the national utopia of building "New Brazils" in Africa after the loss of Brazil, were part of the boosting and maintenance of national pride. Nevertheless, academic and elite discourses, such as anthropology, focused mainly on the definition of Portugal and the Portuguese. A consistent and lasting colonial anthropology was practically nonexistent. This does not, however, preclude that self-representations were also based on representations of the colonial Other, even if there was no miscegenation with those Others. Miscegenation had been useful in the construction of Brazil as a neo-European nation in the Americas but would be contradictory with a notion of Empire in Africa.

We can identify three "periods" in the debates on hybridism and miscegenation. Anthropologists Eusébio Tamagnini and Mendes Correia can personify the first period—which was one of concern with the racial definition of the Portuguese and of opposition to miscegenation. A second, more culturalist period, is personified by Jorge Dias and the influence of Freyre in his work; it is a period of concern with the plural ethnic origins of the Portuguese and with the resolution of the "colonial problem" in the light of the Brazilian experience. Finally, a third period would correspond to the post-1974 era (when democracy was restored) and will remain outside the scope of this essay.

Eusébio Tamagnini and Mendes Correia were the leaders of two schools of anthropology, respectively in Coimbra and Oporto. Their work influenced a period from the late nineteenth to the early twentieth centuries, encompassing the Constitutional Monarchy, the First Republic and the dictatorship of the Estado Novo. In 1902,[2] in a paper on the population of São Tomé, composed of the descendants of slave settlers and indentured laborers, Tamagnini asked: "The crossing between colonizing and colonized races: what is the worth of its products?" (1902:11). His answer was "(. . .) the dialect of São Tomé, being a creole that belongs to the second group, must be seen as a degenerate version of Continental Portuguese" (1902:13). Further on he says that

> . . . Easiness in relationships among the natives resulted necessarily in unfaithfulness and jealousy, which are obviously the causes for most crimes

committed in creole societies: prostitution, indecent behaviour, and its repugnant varieties, such as pederasty, lesbianism, rape and so on, which are practiced in a terrifying way in creole societies, and which are the most obvious evidence of the shameful way in which the European peoples have been civilizing and colonizing the other peoples that they call savages. (1902:39–40 in Santos 1996:49)

Throughout his career, Tamagnini was to publish several studies from 1916 to 1949. Influenced by Broca's and Topinard's work, he was looking for anthropometric statistical averages among the Portuguese, wanting these to coincide with those of the average European. Although after the 1920s he had to take into consideration the developments in genetics, he did so within a Malthusian framework in connection with colonial issues. In the First National Congress of Colonial Anthropology in 1934 in Oporto (one year after the legislation of the Colonial Act), he alerted to the dangers of *mestiçagem*: "when two peoples or two races have reached different cultural levels and have organized completely different social systems, the consequences of *mestiçagem* are necessarily disastrous" (Tamagnini 1934a: 26 in Santos 1996:137). In a panel on population in the Congress on the Portuguese World (at the occasion of the Portuguese World Expo that dictator Salazar set up to promote Portuguese colonialism), he presented a study about the blood groups of the Portuguese and concluded that the Portuguese population had "been able to maintain relative ethnic purity" (. . .) (Tamagnini 1940:22 *in* Santos 1996:145). However, in 1944 he had to acknowledge—albeit with one important safeguard—that

> . . . it would be foolish to pretend to deny the existence of *mestiçagem* between the Portuguese and the elements of the so-called coloured races. The fact that they are a colonizing people makes it impossible to avoid ethnic contamination. What one can not accept is the raising of such *mestiçagem* to the category of a sufficient factor of ethnic degeneration to such a point that anthropologists would have to place the Portuguese outside the white races or classify them as Negroid *mestiços*. . . . (Tamagnini 1944 *in* Santos 1996:12)

In the year following the 1926 coup that established dictatorship, Mendes Correia (head of the Institute of Anthropology and Ethnology in Oporto) had called for the segregation of relapsing criminals, for the sterilization of degenerates, and for the regulation of immigration and the banning of marriage for professional beggars. In 1932 Mendes Correia invited Renato Kehl, president of the Brazilian Eugenics organization to give a conference in Oporto. On the occasion, the Brazilian scientist proposed the introduction of both positive and negative eugenic measures, publicized the advantages of marriage within the same class or race, and condemned *mestiçagem* for being "dissolving, dissuasive, demoralizing and degrading."

Although eugenics was not a successful approach in Portugal, the question of "racial improvement" was much discussed in 1934, in relation to the colonial question and the issue of *mestiçagem*. Although some participants in the First Congress of Colonial Anthropology praised *mestiçagem*, Tamagnini was against it. Based on a study of somatology and aptitude tests done with sixteen Cape Verdean and six Macau *mestiços* who had come to the Colonial Expo of 1934 in Oporto, Mendes Correia concluded that miscegenation was a condemnable practice. In the plenary session Tamagnini reminded everyone that "the little repugnance that the Portuguese have regarding sexual approaches to elements of other ethnic origins is often presented as evidence of their higher colonizing capacity" and asserted that "it is necessary to change radically such an attitude" (Tamagnini 1934b:26 in Castelo 1998:111[3]). He continues: "It is in the social arena that the fact of *mestiçagem* has graver consequences. The *mestiços*, because they do not adapt to either system, are rejected by both . . ." (in Castelo 1998:111). Mendes Correia couldn't agree more: "Being mulatto is longing for oneself . . . just like the despised hermaphrodite cries out the conflict between the sexes . . . the *mestiço* is thus an unexpected being in the plan of the world, an unfortunate experiment of the Portuguese" (Mendes Correia 1940:122 in Castelo 1998:112).

LUSO-TROPICALISM AND THE PORTUGUESE COLONIAL CONUNDRUM

This stand was eventually reversed with Luso-Tropicalism. Any discussion of the trend must be based on a reading of Gilberto Freyre's *Casa Grande e Senzala* (*Masters and Slaves, Ms*), first published in Brazil in 1933. It was first published in Portugal in 1957, with six subsequent editions until 1983. The work's success indicates the circularity of the discourse that links Gilberto Freyre, the bibliography on ethnogenesis and identity in both Portugal and Brazil, and Portuguese colonial ideologies. For that reason my reading of *MS* focuses on the issues of Portuguese identity and the Portuguese colonial "adventure" (for an extended analysis see Vale de Almeida 2000 and 2004).

Freyre argues for the "peculiar disposition of the Portuguese for a hybrid and slaveocratic colonization of the Tropics,"[4] which he explains as a result of the Portuguese "ethnic, or rather cultural, past, as a people undefined between Europe and Africa" (1992 [1933]:5). Then he defines the Portuguese as marked by "a shaky balance of antagonisms" (1992:6). The main antagonism would be rooted on the Euro-African mixture, that is, in the ethnically hybrid character of the Portuguese in the pre-Discoveries period. The scarcity of human capital was supposedly overcome during the colonialization process by "extreme mobility and miscegenation" (1992:8). The Portuguese "joyfully mixed with women of colour . . . and multiplied in mixed children" (1992:9). The colonial system was based on the slaveocratic and patriarchal family that conveyed a *sui generis* sexual morality. Portuguese plasticity—which made the synthesis of miscegenation, mobility, and adaptation—led to a process of non-Europeanization of Brazil; this was largely achieved thanks to the role of cultural mediator played by the Africans.

Freyre's book was to be accused of creating an idyllic image of colonial society, one in which relationships between masters and slaves are not explained in racial and political-economic terms but rather as a culturalist result of the migration of Iberian family patriarchy and patronage to the tropics. Araújo (1994) stresses Freyre's neo-Lamarckian conception of race, thanks to which "the category of biological stock as a race definer becomes malleable by the environment, by climate."

Freyre's purpose was to break with the latent or explicit racism that characterized a good part of Brazilian production on miscegenation up until 1933. Two standpoints were then prevalent: the first one said that the country was not viable; the second refused that condemnation and claimed that miscegenation could be seen as whitening, thus redeeming Brazil (Araújo 1994:29). A third one was Freyre's: it distinguished race from culture and proposed another vision of national identity, one in which the "obsession with progress and reason . . . is replaced up to a point by an interpretation that considers . . . the hybrid and peculiar articulation of traditions . . ." (Araújo 1994:29).

Hybrid ethnic origins; mobility, miscegenation, and adaptation (*aclimatibilidade*), resulting in plasticity; slaveocratic patriarchalism and patronage; and, furthermore, hubris, particularly sexual excess. All these elements in Freyre's canon are to be found in the representations of Portuguese identity before and after Freyre. One can find them in Portuguese social sciences and literature, in official discourses and in common sense identity self-representations with amazing resilience and capacity to adapt to different political situations. That which in Brazil was to become a construction of exceptionality ("racial democracy," "cordiality," "contention of social explosions," and so on) was to become, in Portugal, a construction of exceptionality of the Discoveries and Expansion. Portuguese exceptionalism, as an ideological construct, was actually to increase during the harsher times of the colonial conflict in Africa (1961–1975).

Although the foundations of Luso-Tropicalism are already implicit in *MS* (1933), it was not made explicit until Freyre's lecture in Goa in 1951 called *Uma Cultura Moderna: A Luso-tropical* (A Modern Culture: Luso-Tropical). The doctrine is developed and explained in *Um Brasileiro em Terras Portuguesas* (A Brazilian in Portuguese Lands, 1955, including the Goa lecture), in *Integração Portuguesa nos Trópicos* (Portuguese Integration in the Tropics, 1958) and in *O Luso e o Trópico* (The Luso and the Tropic, 1961).

Um Brasileiro em Terras Portuguesas (*BTP*) is a collection of speeches that were proffered between 1951 and 1952 during Freyre's journeys in the Portuguese colonies, as a guest of Portugal's Minister of the Overseas. In 1952, during a lecture in Coimbra called *Em Torno de Um Novo Conceito de Tropicalismo* (On a New Concept of Tropicalism) Freyre resumes his ideas from the Goa lecture in the previous year:

> . . . I believe that I have found during that journey the expression that I was missing to characterize that sort of Lusitanian civilization which, after being victorious in the tropics, is today still in expansion (. . .) The expression—Luso-tropical—seems to me to reveal the fact that Lusitanian expansion in Africa, Asia and America shows an obvious inclination, on the part of the Portuguese, to an adaptation to the tropics which is not just based on interest, but is also voluptuous. . . . (1955:134)

How was the Luso-Tropicalist program received in Portugal? According to Castelo (1996),[5] the reception was heterogeneous. On the right wing of the political and ideological spectrum, a nationalistic interpretation was made, highlighting the specificity of Portuguese colonization; this position would eventually become the regime's attitude toward Luso-Tropicalism after WWII. On the left, there was more criticism (although never a clear opposition): either by comparing doctrine with historical facts or with the actual policies implemented in the colonies.[6] Castelo says that the imperial renaissance of the thirties and forties could not easily accept Freyre's culturalism; it would rather stress the inferiority of blacks or the superiority of European civilization. This indicates one of the "ambiguous fertilities" of Freyre's work: antiracialist in the Boasian sense, on the one hand, but based on a sort of essentialist culturalism on the other.

The great transformation would happen after WWII. Portugal felt tremendous anticolonial pressure and tried to adapt to it. The main events and reactions were the creation of the United Nations and its Charter; anticolonial conferences of third-world countries (especially Bandung in 1954); the abolishment of the Colonial Act and the change in colonial denominations (from "colonies" and "Empire" to "Provinces" and "Overseas"); and the creation of a rhetoric of the pluri-continental and pluri-racial nature of the nation. Freyre's journey in the colonies took place in 1951, the same year of the Constitutional amendment that tried to refresh colonialism with the above-mentioned changes. Freyre's doctrine then became useful for Portuguese diplomacy between the Bandung Conference of 1954 and Portugal's acceptance as a member of the UN in 1955.

It was in the academic field, however, that the doctrine was more influential. Adriano Moreira introduced Freyre's ideas in his course on Overseas Politics at the School of Overseas Studies. He was backed up by the acceptance of the Luso-Tropicalist criterion by influential scholars such as geographer Orlando Ribeiro, anthropologist Jorge Dias, and human ecologist Almerindo Lessa. The beginning of the war in Angola (1961) and the previous invasion / liberation / reintegration (according to different points of view) of Portuguese India, led the policy makers to an attempt to "Luso-Tropicalize" overseas' legislation and administration. Moreira, head of the *Centro de Estudos Políticos e Sociais*, introduced some reforms when he took the post of Minister of the Overseas (1960–1962): he abolished the Native Status Laws and promoted administrative decentralization—policies that led to his demise as minister owing to the pressure exerted by the integrationist sectors of the regime.

According to Rui Pereira (1986), the dictatorial regime had to rethink the relationship between colonizers and colonized in order to avoid nationalist movements. That was how JIU (the Overseas Research Board) "embraced Malinowski's teachings" (Pereira 1986:219) with a thirty-year delay. Jorge Dias, an anthropologist influenced by American culturalism and by Freyre and who was in charge of new missions for the study of overseas' ethnology, was nevertheless faced with the harshness of colonial reality. Pereira highlights this sentence in the Mission Report of 1957 by Dias: "Blacks . . . fear us . . . and when they compare us with other whites they always do so unfavorably for us" (Dias, in Pereira 1986:223). The following passage is even more revealing:

> . . .We are told time and time again that the natives prefer the Portuguese to the English because we treat them more humanely and take interest in their lives. This tale is repeated just like some errors pass on from one book to another,[7] because the authors prefer to repeat what others have said instead of checking the accuracy of the information. . . . (Dias, in Pereira 1986:224)

Note that the year was 1959, a few years after Freyre's travels in the colonies (in 1951–1952. The written results were published in 1955). Dias's criticisms were a harsh blow to the regime's love for Luso-Tropicalism as defined by Freyre in 1958 in *Portuguese Integration in the Tropics*, published by JIU (and by the Center run by Adriano Moreira). Jorge Dias actually said in the Mission Report of 1957 that "many of those in charge who live in the area believe that we will not be around twenty years from now" (Dias, in Pereira 1986:203). He was right. Armed struggle began in the region in 1964, three years after it had started in Angola—when Adriano Moreira was Minister of the Overseas. It was precisely in this juncture—marked by the first real attempts at colonization and colonial development, on the one hand, and by the beginning of the liberation movements, on the other—that Luso-Tropicalism became useful in helping transform the representations and practices of the anachronistic Portuguese colonialism.

I have already mentioned that Adriano Moreira, besides having been a major figure in the political and social sciences of the late colonial period, was also Minister of the Overseas between 1960 and 1962. During a speech as Minister, in 1961, and while talking about the settlement policies directed at Portuguese soldiers who had been drafted in the beginning of the colonial war, he said that

> . . .We want to make it clear to the commonwealth of nations our national decision to pursue a policy of multiracial integration, without which there will be neither peace nor civilization in Black Africa (. . .) it is a policy whose benefits are proven by the largest country of the future, Brazil. . . ." (Moreira 1961:10–11)

In his *Contribuição de Portugal para a valorização do homem no Ultramar* (Portugal's contribution to the uplifting of Man overseas; 1963 [1958]), he refused to accept the notion of conflict that underlay anticolonial theories, for it did not leave room for human dignity and "polarizes white man and black man, forgetting the universalistic and humanistic message of the Discoveries" (1963 [1958]:12). How could Moreira legitimate this statement? He did so by saying that

> the great sociologist Gilberto Freyre is right when he notes that in Toynbee's oppositional classification of civilizations that peculiar way of being in the world that he fortunately named Luso-tropical is missing. (. . .) It was this conception of egalitarian life, of human democracy, that was the most significant contribution of Portuguese action in the world (. . .) absolutely oblivious to notions of conflict and domination, or to the feeling of racial superiority or inferiority. . . . (1963 [1958]:13)

Luso-Tropicalism was not an anthropological theory or school. It was—and is—a discourse born within a tradition of culturalist essay writing on national identity, specificity, and exceptionalism. And it was so both in Brazil and Portugal. The Brazilian social dynamics—especially in what concerns race and ethnicity—could easily delegitimize Luso-Tropicalism. In Portugal the same could be done by the crisis that put an end to colonialism and the authoritarian regime that supported it and was supported by it.

On the one hand, something that we could call "generic" Luso-Tropicalism remains alive—as an inclination, a common sense interpretation, sometimes as official representation. Luso-Tropicalism has become an ideological social fact. On the other hand, some historical facts of Portuguese colonialism that inspired Luso-Tropicalism are undoubtedly specific from a historical and cultural point of view. This specific reality should be studied within comparative colonial studies. Three concerns should be taken into account, however: critical attention to the resilience of Luso-Tropicalism under the guise of Lusophony[8] and its avatars; complex understanding of historical and cultural transits and traffics between Europe, the Americas, and Africa, thus overcoming a Lusocentric perspective; and comparison with other colonial and postcolonial cases.

THE CAPE VERDEAN CASE: LOCAL ELITES AND THE INVENTION OF IDENTITY IN A COLONIAL CONTEXT

One of Freyre's stops in his journeys across the Portuguese empire was Cape Verde. There he had become the guru of the local literary elite, who saw in Luso-Tropicalism the explanation for Cape Verde's creoleness. In fact, the members of the literary movement named after the journal *Claridade,* notably Baltasar Lopes, thought that Cape Verde was a better example than Brazil of the successes of Luso-Tropical "civilization." Cape Verdeans were in an in-between situation. Officially, they were not classified as indigenous peoples but as Portuguese citizens, as opposed to Angolans, Guineans, and Mozambicans; nevertheless, Cape Verde was, in name and in fact, a colony, not a region like the Azores or Madeira. Authors in *Claridade* developed nevertheless a notion of "regionalism": they saw Cape Verde as a regional variety of Portugal, as much as the North Atlantic islands or any of Continental Portugal's provinces. This, they claimed, was a result of miscegenation and creolization. Freyre's writings on his visit to Cape Verde started a bitter polemic since, instead of confirming *Claridade*'s ideas, Freyre found Cape Verde to be too . . . African. Creole language, in particular, was seen by the Brazilian scholar as a sign of Africanity, not as a sign of a complete synthesis of European and African cultural contributions. That was supposedly Brazil's achievement.

According to Gabriel Fernandes (2002), the literary elite in Cape Verde claimed for itself the role of mediator in the relations between the natives and the colonial power. Throughout the history of Cape Verde this was achieved by means of shifting the border between dispossessed *filhos da terra* (sons of the land) and property owning *brancos da terra* (whites of the land) to a border opposing *brancos da terra* and *brancos metropolitanos* (metropolitan whites, that is, from Portugal), "Cape Verdians" ("civilized") and "Africans" ("indigenous"), colonizer and colonized. There were three crucial moments in this process. The first was the period between the Berlin Conference (1884–1885) and the Republican regime in Portugal (1910–1926). The foundation in 1869 of a Catholic seminar (secondary education did not exist until then) in the island of São Nicolau promoted the education of the elites and fostered the engagement of Cape Verdeans in the administration of the colony of Guinea-Bissau. In the intellectual milieu this was the period of the *Nativistas*, whose claims to Portuguese citizenship went hand in hand with an appraisal of Africa, on the one hand, and the Cape Verde motherland, on the other. The second period goes from the beginning of dictatorship (after 1926) up until 1960. The period was marked by an investment in establishing differences between Africa and Cape Verde (Cape Verde as *not* Africa) as well as by the increasing participation of Cape Verdean elite members and civil servants in "civilizing natives" in mainland Africa. The people from *Claridade* focused on *mestiçagem* as an expression of the cultural Portugueseness of Cape Verde and on the archipelago as an instance of Portuguese regionalism (Fernandes 2002:16). The third period, starting with WWII was the era of stronger colonial presence and institutional work with, for instance, the creation of *Boletim de Cabo Verde* (a journal of colonial studies of the archipelago), calls for the intervention of the local literary elite, and the sending of specialists to study the islands. Fernandes notes that colonial power had left for the local intellectuals the responsibility to prove themselves worthy of differential treatment and that it was now coopting their production in order to avoid the temptations of independence. On the one hand, there was *Claridade*, on the other the youngsters of the Casa dos Estudantes do Império—the so-called "Generation of '50," who were influenced by *Négritude* and called for the "reafricanization of the minds." They were to become members of the independence movement for both Guinea-Bissau and Cape Verde, PAIGC.[9]

Mestiçagem and creolization—as well as creole as a language—are products of a specific history of social relations, social structure, and political economy. I shall follow Fernandes's (2002) outline. The first settlers of the deserted islands of Cape Verde were white men, either single or married, involved in trade with the coast of Guinea. They had to produce in the islands the merchandise for trade. They did so together with those slaves who were allocated to agriculture and cattle raising, and not reexported to the Americas. Small-scale agriculture in the islands was a very different situation from that of Caribbean and Brazilian plantations. The Cape Verdean system soon enabled a rising number of manumissions, as well as a growing number of nonwhite *línguas* (interpreters to be used in mainland Africa) and clergymen. Fernandes claims that the weight of the "ethnic" (that is, "racial") element was minimized by those occurrences and by the increasing moral and economic weakness of the white master owing to agricultural poverty and pirate attacks. The result was a double movement toward creolization and whitening, which led to a desubstantialization of "race," which became more of an indicator of status and power than a criterion for placement in an essentialistic hierarchy.

Slaves were made *ladino* (that is, "domesticated," "europeanized"), whether to be exported or to be used for domestic service. Both slave labor and the female slave were taken possession of, resulting in a growing number of bastard children (2002:36). The category *filhos da terra* (children of the land) began to define children whose legitimacy and social acknowledgment were tied to their organic link with the motherland (2002:42), which amounted to a process of liberation from the condition of "blacks" by means of appropriation of the material or symbolic goods of the (white) father. This process Fernandes calls "socioeconomic whitening." This reinterpretation of race favored a new hegemony, that of the *brancos da terra* (whites of the land, that is, culturally "European," regardless of dark skin colour; 2002:44). Education, emigration, and primitive accumulation led to the ascension of the sons of the land when the whites—faced with droughts, pirate attacks, and low agricultural yields—returned to Portugal taking with them most of the accumulated wealth.

Unlike the Latin America case, in Cape Verde the *mestiços* did not occupy the interstitial social spaces. That sort of mediation was the task of the *brancos da terra* and, later, that of the local literary elites (2002:47). The many *mestiços* were not overcoming the extremes; *mestiço* status was not the escape hatch in some bipolar "racial" system; rather, *mestiços* were the actors in a permanent struggle for the abolition of their "birth defects," that is, in a search for whitening, not a search for creolization. They actively promoted Portuguese culture, not a *mestiço* or black culture (2002:48–9). In sum, Fernandes claims a weak political consistency and weak heuristic dimension of *mestiçagem* in Cape Verde (2002:51): "It was while trying to become a white that the son of the land found out that he was *mestiço*" (2002:51). Instead of the bastards' wish to be recognized as legal consanguine heirs to their white fathers, the *filhos da terra* wished to see their cultural link to the nation recognized. With growing colonial penetration in the nineteenth century, and after the abolition of the remains of feudal land systems, it was increasingly presumed that a common culture was being shared, one that was structured according to the variable of education: "the white father/master is replaced by the teacher/boss" (Fernandes 2002:67).

Gabriel Mariano (1991 [1959]) was pivotal in exploring the hypothesis of the social aristocratization of the *mestiço*, alleging that in Cape Verde the *mestiço* performed the functions that in Brazil were reserved for the whites (Fernandes 2002:86). Mariano's reading of the Cape Verdian *mestiço* was an attempt at defining a *mestiço caboverdiano* (that is, specifically Cape Verdean) who, for Fernandes, was no more than a Portuguese *mestiço*. For the Nativists, however, *mestiço* identity was not central, nor were the ethnic (that is, "racial") differences among members of the creole society. Their taxonomic frame established, rather, a difference between *filhos da terra* and metropolitan agents, between Portuguese civilization and African civilization, between school culture and popular culture (2002:89), while the authors from *Claridade* were building *mestiçagem* when they thought that they were explaining it (2002:90).

By the late 1950s, several Portuguese intellectuals were visiting the islands in an attempt to help the local elite neutralize the sequels left by the detractors of the established non-African and pro-Portuguese identity model. This happened at a time when the Cape Verdeans' position as main helpers of Portuguese colonization in Africa was already consolidated—almost 90 percent of administrative posts in Guinea-Bissau and most of those in Northern Angola were in the hands of Cape Verdeans (Fernandes 2002:137).

The experience of activists and intellectuals from the Generation of '50 echoes that of the French colonized. They were assimilated students, educated in the colonial metropole, where "the presumed *branco da terra* from Cape Verde experiences his most painful blackness" (Fernandes 2002:141). In the Cape Verdean case, as in those of many creole island societies, a "return to roots" as a mechanism of compensation was impossible, and the notion of Africa was necessarily a mystification. Manuel Duarte, one of the protagonists of the Generation of '50, explained his Africanism as a result of the "colonial phenomenon" (Fernandes 2002:147). They *opted* for the political character of their reidentification process. Amílcar Cabral, PAIGC's founder, was to revalue at the same time popular culture and school culture when he stated that "a return to origins no longer means a return to traditions" (Cabral 1977:8). PAIGC, founded in 1956, was to polarize the conflict between colonizer and colonized classes. When it decided to hide in the Guinean countryside in order to start armed struggle, it was faced with tensions between the "assimilated" (the political activists) and the indigenous populations. Another tension was that between founders or leaders of the party, who were mostly Cape Verdeans living in Guinea as civil servants or university students in Portugal, and the Guineans.

Cape Verde was to become independent after the Portuguese democratic revolution of 1974. PAIGC managed to keep the unity between Cape Verde and Guinea Bissau, within an Africanist project. After a coup in Guinea in the 1980s, however, the two countries separated. Cape Verde was to become a multiparty democracy in the 1990s. After that, the trend has been to go back to an idea of specific "Cape Verdeaness." A partial rehabilitation of the legitimizing identity of the colonial period has been under way, resistance identity has been questioned, at the same time that the local economy has become dependent from Portuguese capital investment.

In sum, Cape Verdean creoleness as a product of elite representations has historically depended on a negation of Africa and on a specific Luso-Tropicalist interpretation of the local mixture. Although a certain amount of rehabilitation of African elements has occurred, creoleness is today promoted as a gloss for *national* culture. Instead of a politically charged concept with emancipatory overtones, creoleness tends to mean the same as "Cape Verdean."[10] The emancipatory character of creolization is lost (see Vergès 2001).

CONCLUSION

It is quite interesting that the creole man is anxious to have the anthropologist turn him into the very native that creolization problematizes, in the sense that it estranges him from an origin that can be defined as situated and definable (as native; Silvestre 2002:89). Silvestre analyses how the thought of Gilberto Freyre, Baltasar Lopes from *Claridade,* and Manuel Ferreira produced the category *crioulo* between 1936 (when *Claridade* was first published) and 1967, when Manuel Ferreira's *A Aventura Crioula* was published.[11] He asks why the authors in *Claridade* were so seduced by Freyre's ideas and analyzes the means of translation that turned a theory of miscegenation into a theory of emancipation, especially why it was not discarded after the cooptation of Luso-Tropicalism by the Portuguese colonial and dictatorial regime. His question can be summarized thus: how could a theory of emancipation function at the same time as a theory of colonization?

In *"Uma Experiência Românica nos Trópicos"* ("A Roman Experience in the Tropics," in *Claridade,* 4) Baltasar Lopes used Arthur Ramos's notions (in fact, Herskovits's notions) on acceptance, adaptation, and reaction in the acculturation process.[12] In the essay, Cape Verde is portrayed as a better example of Freyre's ideas on acculturation than Brazil. This would in turn mean that African culture would be more lost in Cape Verde, since acceptance would have gone farther. To help build an emancipatory theory, Freyre's notions had to be hypercorrected, so that they could be adapted to the Cape Verdean case, where miscegenation had supposedly been more complete, especially in language. Silvestre notes that

> This is an intrinsically ambivalent position, since Cape Verde is thus constituted into a subject by means of being dispossessed from the deep logic of colonization that made it into an object. . . . This was implicit in the thought of the *Claridade* authors and was made explicit by Gabriel Mariano in 1959 . . . : "Cape Verde became a Nation in spite of colonialism. It was something that backfired on colonialism." (Mariano 1991 [1959]:61; Silvestre 2002:73)

Since this ambivalence is structural, it is impossible to validate the strategies of Cape Verdean identity that attribute to *Claridade* the role of making a clear-cut separation between a colonial "before" and a postcolonial "after" (Silvestre 2002:74):

> *Claridade* is the critical place of an abrasive juxtaposition—therefore unresolved—of emancipation and colonization. Probably the responsibility for that unresolved juxtaposition is the concept of creoleness [*crioulidade*]. It is curious that *Claridade*'s theorization on the concept has become the official and non official legitimation of Cape Verdean identity. (Silvestre 2002:76)

The concept of culture conveyed by *Claridade* granted central importance to ethnography,[13] owing to the interest in language and national culture of the people. This led to the typically modern gesture of the "fatal junction of the concept of nationality with the concept of culture" (Gilroy 1993:2, in Silvestre 2002:78). Silvestre notes that the fact of celebrating Cape Verdean identity as miscegenated was an important political act in the 1930s and 1940s, since Freyre's conceptions were not yet accepted by the colonial regime. In the process of national identification by the Cape Verdean literary elites, creoleness (*crioulidade*) became a synonym of ethnicity and nationality in a specific territory. Historicity—slavery, colonialism, nationalism, and African socialism after independence—are not forgotten; they are sublimated; they are glossed in the elites' constant debate on the more or less European or African character of the islands.

The iconic cultural product of *mestiçagem* and creolization is Creole language, seen as Cape Verde's most specific cultural product, especially because it is the mother tongue of the "people" (that is, the "folk," or the lower classes). Creole language has a specific history and sociology, though. It was first treated as "the language of the Negro," in a clear opposition to Portuguese. It has been the language of the poor or, in the case of the elites, the language of the domestic space, of interclass interactions, or of intimacy. It is marked throughout by metaphors of gender (as maternal and domestic), space, interaction, class, and race—at least until the people from *Claridade* welcomed it as a regional expression within the Portuguese empire and the precipitate of Luso-Tropical miscegenation.

Although both languages are now official in Cape Verde, a clear demarcation subsists between Portuguese as the official language and Creole as the national language. Braz Dias (2002) says that the use of both languages is permeated by issues of authority and resistance, social identity and distance. If the modern nation-state needs to define a language in a patterned way as a support for its bureaucratic system, bureaucracy in Cape Verde grows with the use of Portuguese and clashes with Creole in the field of identity. A factor of inequality is thus created. A series of oppositions between Portuguese and Creole (also known as *Caboverdiano* or *Kauberdianu*) are outlined by Braz Dias: on the one hand, official, international, formal, written, state and bureaucracy, cultural domination, elites, and modernity; on the other, maternal, national, informal, oral, the Nation, cultural resistance, the masses, and tradition. The outlining of the two fields is of course part of the ideology of language itself, since there is a geographical island variation of the Creole, on the one hand, but any dichotomy is destroyed by considerations of the Creole continuum, on the other. The still subaltern situation of Creole generates diglossia in this continuum.

In Cape Verde, creoleness has come to be the definer of national cultural specificity, not part of a positively valued project of hybridization. This is the result of the work of the elites that built a "regional" identity within the colonial empire, using the resource of their special status as nonindigenous colonials. What seems to be left out of consideration is the projective character of creolization as a form of surpassing nationalism, ethnic exclusivism, and racism. This would takes us to Portugal, where "miscegenation" (the local gloss for creolization) is always discoursed as that which the Portuguese did in the world in the past and elsewhere, not as that which is desirable for a contemporary national society marked by immigration from the excolonies and chauvinistic resistance against multicultural cosmopolitanism. But that would be a whole different story. . . .[14]

Notes

1. Portuguese is the official language of the following countries: Portugal, Brazil, Cape Verde, Guinea-Bissau, São Tomé and Príncipe, Angola, Mozambique, and East Timor. In Cape Verde, Creole is also an official language. In the other African countries and in East-Timor, Portuguese coexists with several other native languages.
2. References to Tamagnini were taken from Santos 1996. Since these are indirect references, I list them here, not in the final list of references: Tamagnini, E., 1902, *Dissertação para a Cadeira de Antropologia e Arqueologia Pré-Histórica*, FCUC; 1934a, "Lição inaugural do ano lectivo de 1934–35," *Revista da Faculdade de Ciências da Universidade de Coimbra*, 5; 1934b, "Problemas de mestiçagem," Porto: Edições da Primeira Exposição Colonial Portuguesa; 1940, "Os grupos sanguíneos dos portugueses," *Revista da Faculdade de Ciências da Universidade de Coimbra*, 8; 1944, "O índice nasal dos portugueses," *Contribuição para o Estudo da Antropologia Portuguesa*, V (1), Coimbra: IAUC.
3. See footnote 2.
4. My translation. The same applies to the rest of the quotes of Portuguese authors.
5. I have used the author's B.A. thesis.
6. Note that there was no freedom of speech in dictatorial Portugal, however.
7. The Luso-Tropicalist theme is endlessly reproduced in travel guides and literature, in pop culture, and so on.
8. Lusophony (*Lusofonia*), similarly to *Francophonie* in France, is the catchword in contemporary Portugal used for describing the Community of Portuguese-Speaking Countries.
9. *Casa dos Estudantes do Império* (Empire Students' Home) was the institution that housed students from the colonies in Lisbon. The fact that the sons (less so the daughters) of colonial elites met in the metropolitan center allowed for the creation of anticolonial thought and networking. A similar situation occurred in the French Empire. PAIGC stands for African Party for the Independence of Guinea and Cape Verde.
10. This is particularly obvious in the Cape Verdean diaspora. Cape Verde's economy depends enormously on emigrants' remittances from the United States, Portugal, France, Italy, the Netherlands, Senegal, and other countries. Cultural products like music play an important role in the definition of a sense of being Cape Verdean. They establish links of "community" among Cape Verdeans around the world, and "talk" more about "home" and "roots" in the archipelago than about any sort of further creolization in the host countries.
11. Manuel Ferreira, Portuguese literary critic who played a central role in defining creoleness as the essence of Cape Verdean literature.
12. Brazilian anthropologist Arthur Ramos was one of the inspirations for Gilberto Freyre's work and was part of the Boas-inspired sort of Brazilian culturalism that countered previous racist interpretations of local society.
13. A significant number of the articles in *Claridade* were ethnographic, in an attempt to systematize "folk" culture.
14. Cape Verdean immigration in Portugal created the first African community in the country as of the 1960s. Processes of racism and scapegoating were soon to build the stereotype of the "Cape Verdean with a knife," an allusion to growing social fears of crime and rape at the time. The postcolonial situation of Portugal is analyzed in parts of Vale de Almeida 2000 and 2004.

References

Alexandre, V., and J. Dias, eds. 1998. *O império Africano 1825–1890*, vol 10 of *Nova história da expansão Portuguesa*. J. Serrão and A. H. Oliveira Marques, eds. Lisbon: Estampa.

Anderson, B. 1983. *Imagined communities: Reflections on the origins and spread of nationalism*. London: Verso.

Araújo, R. B. de. 1994. *Guerra e paz. Casa-grande e senzala e a obra de Gilberto Freyre nos anos 30*. Rio de Janeiro: Editora 34.

Braz Dias, J. 2002. Língua e poder: Transcrevendo a questão nacional, *Mana* 5:352–374.

Cabral, A. 1977. Dignidade e identidade no contexto da luta de libertação nacional? *Raízes* 1 (4).

Castelo, C. 1998. *O modo Português de estar no mundo: O luso-tropicalismo e a ideologia colonial Portuguesa (1933–1961)*. Porto: Afrontamento.

Cohen, A. 1981. *The politics of elite culture. Explorations in the dramaturgy of power in a modern African society*. Berkeley and Los Angeles: University of California Press.

Curtin, P. D., ed. 1972. *Africa and the West: Intellectual responses to European culture*. Madison, WI: University of Wisconsin Press.

Dias, J. R. 1984. Uma questão de identidade: Respostas intelectuais às transformações económicas no seio da elite crioula da Angola portuguesa entre 1870 e 1930, *Revista Internacional de Estudos Africanos* 1:61–94.

——— 2002. Novas identidades Africanas em Angola no contexto do comércio Atlântico. In *Trânsitos coloniais: Diálogos críticos luso-brasileiros*. C. Bastos, M. Vale de Almeida, and B. Feldman-Bianco, eds. Lisbon: ICS, pp. 293–320.

Fernandes, G. 2002. *A diluição da África. Uma interpretação da saga identitária cabo-verdiana no panorama político (pós)colonial*. Florianópolis: Editora da UFSC.

Freyre, G. 1955. *Um Brasileiro em terras Portuguesas. Introdução a uma possível luso-tropicologia, acompanhada de conferências e discursos proferidos em Portugal e em terras lusitanas e ex-lusitanas da Ásia, da África e do Atlântico*. Lisbon: Livros do Brasil.

——— 1992 [1933]. *Casa-Grande e Senzala. Formação da família brasileira sob o regime da economia patriarcal* (Vol. 1 of *Introdução à história da sociedade patriarcal no Brasil*), 29th ed. Rio de Janeiro: Record.

Gilroy, P. 1993. *The black Atlantic: Modernity and double consciousness*. London: Verso.

Haraway, D. 1989. *Primate visions: Gender, race and nature in the world of modern science*. New York: Routledge.

Mariano, G. 1959. *Do funco ao sobrado ou o mundo que o mulato criou*. Lisbon: Junta de Investigações do Ultramar.

——— 1991. *Cultura Cabo-Verdiana*. Lisbon: Vega.

Mendes Correia, A. 1940. O mestiçamento nas colónias portuguesas. In *Congresso do mundo Português*, vol. 14. Lisbon.

Moreira, A. 1961. *"Política de integração," discurso proferido pelo Ministro do Ultramar na Associação Comercial do Porto*. Lisbon.

——— 1963 [1958]. Contribuição de Portugal para a valorização do homem no Ultramar, *Ensaios*, 3rd ed. *Estudos de Ciências Políticas e Sociais* 34. Lisbon: Junta de Investigações do Ultramar.

Pereira, D. 2002. Crioulos de base portuguesa. www.institutocamoes.pt/CVC/hlp/geografia/crioulosbaseport.html, accessed 20 May 2003.

Pereira, R. 1986. Antropologia aplicada na política colonial portuguesa do Estado Novo, *Revista Internacional de Estudos Africanos* 4–5:191–235.

Santos, G. D. dos. 1996. *Topografias imaginárias: As estórias de Eusébio Tamagnini no Instituto de Antropologia de Coimbra, 1902–1952*. B.A. Thesis, Department of Anthropology, University of Coimbra.

Seyferth, G. 1991. Os paradoxos da miscigenação: Observações sobre o tema imigração e raça no Brasil, *Estudos Afro-Asiáticos* 20:165–185.

Silvestre, O. 2002. A aventura crioula revisitada: versões do *Atlântico Negro* em Gilberto Freyre, Baltasar Lopes e Manuel Ferreira. In *Literatura e viagens pós-Coloniais*. H. C. Buescu and M. R. Sanches, eds. Lisbon: Edições Colibri e Centro de Estudos Comparatistas, pp. 63–103.

Vale de Almeida, M. 2000. *Um mar da cor da terra: "Raça," cultura e política da identidade*, Oeiras: Celta.

——— 2004. *An earth-colored sea. "Race," culture and the politics of identity in the post-colonial Portuguese-speaking world*. Oxford: Berghahn Books.

Vergès, F. 2001. Vertigo and emancipation. Creole cosmopolitanism and cultural politics, *Theory, Culture and Society*, 18 (2–3):169–183.

Wade, P. 1993. *Blackness and race mixture: The dynamics of racial identity in Colombia*. Baltimore: Johns Hopkins University Press.

Indian-Oceanic Creolizations: Processes and Practices of Creolization on Réunion Island

Françoise Vergès

In September 2003, the Museum of Contemporary Art of the City of Paris invited me and two other scholars to speak about "creolization" on Réunion Island in conjunction with an exhibition of contemporary Réunion artists. I had already noticed that the notion of "creolization" had seduced many in the art world. I wondered aloud if it was a good thing to be "discovered," to have become the latest site of academic and artistic interest. After "hybridity," "*meztisaje*" or "*métissage,*" *créolité*, creole, and creolization seemed to offer a theoretical frame apt to describe the new cultural emergences produced by migratory flows, transnational encounters, and postnational aspirations. I reminded the audience that on Réunion Island, we had been "discovered" previously—for instance, by the European Left, artists and intellectuals, in the 1970s—and then we had disappeared from their screen. It was a fad, a temporary interest before European desire for the indigenous and the original moved on toward new territories. The phenomenon has been so often described that it looked like nothing new could be said. And once I had said it, what could I add? How could I describe the ambiguous feelings that such interest awakens? I was told that it was a good thing that "concepts traveled" and get adopted and transformed. Was not creolization exactly about this, about opening the cultural space to flows? Yet, the "race for theory" does not occur on an equal field. I felt we were still providing

Europe with concepts without being fully consulted; that even before we had uttered any words, they were seized, scrutinized, analyzed, used, or discarded. Power mattered.

The notion of creolization emerged to describe the situation in territories such as Réunion Island, and it was meant to refer to very specific emergences. Is this context important? Is the genealogy of the notion significant, or should we declare the notion of "creolization" available, regardless of context and genealogy, to any research on intercultural units? I argue that it is important to undertake a careful examination of the situations from which creolization emerged. Rather than trying to transform "creolization" into the next meta-concept, one must clarify the emergences to which it may apply and develop concepts that can describe the diversity of intercultural phenomena that are occurring.

Playing with the concept might be an option, and one might wish the entire world to become creole from Vladivostok to Timbuktu, Lima to Shanghai. But before getting to this one-world dream, I would like to present some conditions of emergence of creolization. I do not suggest, however, that the duplication of these conditions will guarantee the production of similar processes, but they might, and researchers are already arguing that creolization can be observed in megalopolis. It is also important to acknowledge the diversity of creolization processes and practices; what happened in the Indian Ocean profoundly departed from what happened in the Caribbean, Brazil, and the United States, even though similarities exist and a comparison would be fruitful. The marginalization of the Indian-Oceanic formations in postcolonial theory demands, however, that we first present these formations and try to describe their specificities.

I will speak of the *processes and practices of creolization* on Réunion Island, and not of *creole* individuals, languages, cuisine—or of *créolité*, a notion very much connected to the text of Patrick Chamoiseau, Raphaël Confiant, and Jean Bernabé and to the French Caribbean situation.[1] A series of elements must be clear when speaking of creolization on Réunion Island: there was *no native population* on Réunion Island. Once incorporated into the French prerevolutionary colonial empire (1663), the island was populated by extremely diverse groups. The system of slavery and colonialism deeply shaped its territory and its society. It remained a French colony for three hundred years. Creole language remains to this day the main language of communication and is spoken by the majority of the population. Since 1946 the island is a French overseas department, and more recently an administrative region of Europe. It is also a *small* island, often forgotten on the maps of the world. We are used to being confused with the French Antilles—ignored or dismissed because we do not present what is usually seen as a *difference*. Despite current claims,

Figure 1   Children swimming in the harbor

this concept is still understood within the boundaries of binary elements. It is not an African island, nor a French island, nor an Asian island; it is an island of creolization. This existence on the margins (of Africa, of Asia, of France, of Europe) is something that, I argue, must be included among the elements of our problematic. The task is to inscribe the island within the crossroads of Africa, Europe, Asia, and the Muslim world, on the periphery but a periphery that is assumed and problematized.

Creolization on Réunion Island must be understood in the larger context of the Indian Ocean region. If the world of the plantation was its matrix, we must keep in mind that slaves, indentured workers, and settlers arrived on the island with memories, traces of their worlds. For the slaves and the indentured workers, it was not only the traces of their native land but of the Indian-Oceanic world as well, since the Indian-Oceanic world that existed prior to European colonization had transformed the cultures of East Africa, India, the Muslim world and Madagascar, all territories from which forced migrations to Réunion were organized. The Indian-Oceanic world served as the subterranean terrain of creolization. In other words, it was not simply the encounter between African slaves and white settlers that produced creolization (which for Caribbean scholars is the condition of creolization) but the encounter between individuals

Figure 2   Swimming in the harbor

Figure 3   Evening at one of the rare beaches known to cater to *zoreys* (French whites)

and groups already transformed by conquest and exchanges, coming from cultures as diverse as the cultures of Madagascar, the Comoros islands, Mozambique, and the south of India—layer upon layer of significations interacted. The appellations "African" and "Malagasy" are ones for our times—they evoke national or racial identities; but many groups in Madagascar and on the coasts of eastern Africa had already been mixed, affected by other cultures and encounters. The multilayered genealogy of Indian-Oceanic creolization's processes is a fundamental feature. Certainly, this configuration may also apply in the cases of other cultural emergences. Creolization is understood, to borrow an image familiar to islanders, as the endless movement of the waves on the island's coasts, bringing new elements while taking away old elements. The line of the coast is slowly changed, erosion takes its toll, but the ocean with its movement adds new deposits. The tropical winds play a role, bringing seeds of new plants. On Réunion, the physical constraints—hurricanes, fragility of the soil, presence of high mountains that divide the island into discrete territories—and an active volcano also affect the processes of creolization as they are very lively actors of the imaginary.

Loss, exile, traces, inequality, memory, adaptation, borrowing, and masculinity characterized the emergence of creolization processes on Réunion Island, which was apprehended as a local site, yet one deeply connected to regional processes and transformations. I speak of Indian-Oceanic creolizations to capture this multi-layered world. Missing archives could have described the genesis of these processes, but the history of archives on Réunion is one of loss, neglect, and voluntary destruction. However, we are able to retrieve some elements of creolization on Réunion.

INDIAN-OCEANIC WORLD

The Indian Ocean was a site of encounters and exchange long before the arrival of the Europeans in 1498. The cosmopolitan port cities of the Indian Ocean—Monbasa, Calicut—in which Armenians, Jews, Gujaratis, Bengalis, Hindus, Chinese, African, Malagasy, and Muslims mingled, forging a lingua franca, prefigured current cosmopolitan cities. There were wars, conflicts, and slave trade, but there were also practices and idioms of cultural translation that maintained and developed a world of trade and exchange (see Chaudhuri 1990, 1985; Hall 1998; Kearney 2004; Reader 1997; Toussaint, 1966). The arrival of the Europeans deeply affected, but did not destroy, the Indian Ocean world. European imperialism accelerated its integration into a world-system dominated by Europe, but parallel routes of exchange connecting the precolonial world-system of exchange among Africa, Asia, and the Muslim world were maintained.

The forced migrations (slavery, indentured workers) organized by the European colonial powers constructed roads of deportation *and* exchange.

In the second half of the twentieth century, the movement of decolonization produced new links across the ocean. Nationalism and the building of nation-states weakened the Indian-Oceanic world, by seeking first to enforce national identities, marginalize transnational exchange, and control immigration. Institutions such as the Organization of African Unity enforced the respect of national borders, but they also produced new diasporic formations with their own roads of loyalty and exchange (Indian diasporas' connections between Mauritius and Réunion, Muslim diasporas' connections among Madagascar, Mauritius, Réunion, and South Africa). The 1960s dream of South-South political alternatives with its promises of possibilities, of alternative forms of modernity, urbanization, industrialization, and cultural expressions, suggested roads of solidarity between peoples formerly subjugated by Western imperialism. The dream did not become reality: when translated into concrete realizations, the flaws often outnumbered the positive qualities. Modernization was, in most instances, represented in the architecture of the monumental. Dams, cavernous buildings, stadiums, bridges, cities, and universities were erected to affirm the power of the former wretched of the earth.

The Cold War, the enmity between the Soviet Union and China, between India and China, then the collapse of the Soviet Union and the reordering of the world's powers, affected the Indian-Oceanic world. The creation of regional organizations—Indian Ocean Zone of Peace in the 1960s, Indian Ocean Commission (1982), Indian Ocean Rim Association of Regional Cooperation (1995)—testifies to the desire to reinforce the institutional connections in the Indian-Oceanic world. But these institutional formations have not erased the informal roads of exchange.[2]

The effect of multinationals, of policies imposed by the International Monetary Fund (IMF) and former colonial powers on local and regional economies and politics, has marginalized the South-South corridor of flows and connections, Yet, the new forms of globalization—liberalization of market, weakening of national economies, increasing dependency on multinationals, creation of free trade zones with the organization of controlled importation of workforce—have paradoxically reawakened routes of formal and informal exchanges in the Indian Ocean.[3] They have revealed a new cartography of possibilities as well as the formation of new centers and new peripheries. Looking at these new flows and routes, one sees a shift from the focus on a North-South divide and the battle lines left by European imperialism to a focus on South-South flows of capital, cultural exchanges, and an informal traffic of goods and human beings. This shift makes us reconsider the history of transcontinental cultural and political connections past and present, and it can enlighten us about how narratives about peripheries are fashioned, controlled, combined, and marginalized in the non-Western world. Studying the sites of these encounters means studying the social and cultural "production of spaces" across continents, as Henri Lefevre famously showed.[4]

The world of the Indian Ocean was produced by Arab navigators and poets, by Chinese travelers and merchants, by European mythology in the Middle Ages, by African sailors and traders, by slaves, and by European colonizers, and it is currently being redefined by capital, migratory flows, regional cooperation, and cultural exchanges. It was fashioned and refashioned by different social processes, by history, and by waves of meaning and narratives, each erasing or absorbing another, borrowing from another. The narratives of the African-Asian encounters across and on the ocean offer alternative spatializations of contacts and contests to the colonial and national spatializations. Within the historical context of the Indian-Oceanic world, the islands of the southwest Indian Ocean have constituted a zone of contact and contest. Réunion Island, situated on the Asian-African axis, and its processes of creolization cannot be studied outside this larger context.

Figure 4   Tsilaos (Malagasy name given to mountains meaning "the one who is fearless")

RÉUNION ISLAND

Réunion Island, chosen by the French as a stopover on the road to India, had *no* inhabitants when it was colonized in the seventeenth century (1642). Its first inhabitants were French and Malagasy. Slavery was introduced early in the seventeenth century—the first public records of persons registered as "slaves" appeared around 1692—and although the majority of slaves came from Madagascar and the countries of East Africa, there were always Indian slaves. In his study on the slave trade, J.-M. Filliot showed that between 1670 and 1810, of the slaves taken to the Mascarenes islands (Mauritius and Réunion, then Ile de France and Bourbon), 45 percent were Malagasy, 40 percent were from the eastern coast of Africa, 13 percent from India, and 2 percent from the western coast of Africa (Filliot 1974:69). The first women were Malagasy and Indo-Portuguese; the first children born on the island were *métis*. Réunion was never the "jewel" of the French colonial empire in the Indian Ocean. Mauritius was preferred over Réunion as the headquarters of the French colonial presence in that part of the world, and Réunion remained, for quite a long time, the neglected sister of the *îles-soeurs,* as both were called.[5]

Official texts spoke of an unruly population that obeyed neither civil nor religious laws. It took a while to impose colonial order with its rigid social and spatial regulations and control of relations among racial groups. Marooning was severely punished—maroons were hanged or burned alive. Settlers had to go to mass (otherwise they had to pay a fee). They were forced to cultivate coffee and to register with the colonial administration. Réunion was long an "island of men." Women always made up less than 30 percent of the population. Although they have noted it, historians of Réunion Island have never interpreted in terms of cultural expressions and social organization the huge differential between the numbers of male and female slaves, and of male and female indentured workers. Their interpretation focused on the impossibility of marriage and of establishing families (Eve 1998; Fuma 1992). From 1704 to 1848 (date of the abolition of slavery on Réunion Island), the proportion of female slaves was less than that of male slaves: in 1704, 68.8 percent men, 31.2 percent women; in 1708, 73.5 percent men, 26.5 percent women; in 1836, 68.9 percent men, 31.1 percent women; in 1848, 68.7 percent men, 31.3 percent women.

The abolition of slavery did not correct the disparity. In 1851, of 1,334 indentured workers brought to the island, only 199 were women. Plantation work—growing and processing coffee and especially sugar—required physical strength, and since the supply of slaves and then of indentured workers seemed endless, the masters never felt the need to encourage a local reproduction of the bonded workforce. For instance, on the Kveguen plantation, one of the most important on the island, there were in the 1850s 487 men and 12 women;[6] on the Delangard plantation, 57 men, 6 women; on the Pajot, 56 men, 10 women (Fuma 1992:36). Occasionally not even one woman lived on a plantation (for example, the Biberon plantation: 48 men, no women). In 1828, an observer noted: "The population has not increased since 1824 because of the numerical disproportion between the sexes. Men are more numerous than women" (Thomas 1828:402). The illegal slave trade accentuated the disparity, and, as mentioned, the imbalance continued with the import of indentured workers. Although the agreement between England and France on the import of indentured workers from India to the French colonies required that in each shipment 25 percent would be women (the arbitrariness of 25 percent is something to ponder), that amount was never reached. In her study of Indian indentured workers, Michèle Marimoutou (1989) has shown that the ratio remained one woman for three men. An 1881 census gave the following numbers for indentured workers: 22,291 men and 8,343 women (Marimoutou 1989:168). In 1850, among the African indentured workers introduced on the island, there were 107 women and 604 men. The scarcity of women meant that men often entered into an agreement for sharing a woman.[7]

Why are these data relevant for our purpose? Creolization emerged in a slave society, during the first globalization produced by the slave trade and European colonization. It described a process constantly at work whereby new slaves were integrated and creolized by slaves who had arrived earlier. Masters were careful to diversify their community of slaves in order to foreclose or at least weaken loyalty and solidarity among slaves. Slaves learned to live and work side by side, to understand one another by creating and adopting the creole language, and by adopting and adapting one another's beliefs, rituals, and practices. Newcomers could not survive if they sought to protect the "authenticity" of their beliefs, rituals, and practices. The system of the plantation required slaves to forget the past, their roots, and their culture at the same time that it provided the grounds for preserving bits and pieces of their culture, which were then mixed with already creolized ones. The plantation was the matrix of creolization, the machine through which went slaves, indentured workers (and masters, who were also affected by the machine). But, as we have seen, slave and colonial society was first a *masculine* society. The cultural practices of creolization were produced by *men, young men* (landowners requested young men). The island was a camp of young prisoners, where the majority of men lived under the brutal rule of a few men.

Figure 5   The rugged east near the volcano

PRECARIOUS LIVES

Mostly, the slaves had been ordinary men living ordinary lives who were then fastened by the yoke of history onto the colossal event of slavery. Slavery could not be written as an epic. It was a war of predation in which people could be sold by their families as well as by kidnappers, seized as booty.[8] Blindfolded, taken at night on ships, these men left their land and one day found themselves on a small island, sold and taken to a plantation. Although the images of plantations in the southern United States and in the Caribbean have become common, they do not represent plantations on Réunion, which were neither the fictional Uncle Tom Cabin's kind nor the kind described either by free slaves or by abolitionists. The island was a sum of discrete territories, an *archipelago-island*—the physical geography deeply divides the island, and to this day the main way to go from one place to the other is by the coast road. Just one road in the south connects both sides of the island. The number of poor white settlers with two or three slaves was not inconsequential. The portrait of an island forgotten by history would be false—new technologies and European cultural innovations arrived on the island, if only very slowly. There were transformations and dissemination of ideas, ruptures with the past, and internal political debates, but the isolation of Réunion and the conservatism of its ruling class remained.

Slavery was about fabricating disposable people who *did not count* as social beings. Orlando Patterson (1982) has used the term "social death" to describe what happened to people in the world that slavery made. I would like to emphasize this concept. These were lives not worth noting, that did not qualify for recognition except as objects (*meubles* in the Code Noir that codified slaves' lives in the French colonies from 1685 to 1848), living on a land not worth noting, that did not qualify as central on the French imperial map.[9] The experience of not counting, of living on the margins must be reinterpreted. The subject is never connected to sovereignty. It is a vulnerable subject, whose precarious life's horizon is shaped by the capricious decisions of colonial economy, by the masters' whims and endless appetite for bonded workforce. The dehumanization of the slave was determined not only by the economy of predation but also by the refusal to acknowledge him as human by denying him the rituals that surround birth and death. No individual grave for the slave, no name on the grave. This fact should provide the grounds for a rethinking of what is a subject, an enterprise taken up by feminists and postcolonial thinkers for the past three decades. It should provide the grounds for rethinking freedom outside the frame suggested by Western philosophy. Death and solitude were often the terrain on which freedom could be experienced (bands of maroons were chased to be killed but there are also accounts of lonely maroons). These experiences (not counting vulnerability) suffused the vocabulary of creolization, which we should take as a vocabulary of suffering *and* agency.

Not only slaves and indentured workers were bound to the island by the yoke of history. The whites coming to the island were not all wealthy Europeans or young aristocrats seeking fortune but for the most part, were poor peasants from the poor regions of France and Europe forced to emigrate by the State. They had no choice.

The process of creolization was fragile; it was regularly threatened by new arrivals and weakened by the masters' regulations. It was nonetheless this very fragility that was the condition of creolization. Creolization was a dialectical movement of forgetting, adopting, and transforming what was adopted, of creating rituals and practices that could be shared by diverse groups that had always brought their own singular approach. For instance, death was framed within a mix of Afro-Malagasy and Hindu understanding of filiation, genealogy and time, to which each group added its own contributions. They shared a common language—the first official recognition of Réunion Creole appeared in the accounts of a trial at the beginning of the eighteenth century, and in 1828, a book of folktales was published in Réunion Creole.

INDIAN-OCEANIC CREOLIZATIONS

There is *no creolization without conflict* between affirmed contrasts and the movement toward unity. Through a dialectical movement of borrowing from one another—beliefs, rituals, cuisine, aesthetics—and keeping alive certain traditions, enslaved men negotiated their inclusion into the group. The group of slaves was never constituted along rigid limits; it was reconfigured by force, and yet transmission occurred. When Indian indentured workers arrived on Réunion, they clashed with the emancipated slaves and sought to distinguish themselves from bonded workers: they were free, they claimed, and not blacks. And yet they adopted creole ways of being and living while bringing their own rituals, practices, and beliefs, which the population creolized before adopting. The coexistence of conflict, tension, and cohabitation produced a unity, the creolized world, that was, in turn, tested by new contrasts. Both plurality and unity were produced by the same structures: slavery and colonialism.

The fragility of the creolization processes raises questions for the researcher: How were rituals transmitted? How was any solid ground established? Creolization as a process of creating structures of identification, cultural practices, and ways of being and understanding time, space, and the world was not forged in relation to a sovereign territory. Creolization began with displacement and exile creating other forms of inhabiting the territory. It was the experience of *being a foreigner*. The new country was a territory of enslavement, deportation, and exile, but it was also a new world with an evolving culture. Cultures arrived in bits and pieces. The alienation of slavery, the "social death" of slavery, the forced relocation, and the fact of having no ongoing choice produced a radically different relation to the territory.

Figure 6   Manmade dry landscape on the west coast

Processes and practices were produced from loss, memory, translation, and the experience of living on an island, which is also the experience of solitude. Imagine a slave living on a plantation at St. Philippe, a city on the southern coast of the island, where black jutting volcanic rocks sharply contrast with the blue expanse of the ocean. The ocean always seems uninhabited; not a ship, not a boat, not any land in sight, just the expanse of water to the horizon. The night falls; he is alone. Everything that was familiar is gone, and he sings; others join him. I am not being romantic, I am trying to reconstruct the moment when *maloya* (the traditional music of Réunion, sung by slaves, transformed by indentured workers and transmitted to this day) was created—a melancholic music, a "blues." The process of creolization, in spite of its creativity, originality, and innovation, carried with it the memory of brutality and violence; the solitude of men separated from their lands and living without women, without tenderness.

Of course, it is not that men without women could not experience love and tenderness. Homosexuality certainly existed on the plantations, but the brutality of slavery and indenturing evoked the world of camps and prisons rather than the world of love; the world of the strong preying on the weak. The desire to escape punishment, to scrape by a little better, to be distinguished by the master or the *commandeur*—the overseer in the fields—as a "good, compliant" worker was certainly there. How could it have been otherwise? Could we truly believe that the world of slaves was only a world of revolt and heroism? It was a world of accommodation, of small victories, and a world that produced strong individualism, a world of "each for himself."

The precarious life of the plantation system, which on Réunion ended only in the late 1960s, and the organized vulnerability of the population raise a series of questions. How can we explain that brutality, violence, inequality, and survival under extreme conditions bred a culture that has shown an incredible capacity to adapt and adopt? It is as if peaceful conditions would not produce creolization. But peaceful conditions do not entail forced migrations, exile, deportation, dehumanization, and denial of rights. Slavery and the system of indentured work did not last ten, twenty years. Slavery lasted 174 years, and indenturing, 98. Month after month of social death, vulnerability, and organized predation shaped the world of Réunionnais.[10] The state of exception was the norm; even after abolition, the new free "citizens" remained colonized—Réunion was a colony until 1946. Post-abolition Réunion colonial society redefined the techniques of discipline and punishment. Indentured workers complained about the working and living conditions. Poor whites, impoverished by the concentration of land in the hands of only a few landowners and whose number was not negligible, were also subjected to the colonial order. The arrival of new groups—Indo-Muslims and Chinese—by the mid-nineteenth century added to the complexity of Réunion society. Both groups also experienced a great disparity in the numbers of males and females (in 1897, for instance, women constituted only 16.7 percent of the Indo-Muslim migrants). Immigrant males had to marry outside their group, but native women, as we have shown, still constituted only a third of the total population. Both groups experienced what previous groups had experienced: rejection by Réunion's established society. Newspapers spoke of the *péril jaune* (yellow scare), of the threat that these new migrants embodied. (Réunion Creole is still full of expressions that stereotype the different groups constituting the population.)

So, as we have seen, the world that gave birth to creolization processes was a world in which the majority of the population was poor, rural, and deprived of women. It was a world in which the arrival of groups only maintained the population level; there was no indigenous population increase because of the high mortality rate and the low birth rate, owing to the low ratio of females to males. It was a world in which men died young after a harsh life. Yet, it was also a world that invented a unique

Figure 7   Anse des cascades, southeast coast; a favorite spot for families on Sunday outings

aesthetics—for example, modern architects are looking at the inventiveness of vernacular architecture, at the creolized space of habitat that mixes inside and outside in a very original fashion—and a new cuisine, that maintained and reinvented rituals, that developed a rich traditional ethno-medicine and distinct music that borrows from diverse sources, instrumentally, vocally, and compositionally. This world's philosophy rests on different sources, as does its language.

The tales told by the grandmothers of *créolités* belie the short history of their presence. We are not used to thinking of a culture mainly shaped by men. The world of subjugated men is usually a world of violence and brutality, in which the strong rule. On Réunion, violence and brutality are present in the gendered vocabulary of Réunion Creole, in the ways in which female gender, biology, and sexuality are described (with unrepressed rage and aggressivity). The high number of insults aimed at mothers signifies a deep anxiety. If a woman was shared by many men, how could one man trust her to deserve his love? And for the child, who was the father? The practices of creolization incorporated the history of inequality and brutality, and the melancholy of lonely men. Yet, and this deserves our attention, these men, slaves, indentured workers, and poor whites gave us the world that today offers us the capacity to adapt and adopt, to be flexible, decentered and able to develop a theory of the subject which is not contained within the limits of imperial sovereignty.

CREOLIZATION AND POSTCOLONIALITY

Creolization is a process constantly at work, in which "diffusion" and "spread" of elements accompany appropriation and adoption; a process that necessitates the agency of the recipient. Of course, many of the interactions involved in the creolization process do not take place between equals. Creolization is not a harmonious process; it involves exclusion and discrimination. It is, as Aimé Césaire proposed in his letter to Maurice Thorez, about finding a viable way of avoiding "two paths to doom: by segregation, by walling yourself in the particular; or by dilution, by thinning off into the emptiness of the 'universal.'" It is about *not* having the choice to share a territory with others, people whom we have not chosen and whose ways of being and living are not "ours." Creolization challenges the "truth" of identity. It suggests that loss is not necessarily a lack. It does not comprise a series of homogeneous parts that can be subtracted or added at will; it is a dynamic process, a movement. Not from A to B, or A plus B, but bits of A plus altered A plus bits of B. All this may look rather abstract, but it was brought home to me by the experience of living on a land without a precolonial past, a land of estrangement for each inhabitant, who had no roots and no origin but the fact of colonization.

To Édouard Glissant, the *relation* is central to creolization, and he takes the notion of creolization to a new global level. Widespread cultural encounters, fragmentation of cultures, "extreme multilingualism is the inevitable destiny of all countries. Modern communications further exacerbates contact and diversity" (Dash 1995:179). Glissant (1996:19) argues that it is inevitable that increasing "chaos" (increasing encounters of cultures, in which no culture can claim to represent a totality) will lead to creolization. Creolization always contains a part of the unexpected (whereas the outcome of *métissage* can be calculated). Creolization "demands that the heterogeneous elements in relation valorize each other, in other words that there is no degradation or diminution of the subject [*de l'être*] through this contact, this mixing" (Glissant 1996:18).

Though I share with Glissant a good part of his analysis of creolization, I do not think that the process of creolization is the rule in situations of contacts between cultures (historically, it was rather the exception). Contacts between cultures do not necessarily produce creolization; they can produce apartheid, separatism, multiculturalism, and indifferent cohabitation. Creolization requires the forgetting of origins, which survive only as reconstructed and transformed. In the current era of globalization, the politics and economy of predation, trafficking in human beings, brutality, and force are organizing new territories of power and resistance. There are new global cities. Are we witnessing processes of creolization in these territories? They are not exactly reproducing the conditions of the plantation by which the process of creolization emerged. If creolization is understood as a process of mixing, we can certainly argue that we are witnessing such processes. They might produce a unity as well (creolization = diversity *and* unity challenged by diversity, which in turn experiences a process of unification). However, creolization is not a *global* process. I think that we are witnessing processes of creolization along with processes of contact, apartheid, indifferent multiculturalism, and new forms of contact and conflict. Within the same territory—a city, a region—these different processes may coexist, overlap, or be in conflict. Further, it remains to be seen to what extent processes of creolization can resist the pressure of the politics of identity. Is creolization still at work in the current era of liberal globalization? Can it be extended to current situations of contact? Is current globalization producing situations similar to those of the era of slave trade, characterized by trafficking in human beings, predation, brutality, and force?

On Réunion Island (and in the Caribbean), creolization is under attack. It is threatened by the ethnicization of memory, in which each group claims a memory connected to an ethnic group—for example, the memory of slavery connected to *Kaf,* the black population; the memory of indentured work to Malbars, the name given to the Hindus—regardless of the complex history of groups, the inevitable mixing, and the diversity of origins. The shared narrative of creolization is contested by the privatization of narratives. It is also threatened by the dominant discourse of identity formation, whereby the self is understood as self-sufficient, detached from the web of debts, relations, and networks of filiation that contribute to its sense of being. It is threatened by the aspirations of a local petty bourgeoisie that wishes to be recognized as "French" and that often opposes the teaching of Réunion Creole language and history in the schools. It is threatened by local conservatives who are so afraid of local initiatives and creativity that cut across social and ethnocultural groups that they support either an ethnicization of culture or a managed folklorization. It is threatened by liberal globalization and its intent to manage difference and package it for consumption.

However, despite these assaults, creolization processes suggest alternatives to interpret conflict and negotiation, interculturality and difference. The novelty comes from inhabiting a small country with no national traditions, less frightened therefore of losing a "status" among the nations that "count." It comes from the experience of a people who had no pretensions to setting itself as a model and who went into the world not to take possession but as exiles and migrants. The creolization experience—which, again, was not and is not without conflicts arising from being forced to live together, to share a territory with groups from extremely different cultures, religions, and beliefs—constitutes an experience that protects us against the temptation of making ourselves too visible, the temptation to impose our values, our ways of being on other peoples.

The paradigm of Indian-Oceanic creolization suggests a problematic of loss and reappropriation. We look back to the countries of origin to overlay the roads of deportation and forced migrations with new roads of solidarity that do not convey nostalgia for the past. We are open to new emergences, new forms of creolization, new vernacular expressions.

amwin m'la pa bézwin rodé
amwin férblan mon kalité
i débord i koul atèr
sanm tout mon batarsité
amwin m'la pa bézwin rodé
amwin ganblo mon kalité
i débord i koul atèr

Danyèl Waro, Batarsité[11]

Notes

1. On Réunion Island, people do not call themselves "Creoles" but "Réunionnais," to indicate the community to which they belong that transcends ethnocultural connections.
2. See Thierry Malbert's essay in Vergès (2000).
3. A few years ago, Beijing signed an agreement with the Mauritian government, which needed workers for its free-trade zone. Female Chinese workers were sent to work in the factories—living and working under very strict rules (Kothari & Nababsing 1996). Unions could not make contact with them. The local newspapers printed negative reports about the Chinese female workers who "prostituted themselves and brought AIDS." Capital from Singapore, Hong Kong, and South Africa has financed projects in the Seychelles, Mauritius, and Madagascar. Insisting on the common bonds between Madagascar and Japan (islands with an enlightened monarchy in the past, carriers of a distinctive culture and civilization), Japan has established a number of programs on the island (teaching Japanese, exchanges of students, cooperation). The restructuring of the Indian Ocean space has facilitated the emergence of informal routes as well, which are either reconstructing ancient routes of exchange or creating new ones. Direct flights between Antananarivo and Singapore twice a week have reinforced informal economic connections between the two countries. The Malagasy middle class now shops in Singapore, and new networks of informal trade have emerged between Madagascar and South East Asia. Diasporic groups in South Africa, Réunion, Comoros, Mauritius, and Madagascar have seized the new opportunities.

4. Doods and Atkinson 2000; Harvey 2000; Lefevre 1976; Soja 1988. The work of Yves Lacoste and his review *Herodote* is also useful for the understanding of space as socially and politically produced.
5. In 1815, Mauritius was integrated into the British colonial empire. Réunion remained a French colony.
6. Data given in Eve (1998). To Eve, the imbalance meant that women could exercise "their power" on men.
7. The disparity between numbers of women and men was lessened only at the beginning of the twentieth century.
8. On the economy of slavery in Indian Ocean as an economy deeply connected to social organization, see Campbell (2004).
9. I have written elsewhere of the lamentations of the white colonists, who always felt ignored, dismissed, and marginalized in comparison with Mauritius, Madagascar, and India. They always sought to be noticed by the French State, by depicting Réunion as a dutiful daughter, the "colony that colonizes."
10. On the living and working conditions of indentured workers, see Fuma (1999) and Marimoutou (1989).
11. "I do not have to seek/The watering can is my identity/It leaks, it waters the soil/All of it is my "Bastardity"/ I do not have to seek/My watering can is my quality/It leaks, it waters the soil." Song of Danyèl Waro, one of the most famous singer/poet/composers of *maloya*. The song is about the multiplicity of origins that belie the illusion of purity, and it introduces the notion of *batarsité* (from *batar*, bastard).

References

Campbell, G., ed. 2004. *The structure of slavery in Indian Africa and Asia*. London: Cass.

Chaudhuri, K. N. 1985. *Trade and civilisation in the Indian Ocean: An economic history from the rise of Islam to 1750*. Cambridge: Cambridge University Press.

———— 1990. *Asia before Europe: Economy and civilisation of the Indian Ocean from the rise of Islam to 1750*. Cambridge: Cambridge University Press.

Dash, M. 1995. *Edouard Glissant*. Cambridge: Cambridge University Press, 1995.

Doods, K., and D. Atkinson. 2000. *Geopolitical traditions. A century of geopolitical thought*. London: Routledge.

Eve, P. 1998. *Variations sur le thème de l'amour à Bourbon à l'époque de l'esclavage*. St-Denis Réunion: Océan editions.

Filliot, J.-M. 1974. *La Traite des esclaves vers les Mascareignes au XVIIIe siècle*. Paris: Office de la recherche scientifique et technique outre-mer.

Fuma, S. 1992. *L'esclavagisme à La Réunion, 1794–1848*. Paris: L'Harmattan/Université de La Réunion.

———— 1999. *De l'Inde du sud à l'île de La Réunion. Les Réunionnais d'origine indienne d'après le rapport Mackenzie*. St-Denis Réunion: Université de La Réunion/GRAHTER.

Glissant, E. 1996. *Introduction à une poétique du divers*. Paris: Gallimard.

Hall, R. 1998. *Empires of the monsoon: A history of the Indian Ocean and its invaders*. London: Harper Collins.

Harvey, D. 2000. *Spaces of hope*. Edinburgh: Edinburgh University Press.

Kearney, M. 2004. *The Indian Ocean in world history*. London: Routledge.

Kothari, U., and V. Nababsing. 1996. *Gender and industrialization*. St-Denis, La Réunion: Éditions de l'Océan Indien.

Lefevre, H. 1976. *The survival of capitalism*. London: Allison & Busby.

Marimoutou, M. 1989. *Les engagés du sucre*. St-Denis Réunion: Éditions du Tramail.

Patterson, O. 1982. *Slavery and social death. A comparative study*. Cambridge, MA: Harvard University Press.

Pearson, M. 2004. *The Indian Ocean*. London: Routledge.

Reader, J. 1997. *Africa: A biography of the continent*. London: Penguin Books.

Soja, E. W. 1988. *Postmodern geographies: The reassertion of space in critical social theory*. London: Verso.

Thomas, P. 1828. *Essai statistique de l'Ile Bourbon*. Paris.

Toussaint, A. 1966. *History of the Indian Ocean*. J. Guichranaud, trans. London: Routledge.

Vergès, F., ed. 2000. Mapping a contact-zone. Unpublished report for CODESRIA-MacArthur Foundation.

8 Creolization in Anthropological Theory and in Mauritius

Thomas Hylland Eriksen

A great amount of intellectual energy has been invested in cultural mixing during the last decades. Reacting against an idea of boundedness, internal homogeneity, and stability that has been associated with mainstream twentieth-century anthropology, hundreds—possibly thousands—of anthropologists have tried to redefine, reform, revolutionize, or even relinquish that abhorred "C" word— "culture." The range of engagement is suggested in the apparent congruence between postmodernist American anthropologists (for example, Clifford & Marcus 1986) and their now classic critique of the Geertzian notion of cultural integration, and the older European critique of the structural-functionalist idea of social integration, which was led by people such as Barth (1966), whose rationalism and naturalism is everything but postmodernist. In both cases, presuppositions of integrated wholes, cultures or social structures, have been debunked.

From being a discipline concentrating its efforts on understanding nonliterate societies, often implicitly positing the uncontaminated aborigine

Different parts of this chapter have been presented at the Transnational Communities Programme, Oxford University in 1999, at the Creolization workshop at University College London in 2002, and at the Department of Social Anthropology, University of Cape Town in 2003. Thanks are due to the convenors and participants at these events, and in particular Charles Stewart, Zimitri Erasmus, Steven Vertovec, Laurent Medea, and Rose Boswell, for helping me to clarify the argument.

as its hero, anthropology increasingly studies cultural impurity and hybridity, and the dominant normative discourse in the field has shifted from defending the cultural rights of small peoples to combating essentialism and reifying identity politics. While this development has been important and necessary for a variety of reasons, the perspectives developed risk being one-sided and inadequate.[1] A focus on mixing and flows that does not take continuity and boundedness into account ends up undermining its own social theory: Every social scientist knows that cultural meaning is being reproduced and transmitted between generations and that natives do classify and create boundaries, often amidst powerful tendencies of cultural mixing. The views of culture as continuum and variation as endemic are uncomfortably uncontroversial today (see Fox & King, 2002, for a state-of-the-art overview). These views are problematic because the processes associated with socialization and institutional continuity in societies presuppose a wide range of shared understandings, which are often implicit and do not enter the arena of identity politics, and because groups remain bounded in a variety of different ways.

It is a trivial fact that variation within any group is considerable, and cultural flows across boundaries ensure that mixing, in the contemporary world, is everywhere. However, the impression sometimes given that "everything" seems to be in continuous flux, that an infinity of opportunities seems to be open and that no groups, cultural identities, or ethnic categories are fixed, is due to a conflation of discrete phenomena.

First: Strong identities and fixed boundaries do not preclude cultural mixing. Ethnic variation may well exist without significant cultural variation. Processes of cultural mixing say nothing about group identities and degrees of boundedness.

Second: Fluid identities, conversely, do not preclude cultural stability or continuity. Cultural variation can exist without ethnic variation or other kinds of strong group boundaries. Culture is caused by varying degrees of shared meaning, whereas group identities result from clear, if disputed, social boundaries.

Third: The political usages of cultural symbols do not mean that the people in question do not necessarily have anything in common. (Being paranoid is no guarantee that nobody is after you.) Historiography, it has been shown time and again, is necessarily a selective and biased discipline simply because far too many events have taken place in the past for any historian to give all of them a fair treatment. Yet its slanted narratives may become self-fulfilling prophecies in that they give people a shared frame of reference. Besides, the people described by nationalist historians or ideologists of group boundedness may not have that in common which their ideologists ascribe to them, but they may have other cultural elements in common, such as shared jokes and ideas about kin relatedness. What has interested writers on cultural mixing are the situations in which these frames of references do not function; where they are contested, nonexistent, or are being continuously rebuilt. But it may just happen to be the case, in other words, that ethnic boundaries coincide with certain cultural ones. (Moreover, the fact that something is socially constructed does not, of course, imply that it is unreal.)

This means that the ambiguous grey zones, which can be located in the space between categories and boundaries under pressure, are privileged sites for studying the interplay between culture and identity. This is not because all boundaries eventually disappear, but because they are made visible through their negotiation and renegotiation, transcendence, transformation, and reframing. A world without social boundaries (a neoliberalist's dream?) is sociologically unthinkable.

THE TERM "CREOLIZATION"

One of the more popular concepts used to deal with the increased complexity of the empirical fields now studied by anthropologists, is creolization (Drummond 1980; Hannerz 1992, 1996). Creolization is often used merely as a synonym for mixing or hybridity, but from the discussion below, it will become apparent that both the historical origins of the term and its contemporary usage in societies containing self-designating creoles suggest that a more restricted use of the term might be both necessary and analytically helpful.

"Creolization," as the term is used by some anthropologists, is an analogy taken from linguistics. This discipline in turn took the term from a particular aspect of colonialism, namely the uprooting and displacement of large numbers of people in colonial plantation economies. Both in the Caribbean basin and in the Indian Ocean, certain (or all) groups who contributed to this economy during slavery were described as creoles. Originally, a *criollo* meant a Spaniard born in the New World (as opposed to *peninsulares*); today, a similar usage is current in La Réunion, where everybody born in the island, regardless of skin color, is seen as *créole*, as opposed to the *zoréoles* who were born in metropolitan France. In Trinidad, the term "creole" is sometimes used to designate all Trinidadians except those of Asian origin. In Suriname, a creole is a person of African origin, whereas in neighboring French Guyana a creole is someone who has adopted a European way of life. In spite of the differences, there are resemblances between the conceptualizations of the creole. Creoles are uprooted, they belong to a New World, and are contrasted with that which is old, deep, and rooted.

A question often posed by people unfamiliar with these variations is "What is *really* a Creole?" They may have encountered the term in connection with food or architecture from Louisiana, languages in the Caribbean, or people in the Indian Ocean. The standard response is that whereas vernacular uses of the term "creole" vary, there exist accurate definitions of creole languages in linguistics and of cultural creolization in anthropology. There are nevertheless similarities, although there is no one-to-one relationship, between the ethnic groups described locally (emically) as creoles and the phenomena classified as creole or creolised in the academic literature. A motto for the present exploration could therefore be Gregory Bateson's admonition that if one uses creative analogies, one ought to go back to the field from which the analogy was taken to investigate its internal logic. As he puts it: "the moment I begin to work out the analogy, I am brought up against the rigid formulations which have been devised in the field from which I borrow the analogy" (Bateson 2000b:75). In other words, it is worthwhile to take a close look at Mauritian creoledom to see if it could shed light on the theoretical applications of the term "creolization."

MAURITIUS AND ITS CREOLES

Mauritius, located near the Tropic of Capricorn eight hundred kilometers east of Madagascar, is a crowded, bustling, complex, democratic, hierarchical, and, of recent, prosperous island. Its total population is slightly over a million, giving it a population density of about 550 inhabitants per square kilometer. All the inhabitants are descendants of immigrants who have arrived during the last three centuries, from France, China, Africa, Madagascar, and India. About half the population are Hindus, but they are subdivided into North Indians ("Hindi speaking"), Tamils, Telugus, and Marathis, who function politically and culturally as separate ethnic groups. The largest ethnic group are North Indian Hindus, constituting about 40 percent of the population. Seventeen percent are Muslims of Indian descent, around 28 percent are Creoles or nonwhite Catholics of African, Malagasy, or mixed descent, about 7 percent are Tamils, and 3 percent are Chinese and less than 2 percent Franco-Mauritians.

It may be said that all the cultures of all the ethnic groups in Mauritius have been culturally creolized—uprooted and adapted to local circumstances—to a greater or lesser extent. For example, the Bhojpuri spoken by many of the Indo-Mauritians has been so strongly influenced by other languages that it is scarcely intelligible to modern Bhojpuri-speakers in Bihar, and the Franco-Mauritians—like other Mauritians—eat spicy curries and lots of rice. Nearly every Mauritian speaks the local French-based Creole language (*Kreol* or *Morisyen*) fluently, and it is the mother tongue of a substantial majority. Regarding lifestyle, consumption, and way of life in general, it is easy to demonstrate the effects of mutual influence among the ethnic groups that make up the Mauritian population, as well as cultural influence from the outside world—not merely from the West but also from India and East Asia.

In spite of obvious cultural creolization evident throughout Mauritian society, it is chiefly the Mauritians of African and/or Malagasy descent who are classified locally as Creoles. Already in the 1850s, the Rev. Patrick Beaton entitled his book on Mauritius *Creoles and Coolies* (Beaton 1977), contrasting the two major groups of African and Indian descent, respectively. The ancestors of Mauritian Creoles were slaves from different parts of Africa and Madagascar, brought there between 1715 (the beginning of French colonization) and 1810 (when the slave trade was banned). As in other plantation colonies based on slavery, slave owners in Île-de-France (as Mauritius was called during French rule) mixed individuals from different ethnic groups, dissolving family structures and political organization. As a result, in a given compound, there were few shared collective cultural resources; no shared language, no shared kinship structure, cosmology, or traditional system of social organization that might have been transplanted and eventually reproduced. Thus the degree of cultural continuity in the slave groups was by default limited. As in similar setups in the Caribbean, a creole language developed quickly, using French vocabulary, a modified pronounciation and a simplified grammar. In Bernardin de St. Pierre's travel book from 1773, *Voyage à l'Île de France*, fragments of the so-called patois spoken by the slaves are cited in a few places, and they appear to be similar to the creole spoken in Mauritius today.

Some religious beliefs and practices have survived, in modified forms, although the slaves were converted to Christianity and their descendants are Catholics. However, the most significant "African survival" is in music and dance, where the *séga*, which has obvious African forebears, has attained a status as a national music of Mauritius.

In other words, like groups known as Creoles in other parts of the world, Mauritian Creoles have a history of uprootedness, and the connection with their places of origin was severed on arrival in the colony. This entailed the urgent necessity of crafting new cultural and social forms under conditions of extreme hardship.

THE NON-CREOLES

Let me now briefly contrast the situation of these Creoles with that of other Mauritian groups. The Sino-Mauritians, the most recent arrivals to the island (most arrived during the first half of the twentieth century, a few after the Chinese Revolution), have changed their religion (to Catholicism) and to a great extent their language (to Kreol) but have retained both their kinship organization, many aspects of their material culture and important rituals, as well as active links with relatives in east Asia. Regarding the Franco-Mauritians, most of whom are descendants of Frenchmen who arrived in Mauritius in the eighteenth century, their kinship links with Europe have in most cases waned, yet they have always been the economically and culturally dominant group in the island. Even when the British conquered Mauritius during the Napoleonic wars, the Franco-Mauritians were promised the right to retain their customs, language, and religion.

Regarding the ethnic groups originating from the Indian subcontinent, the conditions of their arrival could be said to resemble those of slavery (cf. Hugh Tinker's influential book on the indentureship system, *A New Form of Slavery*, 1974). They were brought from Madras, Calcutta, and Bombay from the 1840s onward in order to replace the liberated slaves as plantation labor. When they arrived in the colony it turned out that they were interned in camps with restricted freedom of movement, and although they were nominally free, their situation may well justify the term "a new form of slavery." However, relevant differences existed between slaves and indentured laborers. These people came from various parts of India: Bihar, eastern Uttar Pradesh, Andhra Pradesh, Tamil Nadu, and Maharashtra. They transplanted their beliefs and ritual practices, languages, kinship structures, food habits, a simplified caste structure, and rudiments of their political organization (including *panchayats*, village councils) to their new home, and even—in the case of the north Indian Hindus—invented a myth to the effect that the small, secluded lake Grand Bassin in southern Mauritius contained the holy waters of the Ganges. (Today, the largest Hindu festival outside India is said to be the annual Maha Shivaratree pilgrimage to Grand Bassin.) Soon after the arrival of the first batches of indentured laborers, temples were built, and as the indentureship period ended, they developed rural villages, replicating in no small degree the Indian countryside.

In spite of this continuity, several aspects of Indo-Mauritian culture and social life result from cultural creolization—from aesthetic details such as clothing to more fundamental issues such as the omnipresence of the monetary economy and wage work; the *jajmani* system, important in rural India, vanished, and the caste system thus lost one of its most important functions. (There are only four operative castes among Hindus in Mauritius, and although politics, marriage, and interpersonal networks have a caste aspect, it is less important than in India.)

Within the Indo-Mauritian communities, notably North Indian Hindus, North Indian Muslims, and Tamils, there are ongoing controversies regarding "cultural purity," the relationship to Kreol and European languages (English and French) and Western culture in general, questions of "roots," and so on. More relevant in the present context are the different implications, at the level of political and cultural identity, of the histories of Creoles on the one hand, and the non-Creole Mauritians on the other.

Non-Creole Mauritians have the opportunity to draw on enormous non-Mauritian cultural traditions in order to make political or existential statements about themselves. Although they, like the Creoles, can be seen as diasporic populations—uprooted, exiled, and homeless—their genealogical and cultural links with their ancestral country enable them to construe their past as an unbroken and continuous narrative that harks back to the mists of prehistory, and, even more importantly in an age of identity politics, their identity can be metonymically linked with a prestigious civilization—Chinese, Indian, Islamic, or European. These links are being reactivated in several ways, increasingly so since the early 1990s, which was not only a period of revitalized identity politics but also one of considerable prosperity in Mauritius. For example, the country has seen the rise of a moderately successful political Hindu movement along the lines of the Bharatiya Janata Party (BJP) in India itself; the Muslims, generally opting for an Islamic identity rather than an Indian (or Pakistani) one, have for years groomed their relationship with the Arab world and Mauritian Tamils, whose organisations have recently been very active in identity politics at the national level, employing architects and craftsmen from Tamil Nadu to build a spectacular Tamil temple near Grand' Baie in northern Mauritius at the turn of the century. While Franco-Mauritians have always traveled regularly to France, Indo-Mauritians also increasingly travel to ancestral countries or spiritual homelands (in the case of Muslims), sometimes in search of their ancestral village.

LE MALAISE CRÉOLE

Such practices, which emphasise the organic connection between diaspora and metropole, simultaneously serve to strengthen group cohesion within Mauritius and to counteract a feeling of uprootedness or *créolité*. Regarding the Creoles, they have few opportunities to match the efforts of the other groups. To begin with, few Creoles recognize and cherish their African origins. Some intellectuals have tried to redefine the Creoles as "Afro-Mauritians" (Benoît 1984 see also Boswell 2003) along the same lines as "Sino-Mauritians," "Indo-Mauritians," and so on , but with limited success. A handful of politically conscious parents have given their children Ashanti or Yoruba names, but French first names predominate massively. Direct contact between Creoles and Africans is limited, and although the booming Mauritian textile industry is now investing in Madagascar, the investors belong to non-Creole ethnic groups.

Even if the effort to provide the Creoles with an African identity had been successful, it would have been difficult to give it a substantial content. Since the slaves came from different parts of West and East Africa, no Creole is able to point out where his or her ancestors came from. The Creoles lack a tangible precolonial past and are unable to draw on close links with a major civilization in their identity politics.

Throughout the 1990s, one of the most pressing public issues in Mauritius was the cluster of social problems called *le malaise créole*, the "Creole ailment" (see Boswell 2003 for a systematic treatment; see also Eriksen 2004). Social change has been rapid in Mauritius since the mid-1980s, leading to a significant improvement of standards of living and educational achievements. In this process, it has become clear that the Creoles have been lagging behind. It has also been argued that the reasons for this can be found in Creole culture, which places a great emphasis on individualism, freedom, and consumption, and in Creole social organization, which lacks the strong kinship obligations characteristic of the other groups. These accounts are one-sided in that they fail to consider, among other things, the connections among Hindu political hegemony, kinship obligations, nepotism, and Hindu dominance in the state sector. Yet it must be conceded that their description of Creole values and way of life are not entirely inaccurate. As I have shown earlier (Eriksen 1988), moreover, that the powerful individualism among the Creoles has nothing to do with "African roots" but can be traced back to the social conditions under slavery, when family and kinship systems were destroyed, individual freedom emerged as the paramount value, and social relations were individualized and became contractual in nature. In the contemporary context of a democratic, competitive capitalist society, the Creoles are at a clear disadvantage because of their loose social organization and their relative lack of symbolic capital in Mauritian identity politics.

TWO WAYS OF BEING CREOLE

Some of the individuals who might seem the very embodiments of cultural creolization (genetically mixed, culturally familiar with several traditions, and frequently rejoicing in the cultural "mosaic" of Mauritius) are not defined as Creoles locally. However, there are also tendencies to the effect that local classifications more closely approach the analytical concept of creolization as it has been developed, for example, by Hannerz. A good example is offered by a ten-year old schoolboy of my acquaintance, who lives in a middle-class neighborhood in a Mauritian town. His father is a Tamil and his mother is a north Indian Hindu; he is, in other words, the offspring of a mixed marriage, although it would be considered "less mixed" than, say, a Hindu-Creole marriage. Since his father is a Tamil, the boy is expected to take Tamil lessons at school. This is not a language that has ever been spoken in his home. The way of life in his family could be described as very creolized; with regard to food, clothes, interior decorating, ritual, and music, both Indian and European influences are clearly present and are routinely and unquestioningly mixed. Not surprisingly, the boy did not want to take Tamil lessons and argued that he considered himself a Creole since his first language was Kreol. The parents, telling me about the son's predicament, had no objections to his line of reasoning; to them, ethnic labels were unimportant and ancestral languages irrelevant; what mattered was the quality of the boy's education. The boy, like many other Mauritians of non-African origin—and not just children of mixed marriages—saw himself as a Creole by virtue of speaking Kreol and not belonging to one of the distinct Asian or European communities in the island. This kind of process, which has been spoken of as "creolization" a few times in Mauritius, corresponds well to the anthropological concept of creolization, but not with standard ethnic classification in Mauritius, where Creole still means "a person of African/Malagasy or mixed descent."

A relevant aspect of Creole identity, as opposed to other ethnic identities in Mauritius, is its fluidity and openness. It is sometimes said that "many Creoles look like Indians nowadays," and it is true that many Mauritians with Christian names and a "Creole" family structure, Creole networks and a creole way of life do look vaguely Indian. This is presumably caused both by conversions and by intermarriage. In general, Creoles are more tolerant of intermarriage than are other Mauritian groups, and it is to some extent possible to *become* a Creole within one's own lifetime—while one cannot conceivably become a Hindu, a Sino-Mauritian, or a Franco-Mauritian. The fuzzy category of Mauritian Creoles thus includes both the traditional Creoles, that is, dark-skinned working-class people most of whose ancestors were slaves, and a residual category of modern or postmodern Creoles, who are Creoles because, for various reasons, they do not fit in elsewhere. On this background, and given the increasing numbers of mixed marriages, some Mauritians actually envision a future when *tu dimunn pu vini kreol*—when everybody becomes a Creole. The notion of cultural mixing or impurity is important here, as is the notion of individualism.

The language *Kreol* (or *Morisyen*) must also be considered. Kreol, which evolved during slavery in the eighteenth century, was created by the ethnic category now called Creoles, but it is the lingua franca of all Mauritian communities as well as the mother tongue of most Mauritians. Attempts at making Kreol an official language have nevertheless failed; in 1982, the radical Movement Militant Mauricien (MMM) party, then in power for the first time, tried to implement it in the media and in schools but were met with massive resistance—not only from Indo- and Franco-Mauritians but also, perhaps surprisingly, from Creoles. In general, the groups working for a wider recognition of Kreol are small and considered left-wing. French and English predominate in the media, in the educational system, and in public administration, French being the main language of culture and English the main language of administration. The resistance to Kreol can be traced to three causes: First, it is still widely regarded as "the poor cousin of French," as an impoverished, shallow, and context-dependent idiom. Secondly, its wider use at the expense of French and English might strengthen Mauritius's isolation, since it is spoken only in Mauritius, Rodrigues, and the Seychelles. Thirdly, Kreol is still associated with the Creole ethnic group and/or creolization as it is understood locally, and Kreol has connotations of impurity and uprootedness. Interestingly, few of the activists who have struggled for recognition of Kreol are Creoles in ethnic terms; they must nevertheless be seen as Creoles in analytical terms—like the European left, some are in favor of strong versions of multiculturalism, whereas others reject cultural tradition altogether as a source of personal identity.

Mauritian society is changing, and so are local perceptions of Creoles. While the standard definition of a Creole remains essentialist and racial, society currently accepts that particular forms of mixing may create new Creoles. Conversion to Christianity, commitment to mixing through marriage, and mixed parentage may, under certain circumstances, make a person Creole. During the last decades, there has been a tendency in the population censuses that increasing numbers state that both their commonly spoken language and their ancestral language is Kreol. This is significant in so far as a person whose ancestral language is Kreol (and not an Oriental language or French) identifies him- or herself as someone rooted in Mauritian society and not in an old world civilization; in other words, as someone belonging to a new society founded on the premise of uprootedness.

CREOLE ESSENTIALISM

Mauritian notions of creoledom are traditionally associated with language and origins, which only partly overlap. Although most Indo-Mauritians speak Kreol, their language of reference still tends to be an Indian language, which means that although they live in a society based on uprootedness, migration, and mixing, they retain a rooted self-identity based on notions of purity, continuity, and boundaries.

Creoles as an ethnic group have no fixed criteria for membership. Creoledom means impurity, openness, and individualism.

The Kreol language is seen as an oral idiom lacking history and literature, and as rather superficial and limited compared to the great civilizational languages of English, French, Hindu, Urdu, and Mandarin. Its utility lies in its ability to unite otherwise very different groups in a shared field of communication.

Now, the anthropological use of the concept cultural creolization closely approximates Mauritian usage. Creolization is seen as a process whereby new shared cultural forms, and new possibilities for communication, emerge owing to contact. It highlights the open-ended, flexible, and unbounded nature of cultural processes, as opposed to the notion of cultures as bounded, stable systems of communication.

In Mauritian public discourse, notions of change, flux, personal choice, and hybridity are routinely contrasted with tradition, stability, commitment to fixed values and purity. These debates closely resemble the aforementioned debates in the academic community regarding stability and change, boundedness, and openness. In the Mauritian context, the phenomena classified as creole—whether the ethnic group Creoles, the language Kreol, or people who have been "creolized"—nearly always represent points of view that are consistent with the creolization perspective of culture. As I have shown, the problems faced by Mauritian Creoles, in a society dominated by essentialist, "rooted" identities, are weak internal organization and a chronic problem of leadership, lack of myths of origin that can match the others, as well as external stereotyping as being morally and culturally opportunistic. There are tendencies for Creole organizations to try to match the other ethnic groups by fashioning a Creole identity that is no less essentialist, no less rooted and bounded than the others. Simultaneously, a movement in the opposite direction amounts to the creolization of non-Creoles—that is, a growing commitment to the "mongrel" culture of Mauritius itself, borrowing and new juxtapositions—at the expense of "ancestral cultures" (for example, some Indo-Mauritians nowadays play the *séga*) and openness to change. Both tendencies coexist and delineate a major field of political discourse. The relevant parameters are depicted in Figure 1. The debates concern, on the one hand, cultural similarity versus variation—in this regard, Mauritian politicians, unlike their European counterparts, favor difference rather than homogenisation—and, on the other hand, the relationship between notions of purity and notions of mixing. As Figure 1 suggests, this field of discourse extends far beyond Mauritius and could shed light on Western political ideologies as well (plus, perhaps, academic debates on the nature of culture).

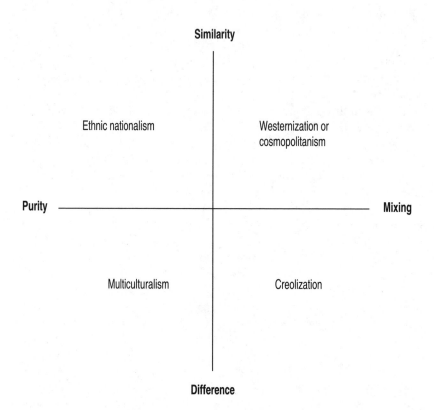

Figure 1   Positions in discourses about culture and identity. In Mauritius, controversies chiefly concern the relationship between multiculturalism and creolization. Ethnic nationalism is scarcely an option, and cosmopolitanism is politically uncontroversial. Seen as an instance of Douglas's (1970) grid-group model, the options can be described in the following way, clockwise beginning in the upper-left corner: low grid, high group; low grid, low group; high grid, low group; high grid, high group. There are Creoles who are against creolization (who favor multiculturalism, that is, strong group identities and clear boundaries), just as there are non-Creoles who favor creolization (mutual influence among cultural groups, individualism).

CREOLIZATION AND DIFFUSION

Creolization, certainly in the Mauritian context, does not refer to any kind of mixing but to those adaptations, dislocations, and cultural dynamics, resulting from contact, that do not result in a fixed belonging to a bounded, historical, cultural tradition. If we want cultural creolization to be theoretically useful, a first step must consist in distinguishing between cultural mixing and collective identities. The second step should consist in distinguishing between different forms of mixing. Terms such as "hybridity," "creolization," "*métissage*," "complexity," and "syncretism" are used by academics to describe processes of mixing, but they are rarely defined in relation to one another. To give an accurate meaning to a term such as "creolization," it is necessary first to study its meaning in linguistics, that is the origin of the analogy of cultural creolization. A preoccupation with cultural mixing is, incidentally, far from new.

The anthropological notion of "cultures in the plural," which has been so severely criticized in recent years, is historically and conceptually related to the biological notion of species. Darwin was himself an eager observer of everything alive (and fossilized), and although he saw the study of culture as an aside from his main work in evolutionary theory, he was fascinated by "pure savages." In his *Voyage of the Beagle* (1997 [1837]), he describes the "Fuegian" (Ona) culture of Tierra del Fuego in Hobbesian terms, seeing the life of the natives as a brutally competitive, and in many ways debased, form of existence. Later visiting Samoa, he was pleased to learn of the civilizing work of missionaries but was otherwise uninterested in the local culture, because it had been contaminated. Just as he was uninterested in the giant tortoises of Galàpagos, believing them to have been imported from Alhambra in the Indian Ocean, he did not view the mongrel culture of Mauritius with the same keen interest as he had observed "savages" in South America. He privileged purity and continuity over mixing and disjuncture (this is discussed in greater detail in Eriksen 1997b).

A key notion in Darwinism is the importance of intraspecies variation for natural selection, yet the boundaries between species are assumed to be absolute. Or are they? In *The Origin of Species* (Darwin, 1985/1859), Darwin writes about animal hybrids that they tend to be sterile if they are crosses between "two animals *clearly distinct* being themselves perfectly fertile" (p. 86). Interestingly, he ends the chapter about variation under domestication by stating that "the accumulative action of Selection, whether applied methodically and more quickly, or unconsciously and more slowly, *but more efficiently,* is by far the predominant Power" (p. 100, my italics).

The problem of distinguishing between varieties and "true species" is a main issue in *Origin*, for obvious reasons: the book's theoretical agenda consists in accounting for "biological decreolization," that is, the emergence of new, fixed species through interaction between varieties of old species under shifting environmental circumstances. Where to place the boundary between species was a main problem, and unlike Linnaeus who believed—at least as a young man—that species were created by God, Darwin knew that there were some deeply disturbing continuities between individuals deemed to belong to different species.

One of Darwin's lasting legacies for the working biologist consisted in developing a new set of criteria for classifying plants and animals and mapping out their mutual interrelatedness, replacing morphology with evolutionary lineage. One of the contributions of classic, Boasian, cultural anthropology a few decades later consisted, similarly, in replacing a racial classification of humans with a cultural one. Today that model seems to be exhausted because of overwhelming internal variation and boundary breakdown, but it has not been superseded by an alternative model simple enough to account for the increasingly complex facts that are now collected by ethnographers.

Already in the generation after Darwin (and Tylor), alternative models of cultural dynamics were developed. Classic diffusionism, informed by the nineteenth-century German humanist tradition including comparative linguistics, problematized the idea of autonomous, relatively closed cultures—and it is reminiscent of, and encounters some of the same problems as, current research on globalization. But the American notion of the melting pot goes even farther back. It seems to have been used first in Crèvecoeur's *Letters from an American Farmer* (1904 [1782]), where the author asked "What is the American, this new man?" and answered "here individuals of all nations are melted into a new race of men, whose labours and posterity will one day cause great changes in the world."[2] Emerson spoke about "the smelting pot" in the mid-nineteenth century, and with Israel Zangwill's popular drama "The Melting Pot" from 1908, the term became a label of self-description for many new Americans. The members of the Chicago school of urban sociology, who set out to do research soon after the staging of Zangwill's play, generally assumed that "acculturation" would eventually replace ethnic entrenchment, except in the case of the blacks (see Hannerz 1980). Another famous analysis of "acculturation" from the same period is Bateson's article about culture contact and schismogenesis, published in 1935 (Bateson 2000a), where Bateson argues that contrary to what many expect, group differences may just as well be accentuated as reduced in situations of contact. Neither the Chicago school nor Bateson discussed mixing. Ralph Linton, in his introductory textbook from 1936 (*The Study of Man*), talks about hybridity first in a biological sense (noting that human hybrids are viable and fertile creatures) and, later, with reference to culture. Showing that virtually everything that is usually seen as "100 percent American" is imported, he nevertheless presumes that this does not affect group identity, cohesion and boundedness.[3]

The issues that have been raised recently under labels such as "creolization" and "hybridization" have been more actively debated in earlier periods than commonly assumed, often in similar ways. Although he does not develop the point, Linton clearly distinguishes between culture and identification. To him, there is no contradiction between cultural diffusion and a strong sense of group identity, although he was concerned that his compatriots were becoming nationalist bigots because they failed to recognize the extent of foreign influence on their everyday lives.

In other words, cultural diffusion and the recontextualization and reintegration of "borrowed items" into preexisting cultural repertoires have long been recognized, even if the dominant research agendas of the mid-twentieth century tended to bracket diffusion. It is not sufficient to point out that mixing does take place; it is necessary to distinguish between different forms of mixing.

Notwithstanding cultural diffusion, which in the era of mass communication often takes place without encounters between groups of different origins, there are a number of different outcomes from long-term encounters between distinct groups. Sometimes, one group is absorbed into the other; sometimes it is absorbed culturally but not socially (the ethnic boundaries remain intact); sometimes the groups merge to create a third entity; sometimes a hierarchical complementary relationship or a symmetrical competitive relationship occurs; sometimes, again, one group eventually exterminates the other (see Harris 1995 for a typology of forms of mixing in the New World).

THE LINGUISTIC SOURCE

The term "cultural creolization" is associated with Hannerz's (1992; 1996) important contributions to an anthropology of global flows from the mid-1980s onward. However, the analogy between linguistics and anthropology implied by the term was, as acknowledged by Hannerz, explored earlier by Lee Drummond (1980) in a study from Guyana. In his article about the "cultural continuum" in polyethnic Guyana, Drummond (1980) notes that Guyanese routinely apply ethnic ascription in social classification and cultural stereotyping. He then shows that their usage is situational and often self-contradictory (Drummond 1980:368). Rather than accepting the emic view (which is shown to be inconsistent) of a society made up by distinctive ethnic-cum-cultural groups, Drummond proposes a view inspired by creole linguistics, arguing its relevance for culture theory in general:

> If variation and change are fundamental aspects of cultural systems, then we must consider the possibility that ethnographic studies of small, post-colonial, ethnically fragmented societies such as Guyana illustrate creole processes found in societies everywhere. (Drummond 1980:370)

The main problem arising from use of the creole metaphor, Drummond then notes, is that of descriptive fragmentation, leading the ethnographer to "exhaust himself describing and comparing every little pocket of informants" (p. 371) —a problem that would soon become familiar in post-modern anthropology, and often resolved through recourse to terms such as "multiple voices," "polyphony," "discourses," and the like. Drummond's own solution, drawing on Derek Bickerton's creole linguistics, consists in seeing culture as a single entity that cannot be pluralized; as "overlapping sets of transformations or continua" (p. 372). A similar view is voiced by Hannerz when he states:

> A cultural theory adequate to the task of understanding complex cultures must be able to deal with the fact that the division of labor is in large part a division of knowledge, making very problematic the notion that culture is by definition shared. (Hannerz 1986:363)

This view represents an advance over the earlier view of the world as an archipelago of cultures (Eriksen 1993, 1994). However, it remains to be explained why boundaries continue to be reproduced through reflexive identity politics, movements aiming to purge local culture of insidious influences from outside, and through everyday practices that are often not verbalized. Cultural flows may be everywhere, but so are cultural continuities. Likewise, hybrid and anomalous identities presuppose the existence of bounded, unambiguous identities. A similar point is made by Hannerz (1990) when he points out that cosmopolitans depend on locals in order to be cosmopolitans. Transgressing boundaries is impossible unless boundaries are being diligently reproduced.

Now recall Bateson's advice to go back to the context the analogy was taken from, looking for unresolved problems in the original context, assuming that similar problems might arise in analogous usage. In order to assess the significance of the term "cultural creolization," it is therefore necessary not only to look at the emic uses of creolization, as I have done in the first part of the chapter, but also to examine the original linguistic usage of the term.

Bickerton once distinguished pidgins from creoles by stating, bluntly, that "pidgins constitute a grossly handicapped case of second language learning while creoles show a partial recourse to the *faculté de langage*" (Bickerton 1976:183–84). In general, linguists have defined creoles as former pidgins that have become mother tongue to a group of people, thereby increasing in structural complexity and semantic richness. Creoles, moreover, are standardized to a certain degree, given that they are the main language of a community of people (and often the lingua franca of a larger population). Another process that may take place in linguistically complex situations with creoles and standard languages existing side by side is decreolization, whereby the creole increasingly approximates the standard form. The Guyanese situation described by Drummond may, by virtue of being a cultural *continuum*, be seen as a postcreole one, where boundaries have already become fuzzy.

The question that remains to be explored is whether these terms—creolization, standardization, decreolization, postcreole continuum—may be helpful in refining the anthropological usage of "creolization" and related terms.

CULTURAL DECREOLIZATION?

Decreolization is the process whereby the boundary between the standard (written) form of a language and the creole is gradually blotted out, and an analogic range of intermediate forms replaces the digital either-or; the boundary is replaced by a frontier area, and the creole forms begin to approximate the standard form. The result can be a postcreole continuum, as can be witnessed in parts of the English- and French-speaking Caribbean, where the distance between standard and creole varieties is fluid, and where spoken language is not necessarily farther removed from the standard language than are certain dialects and sociolects in the metropolitan countries. Another possible outcome of decreolization is the eventual obliteration of the creole forms, sometimes applying only to a particular segment of the population, and a resulting strengthening of boundaries between that segment and the rest of the population.

Cultural decreolization evidently occurs; the first kind of example that comes to mind is that of identity politics seeking to purify cultural forms "contaminated" by foreign influence—sometimes, as in the cases of France and Iceland, focusing on language, but more often pertaining to physical markers of identity (clothes, food and so on), norms (often relating to religion), and knowledge (of, for example, history). Such efforts at cultural purification do not result in a postcreole continuum but rather to the strengthening of boundaries and removal of ambiguity.

We seem to be faced with three typical phases in linguistic creolization: the development of creoles; a stable situation of diglossia with fixed creole and standard forms; and the eventual dissolution of fixed boundaries, that is, decreolization and the emergence of postcreole continua. These stages can rarely be identified in cultural processes, where the cultural continuum is a fact from the beginning, notwithstanding the possible existence of strong *social* boundaries.

A related question is that of standardization. Creole languages historically did become standardized even if they remained oral. As noted earlier, historical sources documenting usage of a French-based Creole in Mauritius (for instance, Beaton, 1977 [1859]; St. Pierre, 1983 [1773]) indicate that there has been considerable continuity in the language for two hundred years up to the present. Although creole languages tend not to be standardized with respect to spelling conventions, state-sanctioned grammars, and so on, their ability to change is clearly restricted by their conventionalized everyday usage by the community of native speakers.

Regarding cultural creolization, we may ask, similarly, under which circumstances the process of mixing ends and standardized, reified idioms are established. Some may react against this way of phrasing the problem, claiming with Deleuze and Guattari (1980), Urry (2000), and others that *the* main characteristics of the human condition consist in movement and change. This position must be resisted. Of course, there is movement, mixing, and change; but there is also stability and continuity. The systemic model developed by Morin (for example, 2001), where organization emerges in the interface between order and chaos through the self-organizing properties of recursive interactions, covers the facts better than does any proposition to the effect that either everything changes or nothing does. There are everywhere degrees of boundedness and stability, just as there are degrees of openness and change.

Standardization of cultural forms can be presumed to happen through political agency, through the sudden isolation of a group or through its externalization in writing, museums, or similar institutions. The cultural form in question will then (again presumably) have been codified in a certain, authoritative way recognized as a standard. Typical examples from European cultural history are linguistic standardization via the printing press and nationalism (Anderson 1983), and standardization of musical expression through notation (Treitler 1981), which served to enhance complexity at the cost of "freezing" evolving traditions.

The parallel between musical notation and linguistic standardization (or decreolization) are evident, just as there is much evidence of musical (and linguistic) "recreolization" taking place as global communication and migration to the West set the stage for intensified contact across boundaries and a consequent weakening of the national project of cultural homogenization.

TOWARD A DEFINITION

In many anthropological writings on creolization, including some of my own, the term is used more or less interchangeably with hybridity and *mestizaje/métissage*: it refers to displacement or mixing. Sometimes it results from the enforced or voluntary displacement of groups or individuals; sometimes it simply amounts to the local appropriation and incorporation of foreign influence. The incorporation of Country & Western music into the standard cultural repertoire of rural southern Norway can accordingly be described as a process of creolization, just as the complex cultural dynamics, involving interaction among various groups of Europeans, Asians, Africans, and Native-Americans, leading to the emergence of a distinctive Caribbean cultural intersystem during and after slavery.

The concept of cultural creolization has been criticized from two perspectives: it is accused of being too wide and general—if every cultural process is creole in character, the term seems superfluous—and for implicitly positing the existence of pure forms existing prior to creolization. Neither Boas nor Kroeber, neither Malinowski nor Mauss was a stranger to the idea of demographic movement and cultural mixing. The assumption of the relatively isolated society was chiefly a methodological device, and Radcliffe-Brown himself worried about the increasing difficulty of isolating the entities for study (Radcliffe-Brown 1952:193). Network analysis, multisited fieldwork, and similar methodological reforms have responded to this challenge without changing the basic premises—the Manchester school, to mention an obvious example, remained loyal to the Evans-Pritchard who wrote *The Nuer*. The recent emphasis on flows, change, variation, and mixing may therefore be seen as less radical than often assumed. An important point made by Hannerz (1996:67), however, is that there are important differences in degree, and that the choice of terminology directs the attention toward processes of particular analytic interest. Nobody would deny that it enhances our understanding of, say, contemporary immigrant life in Berlin to look at the cultural dynamics of Turkish-German relationships, or that contemporary black British culture is an outcome of a dynamic relationship among Africans,

West Indians, and native Britons. In other words, creolization (or a similar term) is useful for describing a certain kind of cultural process, which has proven to be rather common, in all probability increasingly so in the present era of accelerated communication and demographic mobility.

In addition to the aforementioned, creolization can also be taken to refer to dislocation, alienation, localizing foreign influence, anomalous or ambiguous ethnic groups such as *douglas* (people of mixed African-Indian origin) in Trinidad and Guyana, or traveling groups (*tatere*) in Norway and Sweden (people of mixed Gypsy-Scandinavian origin).

Different parts of a cultural environment, and of people's life-worlds, are being affected by influence from outside at different speeds and to differing degrees. Sometimes people are acutely aware of changes taking place in their immediate environment and take measures to stop them, to enhance them, or to channel them in their preferred direction. At other times, people may be unaware of these processes, even if foreign influences and cultural mixing may change their cultural environment profoundly. These are some of the intricacies of contemporary cultural processes that need disentangling if we are to be successful in studying them accurately. Merely stating that mixing is an inherent feature of contemporary culture is no more enlightening than saying that cultural diffusion is a fact. More precision is needed (see Khan 2001). Thus:

- *Cultural pluralism* directs the attention of the researcher toward the relative boundedness of the constituent groups or categories that make up a society. It is a close relative of multiculturalism.
- *Hybridity* directs attention toward individuals or cultural forms that are reflexively—self-consciously—mixed, that is, syntheses of cultural forms or fragments of diverse origins. It opposes multiculturalism seen as "nationalism writ small."
- *Syncretism* directs attention toward the amalgamation of formerly discrete world views, cultural meaning, and, in particular, religion.
- *Diasporic identity* directs attention toward an essentially social category consisting of people whose primary subjective belonging is in another country.
- *Transnationalism* directs attention, rather, to a social existence attaching individuals and groups not primarily to one particular place but to several or none.
- *Diffusion* directs attention toward the flow of substances and meanings between societies, whether it is accompanied by actual social encounters or not.
- *Creolization*, finally, directs our attention toward cultural phenomena that result from displacement and the ensuing social encounter

and mutual influence between/among two or several groups, creating an ongoing dynamic interchange of symbols and practices, eventually leading to new forms with varying degrees of stability. The term "creole culture" suggests the presence of a standardized, relatively stable cultural idiom resulting from such a process. *Cultural de*creolization occurs when, in the case of group-based power differentials and inequalities, the subordinate group is socially or culturally assimilated into the dominant one (for example, *cholos* becoming *mestizos* in Latin America) or when a creolized idiom is "purified" and made similar to a metropolitan or "high culture" form.

I propose a definition of cultural creolization, thus, that is faithful to its linguistic origins but that does not restrict itself to societies where "creole" is an emic term or where linguistic creolization has taken place (see, for example, Willis, 2002, on creolization in the Pacific; Archetti, 1999, on creolization in Argentina). The Mauritian example presented in some detail above nevertheless refers to a society where the term "Creole" (*kreol*) is commonly used to designate both a language and a cultural group.

MAURITIAN MEANINGS OF CREOLIZATION

In Mauritian society, a main tension is that between creolization and multiculturalism (Eriksen 1997a). The Catholic Archbishop of the Mascareignes expressed a common view when he said, in the early 1990s, "Let the colours of the rainbow remain distinctive so that it can be beautiful." Opposition to cultural mixing and mixed marriages within Mauritian society is strong. In the eyes of many Mauritian politicians as well as ordinary citizens, peace is maintained on the crowded, culturally heterogeneous island only because there is a precarious numerical equilibrium and functioning politics of compromise between the ethnic groups. Any "upsetting of this balance" would ostensibly threaten the peace.

An alternative view is posited by Mauritians who reject ethnic classification as a set of primordial identities and who demand the right to be mixed in every sense. In the 1970s, this view was forcefully developed by the politician, scholar, and poet Dev Virahsawmy, who wrote poetry and plays in Kreol in spite of his Telugu origins, and who even devised his own religious rituals blending influences from the great world religions present in the island.

The term "creole" itself has a fairly unambiguous meaning in Mauritius. It refers to those Mauritians who are Catholic and have African, Malagasy, or mixed origins and/or who are seen by others and see themselves as Creoles. As shown in earlier ethnographic work on Mauritius (Boswell 2003; Eriksen 1988, 1998), Creole culture is perceived as stable and fixed, although it lacks—unlike the other cultural groups of the island—an illustrious past. At the same time, the Creole ethnic category is more open to new recruits than other ethnic groups in the island.

Let us now consider the four main features of creolization identified above, in the context of Mauritian society: New forms resulting from contact between/among two or several groups; eventual standardization; decreolization; and the postcreole continuum.

New cultural forms clearly have arisen, and continue to arise, out of intergroup contact. This is evident, among other places, in food, music, religious beliefs, and linguistic practice, if not necessarily at the level of identification.

Standardization has partly taken place in Kreol, but there is no commonly agreed-on orthographic standard. At the level of culture, some effort has been invested into creating a standard Creole high culture on a par with the Asian and European cultures already recognized in Mauritius. There is no general agreement as to its content, however. Some argue that it ought to have strong African elements, while others argue that the history of slavery and mixing is what constitutes the unique Creole contribution to Mauritian culture (Boswell 2003). Some Mauritian Creoles even search for cultural authenticity in Rastafarianism—a Jamaican religious movement (Wathne 2003).

Creole essentialism is far from unknown in Mauritius. Occasionally, Creoles claim that they are the only *vrais Mauriciens*, real Mauritians, since they are the only group who, as it were, emerged from the Mauritian soil. As is evident, this version of Creole identity is different from the attempt to anchor it in an African past, but both are attempts to fix and standardize a collective identity.

Decreolization takes two forms in Mauritius: the "purification" of a cultural form perceived to have been creolized in the past, and attempts to fix and anchor cultural forms and social identities hitherto associated with mixing and impurity. Many urban middle-class Mauritians of French or mixed origin are worried about the Kreol (and more recently English) influence on Mauritian French, and try to purge their language of *mauricianismes*, that is, Creolisms. Similar concerns are voiced regarding the "contagious" effects of other aspects of Creole culture. Similarly, Mauritian Hindus emulate metropolitan forms by bringing pandits from India to "purify" their ritual practices; while Mauritian Tamils have taken steps to ensure that their new temples conform to the standard in Tamil Nadu. The most widely acknowledged form of decreolization in Mauritius is nevertheless the process sometimes disparagingly described as *fer blan* ("to make white"), whereby people with a Creole background "Gallicize" their way of life, begin to address their children in French and change their lifestyle to make it conform to the norms of the dominant Franco-Mauritian group.

The other, rare, form of decreolization consists in Creoles insisting on representing a rooted, uniquely Mauritian culture with a respectable peerage and no present indebtedness to foreign influences. They would argue that creolization, in the sense of borrowing, has ceased and that Creole culture is no longer a *creole* culture but a standardized form.

The remaining question is whether the notion of the postcreole continuum makes sense in the Mauritian context. I should argue that it does, existing alongside and often predominating in relation to, processes of decreolization. Creole identity is associated with mixing, diffusion, and borrowing, and many Creoles have manifestly mixed origins. This implies that any Mauritian who does not obviously belong to one of the bounded, historically anchored communities will be seen as belonging to the residual category of Creoles. Notwithstanding the minority view that Creole identity has been or should be decreolized, there are in fact multiple points of entry into the category and no fixed essence in Creole identity.

* * *

I hope the foregoing discussion has shown that the linguistic analogy is useful, but paradoxically, this is not least the case when flows are stemmed and fixity is implemented, either at the level of reified culture or at the level of group boundaries. The concept of cultural creolization not only tells us about mixing and boundary transgression but also calls attention to the formation of new standardized forms and new boundaries. As the Mauritian material shows, there are many points of entry into Creoledom. Some are born creole, some achieve creoledom and others—such as the children of certain mixed marriages—have creoledom thrust upon them. The key terms are "dislocation," "fuzzy boundaries," and "intergroup cross-fertilization."

Notes

1. See Sahlins (1999), de Heusch (2000), and Bader (2001) for critiques which are, incidentally, less charitable than the perspective I am developing here. I nevertheless agree with these authors that it is a travesty to reduce culture to the politics of culture, since culture is largely implicit, embodied and nonverbalised. This does not imply that studying the politics of culture is uninteresting, only that it does not tell us much about that which "goes without saying because it comes without saying."

2. I owe this example to John Davidson.

3. Linton's justly famous ethnographic vignette begins thus: [D]awn finds the unsuspecting patriot garbed in pajamas, a garment of East Indian origin; and lying in a bed built on a pattern which originated in either Persia or Asia Minor. He is muffled to the ears in un-American materials: cotton, first domesticated in India; linen, domesticated in the Near East; wool from an animal native to Asia Minor; or silk whose uses were first discovered by the Chinese. All these substances have been transformed into cloth by methods invented in Southwestern Asia. If the weather is cold enough he may even be sleeping under an eiderdown quilt invented in Scandinavia.

References

Anderson, B. 1983. *Imagined communities*. London: Verso.

Archetti, E. 1999 *Masculinities. Football, polo and the tango in Argentina*. Oxford: Berg.

Bader, V. 2001. Culture and identity, *Ethnicities* 1(2):251–273.

Barth, F. 1966. *Models of social organization*. London: Royal Anthropological Institute, Occasional Papers, 23.

Bateson, G. 2000a [1972a]. Culture contact and schismogenesis. In *Steps to an ecology of mind*. Chicago: University of Chicago Press, pp. 61–72.

———— 2000b [1972b]. Experiments in thinking about observed ethnological material. In *Steps to an ecology of mind*. Chicago: University of Chicago Press, pp. 73–87.

Beaton, P. 1977 [1859]. *Creoles and coolies, or five years in Mauritius*. London: Kennikat.

Benoît, G. 1984. *The Afro-Mauritians*. Moka: MGI.

Bickerton, D. 1976. Pidgin and creole studies, *Annual Review of Anthropology* 5:169–193.

Boswell, R. 2003. Le malaise créole: A critical study of ethnic identity in Mauritius. Ph. D. thesis, Vrije Universiteit Amsterdam.

Clifford, J., and G. Marcus, eds. 1986. *Writing culture: The poetics and politics of ethnography*. Berkeley and Los Angeles, CA: University of California Press.

Crèvecoeur, J. H. St. John de. 1904 [1782]. *Letters from an American Farmer*. New York: Fox, Duffield.

Darwin, C. 1997 [1837]. *Voyage of the Beagle*. London: Wordsworth.

———— 1985 [1859]. *On the origin of species by means of natural selection*. Harmondsworth: Penguin Classics.

Deleuze, G., and F. Guattari. 1980. *Mille plateaux*. Paris: Odile Jacob.

Desmond, A., and J. Moore. 1991. *Darwin*. Harmondsworth: Penguin.

Douglas, M. 1970. *Natural symbols*. Harmondsworth: Penguin.

Drummond, L. 1980. The cultural continuum: A theory of intersystems, *Man* 15(2): 352–374.

Eriksen, T. H. 1988. *Communicating cultural difference and identity: Ethnicity and nationalism in Mauritius*. Oslo: University of Oslo Department of Scocial Anthropology. Occasional Papers in Social Anthropology, 16.

———— 1993. Do cultural islands exist? *Social Anthropology* 2(1):133–147.

———— 1994. *Kulturelle veikryss. Essays om kreolisering* (Cultural crossroads: Essays on creolisation). Oslo: Universitetsforlaget.

———— 1997a. Multiculturalism, individualism and human rights: Romanticism, the Enlightenment and lessons from Mauritius. In *Human rights, culture and context*. R. Wilson, ed. London: Pluto, pp. 49–69.

———— 1997b. *Charles Darwin*. Oslo: Gyldendal.

———— 1998. *Common denominators: Ethnicity, nation-building and compromise in Mauritius*. Oxford: Berg.

Eriksen, T. H. 2004. Predicaments of multiethnicity: Lessons from the Mauritian riots of 1999. In *Ethnicity, nationalism and minority rights*. S. May, T. Modood, and J. Squires, eds. Cambridge: Cambridge University Press.

Fox, R., and B. King, eds. 2002. *Anthropology beyond culture*. Oxford: Berg.

Friedman, J. 1994. *Cultural identity and global process*. London: Sage.

Hannerz, U. 1980. *Exploring the city: Inquiries toward an urban anthropology*. New York: Columbia University Press.

——— 1986. Small is beautiful? The problem of complex cultures, *Comparative Studies in Society and History* 28:362–367.

——— 1990. Cosmopolitans and locals in world culture. In *Global culture. Nationalism, globalization, and modernity*. M. Featherstone, ed. London: Sage, pp. 237–252.

——— 1992. *Cultural complexity*. New York: Columbia University Press.

——— 1996. *Transnational Connections*. London: Routledge.

Harris, O. 1995. Knowing the past: The antinomies of loss in highland Bolivia. In *Counterworks: Managing diverse knowledges*. R. Fardon, ed. London: Routledge.

Heusch, L. de. 2000. *L' ethnie*. The vicissitudes of a concept, *Social Anthropology* 8(2): 99–116.

Khan, A. 2001. Journey to the center of the Earth: The Caribbean as master symbol, *Cultural Anthropology* 16(3):271–302.

Linton, R. 1937. One hundred per-cent American, *American Mercury* 40:427–429.

Morin, E. 2001. *La Méthode V: L'Identité humaine*. Paris: Seuil.

Radcliffe-Brown, A. R. 1952. *Structure and function in primitive society*. London: Routledge and Kegan Paul.

Rushdie, S. 1991. *Imaginary homelands*. London: Granta.

Sahlins, M. 1999. Two or three things that I know about culture, *Journal of the Royal Anthropological Institute* 5(3):399–421.

St. Pierre, B. de. 1983 [1773]). *Voyage à L'Ile de France*. Paris: Maspéro.

Tinker, H. 1974. *A new form of slavery: The export of Indian labour overseas 1880–1920*. Oxford: Oxford University Press.

Treitler, L. 1981. Oral, written and literate process in the transmission of medieval music, *Speculum* 56(3):471–491.

Urry, John. 2000. *Sociology beyond societies*. London: Routledge.

Wathne, Kjetil. 2003. Mauritius, a kaleidoscope of peace? M.A. dissertation, University of Oslo.

Werbner, P., and T. Modood, eds. 1997. *Debating cultural hybridity*. London: Zed.

Willis, D., ed. 2002. *The age of creolization in the Pacific: In search of emerging cultures and shared values in the Japan-America borderlands*. Hiroshima: Keisuisha.

9 Is There a Model in the Muddle? "Creolization" in African Americanist History and Anthropology

Stephan Palmié

Perhaps unsurprisingly, the career of the term "creole" in social scientific discourse begins innocuously enough as a fairly "experience-," or "evidence-near" indexical descriptor.[1] Up until the 1960s, most historians, sociologists, and anthropologists stuck to usages cleaving close to the original sense of "creole" as either (a) designating the social identities and cultural forms resulting from the indigenization of originally allogenic populations, or (b) contrasting these against populations and cultural forms construed as properly "autochthonous" (typically Native Americans) and groups locally accorded the status of foreigners.[2] Historians, in particular, treated the term as largely self-evident and only rarely saw the need to explicate or contextually specify its meaning. A fairly typical example is Richard Pares (1950:348n.9) who, in his study of the Nevisian Pinney dynasty, insisted that in eighteenth-century British Caribbean usage "the word 'creole' in its proper sense does not mean a half-breed; on the contrary, it means a person of pure white blood born in the colonies, as distinguished from one born in Europe. Later the sense was enlarged, to distinguish any person born, or thing produced, in the colonies from a person or thing of the same kind, born or produced elsewhere. Thus 'creole' negroes were distinguished from 'African' negroes."

Whether in adjective or nominalized form, the term "creole" remained close to the way the major eighteenth-century Caribbean planter historians such as Edward Long and Bryan Edwards or contemporary observers such as Moreau de Saint-Méry used them to designate individuals and groups who had become nativized in the New World in the aftermath of the Columbian voyages, in contrast to first-generation European immigrants and African-born slaves.

This usage has endured. And with the advent of the so-called new social history in the second half of the 1960s, it was put to good use by demographic historians such as Higman (1976, 1984), Kulikoff (1986), Bergad (1990), Engerman and Higman (1997), and Walsh (1997), to name just a few. Here the newcomer/creole distinction marks, among other things, certain effects of the sociology of migration, particularly the sex ratio among immigrant groups, and its effect on their capacities for forming relatively stable social structures sustaining processes by which cultural forms (whether of Old World origin or improvised in the face of novel challenges) could solidify into transgenerationally salient traditions. Few of these scholars actually employ the term "creolization" in any other way than to mark the transition from demographically unviable aggregates of first-generation immigrants (plagued, as they usually are, by extremely low fertility and high mortality rates) to "creole" populations whose sex ratios have leveled off (unless, as in the case of many Caribbean slave populations, continued importation of Africans prolonged this process). Nevertheless, as Breen (1984:198) put the matter in an early survey of this literature, which still stands as a model of clarity, the preeminent problem for the study of post-Columbian New World cultures remained "to define with precision the constraints upon [behavioral] choice" affecting members of populations caught up in specific structural dynamics—be they shaped by demography, by the emergence or consolidation of economic or political regimes, or by the evolution of ideological factors impinging on such arrangements (cf. Morgan 1997; Price 2001).

Yet such lines of inquiry are hardly representative of the thrust of "creolization" discourse in contemporary anthropology (or history, for that matter). As Mintz (1996), Price (2001), and Khan (2001) have pointed out, the proliferation of terms such as "creole" and "creolization" in the anthropological literature has been driven less by empirically grounded research than by processes of abstraction. Even more significantly, what one is likely to encounter today are not extrapolations from earlier historical or ethnographic uses and limited generalizations of the term "creolization" (as, for example, in the case of Pearse 1956, Adams 1959, Smith 1965, Goveia 1965, or even Brathwaite 1971) but usages shaped by a series of linguistic analogies. In itself, this may not seem overly surprising, given that the term "creole" has long been associated with the languages spoken by *some* (but by no means all!) of the people to whose social identities the term has historically been applied. But it is clear that the humble term "creole" would hardly have been extracted from a number of fairly unimportant regionalist debates and elevated to the status of a concept capable not just of generalization but of integration into an "au courant" theoretical vocabulary, had it not been for its enhancement with meanings that derive largely, if not wholly, from its history within the discipline of linguistics.

In this respect, the current consensus appears to be that the first consistent use of "creole" to designate languages arising in New World plantation contexts, and perceived as essentially novel linguistic entities, originates with Moravian lexicographical efforts in the Danish Virgin Islands and Suriname in the eighteenth century (Baker & Mühlhäusler, this volume; Holm 1988). But it is important to note that Moravian efforts at codifying languages such as Negerhollands and Sranan Tongu remained largely unaffected by the conceptual linkages among language, culture, and peoplehood that had been gaining ground in Europe since the days of Condillac and Herder. In fact, it took at least another hundred years before scholars such as van Name, Coelho, and Schuchardt would begin to regard the languages developed by subaltern colonial populations as linguistic *anomalies* worthy of special attention. In other words, it was on the grounds of those modern linguistic ideologies[3]—consolidating what Fredrik Barth (1969:11) once summed up as the "traditional proposition that a race = a culture = a language"—that the various "petit negres," "patois," or "broken" versions of Indo-European languages that had arisen in the context of European overseas expansion became visible as representing a problem. Thus, far from prodding a reevaluation of post-enlightenment conceptions of languages as "objective" *entities* discretely distributed in social space, studies of creole linguistics were firmly anchored in precisely such conceptions right from their inception as an academic (instead of pragmatically driven) pursuit. Just as lexical heterogeneity, substitution of nominal inflection or verbal conjugation by analytical modifiers, identity of adverb and adjective, and other "linguistic defects" came to constitute hallmarks of "creole" languages, so did these seemingly anomalous and artificial subaltern vernaculars underwrite ideas about what a proper language should look like, how it ought to be acquired, and who should be speaking it.

Yet while the initial linguistic attention to languages associated with populations designated as "creole" long remained descriptive, and only vaguely typological in orientation, by the middle of the twentieth century a slowly emerging disciplinary focus in linguistics on creole studies transformed the meaning of the term "creole" in at least three distinct ways. It now began to function as a classificatory device for isolating certain types of "hybrid" languages originating in colonial contexts; it became complemented by a novel nominalized verb form in order to represent the linguistic processes from which such languages emerged ("creolization"); and it attained analytical significance as a concept claimed by various theoretical "schools" purporting to explain the structural and phonological features of creole languages in relation to widely divergent hypotheses about their origins. This move from description to analysis may have been fruitful as far as linguistics is concerned. But it proved eminently problematic once anthropologists and historians began to reimport linguistic theory into their studies of what came to be called "creole" cultures and processes of "cultural creolization."

Why this should have been so is fairly evident today. Linguists, at least, seem prepared to acknowledge that their attempts at generalizing about the genesis and the development of creole languages stand and fall with sociolinguistic inferences impossible to draw in the absence of detailed historical data.[4] Referring to the so-called pidginization/creolization cycle that to this day underlies most historians and anthropologists' use of these terms, Jourdan (1991:192) notes that in positing a seemingly predictable transition from highly restricted pidgins developed by speakers of mutually unintelligible languages to full-blown creoles among their descendants, linguists "relied heavily, and of necessity, on 'Just So' stories from the Caribbean and other plantation settings"—contexts, in other words, in which concrete evidence for precisely such transformations is notoriously lacking. McWhorter (2000:38f.) consequently speaks of an "inevitable *post hoc*-ness in tracing the emergence of a creole" and argues that the vague and ambiguous nature of the historical record for the Caribbean has given linguists near-unlimited interpretative leeway in concocting explanations for the presence or absence of creole languages in certain regions. Harris and Rampton (2002:35) likewise argue that the substratist-universalist debate is based in speculative theorizing and ideological contention, driven by a "search for *total* explanation, licensed by the paucity of the historical record"[5] and marked by widespread reification of language as mere "system output" rather than the product of historically contextualized human communicative agency. Their conclusion about the usefulness of creolization as a conceptual tool in social and historical analysis comes as no surprise: "there do seem to be good grounds for doubting the value of traditional creole language study as a ground-breaking model or template for the analysis of cultural contact" (Harris & Rampton 2002:38).[6]

Painful as this may be to those of us who rely on linguistically derived modeling devices for ordering our data, the fact is that linguistic theories of creolization nowadays stand and fall *not* on the kind of abstract predictive potential we expect from them when we import them into our work. They rather thrive on the sketchy and often rather problematic primary data that linguists in turn cull from the anthropological and historical literature. What results is a strange cross-disciplinary feedback loop where anthropologists and historians recycle as theory the speculations linguists generate from anthropological and historical data increasingly produced and organized on the basis of linguistic hypotheses. How has this situation come about? The genealogy of linguistic borrowings Ulf Hannerz (1987) cites as formative for his influential statement is surprisingly shallow, reaching back less than a decade to formulations by Johannes Fabian (1978) who merely suggested *exploring* pidgin and creole linguistics as a source for analogies in the study of African popular culture. But what seemed to have burst on the scene of anthropological theory building in the late 1980s by then had already had a lengthy intellectual history in a particular ethnographic field—viz. the study of African-American cultures, to which I now turn.

* * *

Although Melville Herskovits was certainly not the first anthropologist to analogize culture and language, nor the first to develop what nowadays is known as a "substratist" argument in creole language studies, it probably was he who initially laid out the terms for an analogy between linguistic and cultural processes emerging in this particular field since the 1930s.[7] Somewhat contrary to the major thrust of his research (which, after all, centered on formal "trait" comparison), by 1941 Herskovits had come to argue that studies of linguistic "Africanisms" had so far largely focused on overt lexical correspondences while neglecting grammar and phonology—just as normative and conceptual aspects of culture had been prioritized over the study of such "cultural imponderables" as personal comportment or, as he put it, "retention of Africanisms in motor behavior" (Herskovits 1989:145ff., 275–91, 1966:59f.). More specifically, Herskovits posited that "Negro linguistic expression should everywhere manifest greater resemblances in structure and idiom [that is, phonemics] than could be accounted for by chance" (Herskovits 1989:280). This was so, Herskovits surmised, because

> The Sudanic languages of West Africa, despite their mutual unintelligibility and apparent variety of form, are fundamentally similar in those traits which linguists employ in classifying dialects, as is to be discerned when the not inconsiderable number of published grammars of native languages, spoken throughout the area from which the slaves were taken, are compared. This being the case, and since grammar and idiom are the last aspects of a new language to be learned, the Negroes who reached the New World acquired as much of the vocabulary of their masters as they initially needed or was later taught to them, pronounced these words as best as

they were able, but organized them into their aboriginal speech patterns. Thus arose the various forms of Negro-English, Negro-French, Negro-Spanish, and Negro-Portuguese spoken in the New World, their "peculiarities" being due to the fact that *they comprise European words cast into an African grammatical mold.* (Herskovits 1989:280, emphasis mine)

From there, it was for Herskovits (1989:281) only a small step to asserting the comparability of the "similarities in the grammar of language over the entire West African region with what may be termed the grammar of culture, one finds in a similar situation [that is, in the same 'culture area']."

Here we have one of the earliest examples of an explicit attempt to transfer to cultural analysis what came to be known as substrate theories about how African linguistic structures (of wider or narrower definition) provided the morphosyntactical and phonological molds into which European lexical items were poured ("superlexification") and by which they were phonetically conditioned. Herskovits's formulation quickly fed back into linguistics (for example, Turner 1949, Hall 1950), where, by the late 1950s, the existence, nature, and degree of influence from putative African substrates on creole origins became subject to considerable debate.[8] But it is important to note that for Herskovits and most anthropologists concerned with African American cultures before the end of the 1960s, the "grammar of culture" analogy represented not so much a genuine explanatory tool as a device for circumventing certain analytical problems. For example, those cases where Herskovits's so-called "ethnohistorical" method of identifying specific "Africanisms" by comparing African "tribal ethnographies" with data obtained in particular New World contexts yielded too unspecific or ambiguous results to allow "explaining" the correspondences in cultural form by postulating large-scale slave imports from these African societies into particular New World. Methodologically, the concept of a generalized West African grammar of culture, of course, resulted in as dubious an evasion of genuine historical problems as his parallel concept of a "generalized West African cultural heritage": whereas the latter purportedly "explained" that certain cultural "traits" and "patterns" in African-American societies could not unambiguously be traced to specific African source cultures because of processes of surface convergence, the former did the same questionable conceptual work on a "deep structural" level allegedly common to all West African cultures anyway.

Although by the late 1960s a few anthropologists began to explore newer developments in linguistics such as theories of diglossia, code-switching, and relexification (for example Abrahams 1970; Mintz 1971; Reisman 1970), by and large Daniel Crowley's remarks at a 1967 AAA symposium on Afro-American culture were still largely representative of the field. "Creolization," Crowley argued, "today describes more generally the processes of adaptation [that] Herskovits synthesized as retention, reinterpretation, and syncretism." Interestingly (from our present vantage point, that is) Crowley added that such a concept ought to be "applicable not only in Latin America, the Caribbean, southern Louisiana, and West Africa but also in any area where a culture neither aboriginal nor alien but a mixture of the two, with retentions on both sides and ample borrowing from other outside sources, is in the process of becoming dominant—which is to say, most of the world" (Crowley as cited in Whitten & Szwed 1970:38). But this curiously prescient statement aside, there is little in these formulations that went much beyond Herskovits's programmatic pronouncements concerning what, by then, had become known as "acculturation studies."

This situation changed rather dramatically in 1976 when Sidney Mintz and Richard Price first published a short but forcefully argued essay (Mintz & Price 1992) advocating an analytical shift away from comparing seemingly free-floating units of cultural form to units of historically contextualizable social enactment. Problematizing the historical conditions of social reaggregation among enslaved Africans in the New World, Mintz and Price directed attention not only to—processually induced—discontinuities in cultural transmission but to the theoretical necessity of assuming cultural creativity and large-scale ad-hoc syntheses to have precipitated the institutional crystallization of such cultural forms as were observable in the Americas. In so arguing, they did away with one of the key premises of virtually all previous approaches toward African-American cultural history that did not presume the total insignificance of African influences: the assumption that the transmission and implantation in particular regions of the Americas of "traits" and "patterns" deriving from specific African cultures had been a predictable, quasi-automatic outcome of the forced migration of sufficient numbers of Africans to those regions. Instead, they urged anthropologists and historians to regard the emergence and eventual traditionalization of specific African-American cultures as part and parcel of the emergence of relatively stable *social relations* among—initially largely desocialized—collectivities of slaves under locally specific New World conditions. As they argue (1992:40),

> In attempting to put our emphasis on the social-relational problems that faced the slaves, we do not intend to ignore or to deemphasize the cultural materials that would inform their nascent institutions. But these cultural materials, we submit, are best seen as an aspect of the growth of institutions, the persons involved, and the sorts of coherence they must have come to provide to the slave community as a whole.

Such a perspective shifts the "baseline" of African-American cultural history from the hypothetical realm of African "origins" to those New World settings into which enslaved Africans came to be inserted (Mintz & Price 1992:1) and, therefore, out of the realm of cultural morphology and into that of social history. "It should no longer be sufficient," Mintz and Price (1992:41) remind us, "to maintain that Haiti's twin cult, the worship of Shango (Xango) in Trinidad and Bahia, and the use of oracles in Suriname are simply examples of Africa transplanted, or even of specific ethnic continuities of culture. Our task must rather be to delineate the processes by which those cultural materials that were retained could contribute to the institution-building the slaves undertook to inform their condition with coherence, meaning, and some measure of autonomy." This was not to deny the influence of Africa on New World cultures but to qualify the "Africanness" attributable to individual cases as a product of New World history. It was to transform it from a postulate into a subject for empirical research.

Still, Mintz and Price's essay represented not just a constructive critique of the ahistoricism of previous approaches. (Indeed, it has, unfortunately, not often been read that way!) It also served as a vehicle for an important set of hypotheses that were to have far-ranging impact. One of them has become known as the "rapid early synthesis"-hypothesis. The other one— which is, perhaps, best seen as a subsidiary of the first—revolves around the concepts of "deep structural" or "grammatical" principles operative in the formation of African-American cultures. Almost predictably, both of them opened the door to a massive influx of outdated linguistic theory into anthropological and historical research. As Price (2001) has recently conceded, this may have been due to the fact that the methodological model they presented was insufficiently set off from certain hypotheses he had developed on the basis of his research among the Saramaka maroons of Suriname, who, as Price (2001:44) nowadays puts it, "forged their society via more rapid, smoother creolization processes" than did historically differently situated African-American populations. What he may well be referring to are assertions such as the following passage from his own ambitious synthesis (Price 1976:21) of large amounts of maroon historiography that would find its way into the coauthored essay in minimally altered form:

> We can assert with some confidence, then, that within the earliest decades of the African presence in Suriname, the core of a new language and a new religion had been developed; and the subsequent century of massive new importations from Africa apparently had the effects merely of leading to secondary elaborations.

What follows this passage in the co-authored text is crucial. For here Mintz and Price (1992:50, emphasis mine) suggest "*tentatively* that similar scenarios may have unfolded in other parts of Afro-America, and for other cultural subsystems as well." This modest proposal fell on fertile ground. Particularly in U.S.-slave historiography the "rapid early synthesis model" soon became the theoretical gospel of a new brand of studies of African-American cultural history, conjugating (and often unwittingly so) North American data through Surinamese models.

This was so because the second major hypothesis that Mintz and Price launched in their celebrated essay seemed to ideally fit certain problems that had vexed historians of North American slavery since at least the early 1960s, when the Herskovitsian search for "Africanisms" began to replace earlier "catastrophic" interpretations of African-American cultural history. What these historians encountered was a problem that had already occupied Herskovits himself and had, in fact, occasioned some of his more dubious interpretations. The problem was this: although African-American cultures in the United States seemed palpably "different," there was comparatively little that could be directly traced to any specific African source.[9] And precisely in this respect Mintz and Price's resuscitation of Herskovits's notion of a generalizable "grammar" of West African cultures— once coupled with Price's Surinamese extrapolations—appeared to provide an acceptable alternative to the superficial search for morphological correspondence. "An African cultural heritage, widely shared by the people imported into any new colony," they write (Mintz & Price 1992:9f., emphasis mine), "will have to be defined in *less concrete terms*, by focusing more on values, and less on sociocultural forms, and even by attempting to identify unconscious 'grammatical' principles which may underlie and shape behavioral response." Believing that "for almost any aspect of culture one could probably identify abstract principles which are widespread in the region [that is, West Africa]" (Mintz & Price 1992:10), they hypothesize that

> From a transatlantic perspective, those deep-level cultural principles, assumptions and understandings which were shared by the Africans in any New World colony [. . .] would have been a limited but crucial resource. For they could have served as a catalyst in the processes by which individuals from diverse societies forged new institutions, and could have provided certain frameworks within which new forms could have developed. (Mintz & Price 1992:14)

Of course, they also concede that "anthropologists have given relative little attention" to such matters in general, "and when they have, they have rarely done it well" (ibid.: 12). But this—rather fundamental—caveat went almost entirely unnoticed. Instead, what soon came to be known as Mintz and Price's "creolization" model (they themselves never used the term in the coauthored text!) was rapidly assimilated to oftentimes highly bowdlerized versions of linguistic substrate theory.

In sum, Mintz and Price's tacit endorsement of Herskovits's analogy about a "grammar of culture," their suggestions about the operation of "unconscious 'grammatical' principles" (1992:9, note the quotation marks!), "cognitive orientations" (ibid.:10), or "deep-level cultural rules or principles" (ibid.:53), and their frequent use of language as an illustration of the rapidity with which new cultural forms could emerge, seem to have triggered a fairly systematic misreading of their text.[10] What was meant as a clarion call for the historicization of African-American anthropology turned into the siren's song of a linguistic analogy that effectively undermined efforts to install a genuinely historical methodology in African-American cultural history. What Mintz and Price had suggested was basically a two-part working hypothesis for processual analysis that may be summed up as follows:

1. The documentable rapidity and synthetic nature of change in one "cultural subsystem," language, may be indicative of similar change in other "subsystems" (religion, kinship, and so on);
2. New and hybrid cultures may have been built up from "deep-level principles" common to various African cultures in a manner for which the relation between morphosyntax and lexicon in creole language evolution might provide a heuristic analogy.

What these suggestions were taken for, however, was not a model *for* inquiry but a model *of* processual reality: cultural change works like linguistic change.

* * *

What is ostensibly surprising is how eagerly historians bought into this mistaken equation. Indeed, the problems generated by literalizing the creolization-metaphor are, perhaps, best illustrated in the context of the study of slave cultures. Take the case of Charles Joyner, who complains (1984:246f.n9) that in his important *The Black Family in Slavery and Freedom, 1750–1925*, Herbert Gutman (1976)[11] had used the concept "creolization" not only "always in quotation marks" but "merely [as] a general term to describe the transformation of Africans into Afro-Americans (or 'creoles'). He does not examine slave language, nor does he use a linguistic model of creolization."

Moreover, in Joyner's eyes, even Mintz and Price ultimately failed to make the most of their own suggestions in "merely draw[ing] upon creolization theory to analyze Afro-American linguistic change, but stop[ping] short of proposing an explicitly creolist approach to other cultural formations" (ibid.). How then might these defects be remedied? Predictably, Joyner begins his enterprise by enhancing Mintz and Price's hypotheses about the emergence of African-American speech communities with some (linguistically problematic) notions about lexical expansion as a by-product of the process whereby pidgins are transformed into creoles.[12] The next step is the assimilation of their notions of "'grammatical' principles," "deep structure," and so forth to linguistic substratum hypotheses. This, in turn, results in a program for teasing out the "rules" according to which the culture of South Carolinian Gullah-speakers was built up from an "African grammar." Let us take a concrete example and see how this works.

As had been first suggested by Wood (1974) and Littlefied (1981), there exists a complex historical relation between the emergence of rice plantations in South Carolina and slave imports into that region from areas of West Africa (Senegambia to Sierra Leone) characterized by long-standing patterns of wet-rice cultivation (Carney 2001). What Wood (1974:56) cautiously called a "temporal association between the development of rice and slavery" in the Carolinas is now fairly uncontroversially seen as having involved a substantial measure of agricultural technology transfer from Africa to the New World.[13] Moreover, as Joyner himself usefully suggests, African techniques of sowing, harvesting, winnowing, threshing, and husking rice should be seen as part of a larger complex including, for example, forms of coiled basketry and food preparations, perhaps even styles of musical expression structuring work patterns. Yet instead of asking how precisely the knowledge and skills pertaining to rice cultivation that some Africans undoubtedly brought to South Carolina came to be integrated into, and perpetuated by, an emerging system of plantation production, Joyner appears more interested in driving home the importance of linguistically conceived "creolization theory." In doing so, he foregoes the opportunity for a truly historical explanation of formal stability and change. "More important than such static [!] retentions" of agricultural techniques and practices, he argues (Joyner 1984:58f.), "was the successful imposition by All Saints [parish] slaves of a cooperative work ethos upon the highly individualistic task system through which their masters tried to regulate their labor. This syncretic achievement exemplified cultural continuity with Africa at a deeper and more fundamental level than did simple African retentions. Here the slaves adapted a basic African work orientation to a vastly different labor system and, in the process, adapted the masters' labor system to their own sense of appropriateness. Moving across the fields in a row hoeing side-by-side to the rhythm of work songs, the slaves imposed a group consciousness on their field work. The task system treated them as individuals with individual work assignments; nevertheless, they continued to work in groups, corresponding to cooperative work patterns widespread in West Africa."

Without delving into the problems posed by Joyner's implicit contention that the slaves were resisting something (individualization, an imposed labor regime, the masters' authority, or what have you), one can see several difficulties with the overall picture he paints. The first has to do with the fact that the task system was by no means the only form of organizing plantation labor. Instead, it stood in a historically well-documented opposition to a form of cooperative labor organization most slaves seem to have dreaded: gang work—that is, the strictly regimented deployment of large numbers of slaves working under rigid, and often brutal, supervision for the duration of fixed hours.

As Philip Morgan has shown in a careful comparison of a large body of evidence pertaining to crop-specific plantation regimes in the Americas (Morgan 1982, 1988), slaves can just as well be portrayed as freely embracing task systems. This was not because task systems were individualizing and somehow close to certain capitalistic forms of labor extraction (which was arguably the case). It was because task systems offered the potential advantage of freeing part of the worker's time for other, more autonomous forms of activity—such as, for example, provision gardening, live-stock raising, and gainful exchange. As Morgan demonstrates for the classic rice region of the Carolina low country, evidence from the Reconstruction Southern Claims Commission (as well as earlier sources) shows that the task system had underwritten a slave domestic economy that not only generated adequate nutrition but modest wealth. Nor had the task system been imposed by planter fiat. Instead, it grew out of prolonged struggles between planters and slaves not only over the allocation of the slaves' time and effort but over the structuring of a whole way of life that emerged in tandem with the task system in the first half of the eighteenth century and that included as its central component the slaves' customary rights to subsistence production, exchange of surplus, and accumulation of property (Morgan 1982). Perhaps most important, the task system became linked to customary rights to dispose of such property in the form of bequests to kinfolk and descendants, thus stabilizing transgenerational continuities within a social formation bearing striking resemblance to what Sidney Mintz (1978) in reference to the Caribbean calls "proto-peasantries." As Ira Berlin (1980:66) succinctly puts it, the "autonomy generated by both the task system and truck gardening provided the material basis for lowland black culture." This neither proves nor disproves hypotheses about the role of African "grammatical principles" in shaping Carolina low country slave culture; what it does, however, is provide a heuristic basis for gauging the concrete factors conditioning its emergence.

But this is not the only issue obscured rather than elucidated by Joyner's "explicitly creolist approach." For had he not been more interested in demonstrating the presumed "reflexes" of an (hypothetical) antecedent "deep structural" African communal work ethos, he might have asked himself—as did Bascom (1941:45) some forty years earlier—why co-operative work groups were, indeed, observable *after* the end of slavery.[14] Was this because emancipation had upset a previous proto-peasant adaptation internal to the plantation regime to which they had been legally bound, and had now given rise to a peasantry struggling to maintain itself under the increasingly precarious conditions of landholding in post-Civil War South Carolina?[15] Was it—as a reading of the case through the lenses provided by Richard Price's maroon casuistry might suggest—a latter-day *reversion* to a "structurally" more African pattern? Or were such forms of cooperation, perhaps, a post-emancipation innovation befitting a wide variety of situations in which embattled peasants functionalized work routines to express and defend some measure of communal autonomy—something, in other words, that might have occurred in rural Europe, Southeast Asia, or colonial Africa as well?[16] And if, indeed, we want to book it as a "creolized" reflex of the cultural "grammar" of fundamentally African patterns of organizing agricultural labor, would we want to take into account the tremendous variety of genuinely African situations that might be relevant here? No doubt, slaves in the kin-based villages of the Western Sudan on the plantations of Dahomean nobles, Sokoto religious hierarchs, or Niger Delta merchant princes sang work songs, hoed side-by-side, and helped less-capable fellow slaves along.[17] Is all this then germane to All Saints' Parish, too? Joyner, whose problems are solved by an "explicitly creolist approach" does not tell us.[18]

As this example shows, approaches driven by what is nowadays a veritable machine of creolization[19] run the serious risk of mistaking a metaphor, or, at best, analogy, for the "thing itself." The result is a kind of methodological Gresham's law: bad theory drives out empirical research by substituting purely hypothetical processual models for analyses of documented process. Nor does the confusion caused by the discursive interference between older conceptions of "creolization" and naive linguistic borrowings show any signs of dissipating. In a recent volume entitled *Creolization in the Americas* (Buisseret & Reinhardt 2000) we thus find not only careful empirical reconstructions of the livelihood of settlers and slaves in the Lower Mississippi Valley that entirely dispense with grammars of culture, substrata, lexifiers, target cultures, and other such spurious explananda. We also encounter strained attempts to process a competent documentation of early South Carolinian pharmacopoeia through an unnecessary, and ultimately unhelpful, medicine : lexicon :: illness beliefs : grammar scheme. Perhaps even more exasperating is the recent formation of a self-conscious reaction among historians trying to rescue African-American cultural history from the stranglehold of what Paul Lovejoy (1997) calls the "creolization school."

Proceeding from the assumption that Mintz and Price's ill-labeled "creolization model" minimizes, or, at best, overgeneralizes, the African contribution to New World cultural formations, scholars such as John Thornton (1992), Gwendolyn Hall (1992), Michael Mullin (1992), Paul Lovejoy (1997, 2000), and Michael Gomez (1998) have embarked on a new round of searches for transatlantic cultural continuities, based on assumptions about the relative stability and perdurance of originally African ethnolinguistic identities ("nations"). Yet what Lovejoy (2000:1) confusingly calls "'Africancentric' or even 'Afrocentric'" approaches hardly goes beyond the terms of the fundamentally mistaken linguistic analogy. This is so not only because surprisingly ahistorical views of African ethnic phenomena and processes seriously mar much of this literature,[20] or because the deeply anachronistic (and Eurocentric) term "nation" powerfully resonates with the same linguistic ideologies that gave rise to formal creolization theory in the first place. It is because some of the contributors to this debate are all but reluctant to borrow from outdated creole linguistics themselves.

A case in point is Chambers's (2000) attempt to connect historical New World terminology designating slaves as "ebo," "eboe," "ibo," and so on with what he feels are African forms of "essential" Igbo-ness *avant la lettre*. Obviousy aware that the term "Igbo" came to function as an African ethnonym only in the twentieth century, and so cannot well be retrojected into the era of the slave trade, Chambers recurs to operationalizing an analogy between "Igbo-speaking" and "Igbo-acting" as predicates applicable to enslaved individuals and groups. Given Chambers's (2000:57) dubious interpretative premise that "[s]ocial and cultural artifacts termed 'Ibo' or 'Eboe' in the New World are signs of a historical Igbo presence," he has no qualms about booking yams consumption as a "basilectal" element of an "Igboesque" creole cultural continuum that is beyond all reasonable standards of interpretative license in historical inference, or, for that matter, beyond any kind of theoretical consensus within the donor discipline of linguistics.[21] As a result, the term "creolization" —quite miraculously—turns out to circumscribe a process of "Africanization" (Chambers 2000:60) in which enslaved "Igbo may have tended to copy-translate ancestral cultural forms and functions into creole (or even Euro-American) forms, that is, acted as 'calques'" (ibid.:58). Whatever Chambers may mean by this truly astonishing formulation, we seem to come full circle here: whoever Chambers's yams-calquing "Igbo" were (or thought they were!) has become as irrelevant as the self-conceptions of sixteenth-century denizens of Spanish America whom twentieth-century historians have swept up under the anachronistic label "creoles" (Palmié, this volume). In the end, Lovejoy (2000:23) might well be taken at his word when he closes his introduction to the volume containing Chambers's remarkable insights by remarking that "identity is in any case a shadowy concept, one that is open to interpretation, reinterpretation, and even misinterpretation."

* * *

Such flights of interpretative fancy, however, are merely symptomatic of the (by now) far-reaching confusion of tongues with which I have been concerned all along in this essay. For what we are left with, it seems, is a "concept for all seasons" —let alone projects and purposes. Yet if terms such as "creole" and "creolization" are so clearly overburdened with contradictory historical meanings, overdetermined by differentially politicized local usages, and warped in their anlytical capacity by inappropriate transdisciplinary applications, what—besides sheer intellectual inertia, or discursive fashion-consciousness—makes for their continued use?

In a perceptive essay on the first wave of creolization-theory in anthropology, David Parkin (1993:85) noted that while the concept of creolization appears to remedy some of the defects of the discipline's conception of culture, its applications "neatly reproduce some of the traditional approaches to the study of culture." Like him, Marilyn Strathern (1992) early on pointed out the extent to which the creolization concept remained pegged to the very modernist holist/particularist paradigms it was supposed to help dismantle. Rather than marking a radical departure, for her, the discovery of postplural hybridity merely accentuates the obvious: reproduction of people, cultures, identities, or power structures inevitably involves the creation of new forms from fragments of old materials. Once we let go of an older imagery of objectified cultural parts and wholes, creolization is reproduction, and vice versa. How easily the threshold beyond which the conceptual distinctions collapse is crossed becomes even clearer when we ask ourselves—as Aisha Khan (2001:278, 283) commends— "when does creolization start? And what, then, has ended?" For if "we are to proceed in accord with the axiom that all things exist only in relation to other things, then if there is creole, it follows that there must be un-creole." But what would this be? And where would we locate it except in those patently ideological constructions of ethnic, cultural, and linguistic closure that have been with us since Tacitus's days but are, of course, the hallmark of various post-nineteenth-century racisms and nationalisms?[22]

If so, Robert Brightman (1995) may well have a point when he argues that much of the current rhetoric against the "traditional" culture concept in anthropology is itself a product of processes of "relexification" toward ever newer disciplinary "acrolects." Could we replace the concept of "culture" by that of "creolization"? Of course we could! Calquing our way into new phonological forms, we might perhaps find ourselves repeating Boas's, Goldenweiser's, Lowie's, or Sapir's efforts to divest the culture-concept of its tendencies to bend our thinking in the direction of reifiable, objective wholes beyond the reach of human agency or reflection. If so, little, in fact, might be gained for the discipline, but little lost as well. Things, however, look different for those of us who actually study the region from which terms such as "creole" and "creolization" originally diffused into their current global, transdisciplinary discursive economy. To my idea, Caribbeanists stand much to lose from such disciplinary relexification—and not only in analytical acumen but in political terms as well.

For once we lift these terms out of the concrete local and historic specificity of their Caribbean contexts and turn them into markers of universally applicable "target theories" about human knowledge and practice, the Caribbean, as a region imagined or perhaps even invented under the sign of "creolization," will arguably disappear—if only because it will have been discursively rendered coextensive with the rest of the world. Again, this would not be terribly bothersome, academically. There clearly is no reason why we should continue to carve up the world in the way we do.[23] But what, then, of folks for whom the term "creole" circumscribes significant aspects of their social identity? As a Caribbeanist, I cannot help but ask: if the whole world is in creolization these days, how are we to talk about people whose local worlds are the products of centuries of struggle against those violent and dehumanizing processes out of which the global (post)modernity we currently inhabit ultimately emerged (Trouillot 1998)? Historically, the unstable and fluid Caribbean hybridities and syntheses that nowadays so capture our interest and imagination were achieved at a grueling price. And to dawdle with these well-documented facts is to indulge in an intellectually vapid and politically irresponsible solipsism.

Perhaps we all really *are* Caribbeans now, in our urban archipelagoes, as James Clifford (1988) famously vaunted. Perhaps the world has indeed caught up with a bunch of islands stretching from the Bahamas to the Orinoco delta, belatedly joining them in universal "creolization" (Hannerz 1987). But unlike malnourished Haitian peasants, Cubans reduced to prostituting themselves to hard-currency-carrying tourists, or Jamaican migrant cane cutters toiling away at below-minimum wages in central Florida or Louisiana, perhaps we simply can afford to think so. Creolization theory will surely be with us for considerable time—as a label for a whole array of intellectual pursuits, some of them undoubtedly stimulating and salutary, some contrived and productive of further confusion. But beyond all current fascination with things Caribbean and "creole" we need to keep matters in perspective lest we fool ourselves into believing that slavery was a great chance to be creative, that extreme poverty and hyper-exploitation are conducive to enviable authenticity, or that the Caribbean region's truly dreadful colonial history "somehow" prefigures our existential condition as cosmopolitans economically empowered to pursue hitherto unprecedented forms and degrees of consumptive eclecticism.

Notes

1. Early anthropological attempts to operationalize the term occurred mainly in the context of debates about the conceptualization of large scale "culture areas" in the Americas (for example, Adams 1959; Gillin 1947; Simmons 1955; Tschopik 1948; Wagley 1960) and the so-called "plural society thesis." (For assessments of the issues involved in the latter debate see Mintz 1974b and Austin 1983). However, the manner in which the term "creole" was deployed in these debates remained terminologically and conceptually inconsequential.
2. These include not only first-generation immigrants but also some groups whose arrival (as in the case of Chinese or South Asian population segments in some Caribbean societies) dates back several generations.
3. On which see, for example, Crowley (1990); Olender (1992); Gal and Irvine (1995); Woolard (1998); and Alter (1999).
4. How, for example, could a "universalist" hypothesis about linguistic creativity in the face of multiple interference in first language acquisition hold without precise knowledge of the socialization process the children of dominated or enslaved groups underwent in a wide range of colonial settings? How could a substratist argument about the structuring force that specific African grammars exerted on European lexifiers be sustained without knowledge about how single groups of enslaved Africans might have become enabled to impress *their* version of how humans should communicate on other, linguistically alien slaves? How, finally, might arguments about African (or New World, for that matter) monogenesis be defended against even only modified versions of Bickertonian bioprogrammatics without knowing the precise trajectories along which enslaved Africans traveled—not only from specific locations in Africa to specifically structured New World environments but from one location in the New World to the next?
5. Even less generously, Bakker (2002:75) laments that creole genesis scenarios, in many instances, are "purely speculative, but they are quoted as fact by other creolists." Hence his exasperated plea that creolist linguists "should be forbidden from making any claims on history or life on plantations without reference to the work of historians" (ibid.). The trouble is that those historians may already have been reading creolist texts!

6. This is not to speak about the opinions of those creolists who argue that the creole language/creolization concepts have overreached or exhausted their usefulness for linguists (for example, Jourdan 1991:191; Mufwene 1997; Parkvall 2002).

7. Substrate-influence arguments had been launched at least since the late 1920s, the most spectacular case certainly being that of the Haitian linguist Suzanne Sylvain who, in 1936, famously described Haitian creole as "an Ewe language with a French vocabulary" (Holm 1988:37). Herskovits appears to have been unaware of these studies when he and his wife Frances first approached the issue in the 1936 monograph *Suriname Folk Lore* (Herskovits & Herskovits 1936:114–135). For a fuller discussion of substrate/superstrate theories see the contributions in Muysken and Smith (1986), as well as Baker and Mühlhäusler, this volume).

8. See, for instance, Alleyne (1980); Muysken and Smith (1986); Holm (1988:37–44); Arends, Kouwenberg, and Smith (1995); Arends (2002).

9. I am somewhat overstating the case here. The work of the Savannah Unit of the WPA Georgia Writers Project (1940), Bascom's research among the Gullah (1941), and Lorenzo Turner's *Africanisms in the Gullah Dialect* (1949) certainly demonstrated that in some isolated rural areas of the U.S. South fairly "straightforward" Africanisms could be found. Even Bascom (1941), however, was more inclined to speak of an "African flavor" rather than of "specific correspondences" in respect to the bulk of Gullah "traits."

10. But see Price and Price (1972), where the notion of an African "grammar" of naming practices is, indeed, literalized to a considerable degree.

11. Gutman, in fact, seems to have been the first historian to actually make use of Mintz and Price's essay—and, one should add, in a judicious manner and to good effect.

12. Cf. the following passage: "The earliest African slaves in South Carolina did not constitute a speech community, as the term is used by sociolinguists. The slaves' various African languages were often mutually unintelligible. The common language that they acquired was a pidginized form of English. Pidgins are developed as a means of communication among speakers of diverse languages. A pidgin is by definition an auxiliary language. It has no native speakers. But when the pidgin is [sic] passed on to the American-born children of those enslaved Africans, it became the children's native tongue. If a pidgin acquires [sic] native speakers, it is no longer considered a pidgin by linguists but is said to be a creole language. As a native tongue it has to serve all the functions of a language, not merely the restricted functions of a pidgin. Linguists call the process of change in which two or more languages converge to form a new native tongue 'creolization.' The creole language of the slaves, Gullah, continued to develop—both in inner form and in extended use—in a situation of linguistic contact. There was reciprocal influence of English and African features upon both the creole and the regional standard. The English contribution was primarily lexical; the African contribution was principally grammatical" (Joyner 1984:xx–xxi.).

13. The case is quite convincing because we can assume that the British colonists in South Carolina could hardly have brought an understanding of rice cultivation from their European societies of origin, although they certainly were aware of the commercial advantages of the crop, given its extensive cultivation in parts of southern Europe (for example, Lombardy).

14. The crux of the matter may well be that the term "cooperative" itself remains deeply problematical unless we specify what exactly it is supposed to mean. Viewed from the outside, both gang and task work necessarily involved forms of cooperation among laborers. We may presume that in the first case, cooperation was largely enforced "from above," so to speak, while the degree of cooperation that actually obtained in task work may have been a matter over which the slaves themselves exerted considerable control.

15. Because of Sherman's famous 1861 Field Order No. 15, Sea Island African Americans enjoyed a brief period (ending with the onset of Presidential Reconstruction under Johnson in 1865–1866) of unlimited control over land. Cf. Rose (1964) for a now classical work on the unusual opportunities, challenges, and eventual disappointments war-time emancipation and postwar expropriation brought to Sea Island African Americans. See also Foner (1983) for the bitter struggles that ensued in the process of economic and political marginalization of such "reconstituted peasantries" in the period after Reconstruction.
16. See, for example, Wolf (1966, particularly pp. 77ff.); Scott (1976); and Isaacman (1993).
17. Cf. Meillassoux (1982); Lovejoy (1979); and Northrup (1981).
18. In all fairness to Joyner, I hasten to add that he was neither the first nor the last to be seduced into literalizing the creolization metaphor. In fact, this tendency is, perhaps, most evident in studies of expressive culture. See Rath (1993) for a particularly egregious example.
19. In many ways "creolization" supplanted the older semantic machine provided by the "acculturation" concept that had plainly become obsolete by the end of the 1960s.
20. Cf. Morgan (1997). For a concrete example see Caron's (1997) critique of Hall (1992).
21. Cf. the following passage: "it seems clear that Igbo may have tended to 'calque,' that is, to copy-translate into another cultural code behaviours (including words and phrases and other social ´things´) from the ancestral set. Therefore, even 'basilectal' (root) things such as yam-growing and -eating, especially the reliance on D. rotundata, became identified as of 'Guinea' rather than from Igbo specifically (that is, in the Anglophone Americas)" (Chambers 2000:58).
22. To be sure, our world arguably evidences an unprecedented degree of articulations between heterogeneous cultural forms and practices, a proliferation of seemingly novel forms of identification, and new ways of negotiating difference. It would be hard, indeed, to argue against such a claim. Nevertheless, it is not at all self-evident how we have come to be aware of this, or why it should matter to us. Could it be that Young (1995:4) is right in suggesting that, in contrast to nineteenth-century obsessions with classificatory separations (between, say, nations, languages, cultures, or races), today's "self-proclaimed mobile and multiple identities may be a marker not of contemporary social fluidity and dispossession, but of a new stability, self-assurance, and quietism"?
23. Who knows, Africa, the Middle East, or the curious set of peninsulas jutting out from Western Asia that is known as Europe may well turn out intellectually dispensable one day. "America" and "India", of course, are beautiful cases in point—if only because there really was a time when these terms *were* interchangeable.

References

Abrahams, R. D. 1970. Traditions of eloquence in the West Indies, *Journal of Inter-American Studies and World Affairs* 12:505–527.

Adams, R. N. 1959. On the relation between plantation and "Creole Cultures." In *Plantation systems of the New World*. V. Rubin, ed. Washington DC: Pan American Union, pp. 73–79.

Alleyne, M. C. 1980. *Comparative Afro-American*. Ann Arbor, MI: Karoma.

Alter, S. G. 1999. *Darwinism and the linguistic image*. Baltimore, MD: Johns Hopkins University Press.

Arends, J., S. Kouwenberg, and N. Smith. 1995. Theories focussing on the non-European input. In *Pidgins and creoles*. J. Arends, P. Muysken, and N. Smith, eds. Amsterdam: John Benjamins, pp. 99–109.

Arends, J. 2002. The historical study of creoles and the future of creole studies. In *Pidgin and creole studies in the twenty-first century*. G. Gilbert, ed. New York: Peter Lang, pp. 48–68.

Austin, D. J. 1983. Culture and ideology in the English-speaking Caribbean: A view from Jamaica, *American Ethnologist* 10:223–240.

Bakker, P. 2002. Some future challenges to pidgin and creole studies. In *Pidgin and creole studies in the twenty-first century*. G. Gilbert, ed. New York: Peter Lang, pp. 69–92.

Barth, F. 1969. Introduction. In *Ethnic groups and boundaries*. F. Barth, ed. Boston: Little, Brown.

Bascom, W. 1941. Acculturation among the Gullah negroes, *American Anthropologist* 43:43–50.

Bergad, L. W. 1990. *Cuban rural society in the nineteenth century*. Princeton, NJ: Princeton University Press.

Berlin, I. 1980. Time, space, and the evolution of Afro-American society in British mainland North America, *American Historical Review* 85:44–78.

Brathwaite, E. K. 1971. *The development of creole society in Jamaica, 1770–1820*. Oxford: Clarendon Press.

Breen, T. H. 1984. Creative adaptations: Peoples and cultures. In *Colonial British America*. J. P. Greene and J. R. Pole, eds. Baltimore, MD: Johns Hopkins University Press, pp. 195–232.

Brightman, R. 1995. Forget culture: Replacement, transcendence, relexification, *Cultural Anthropology* 10:509–546.

Buisseret, D., and S. G. Reinhardt, eds. 2000. *Creolization in the Americas*. College Station, TX: Texas A&M University Press.

Carney, J. A. 2001. *Black rice*. Cambridge, MA: Harvard University Press.

Caron, P. 1997. "Of a nation which the others do not understand": Bambara slaves and African ethnicity in colonial Louisiana, 1718–1760, *Slavery and Abolition* 18:98–121.

Chambers, D. B. 2000. Tracing Igbo into the African diaspora. In *Identity in the shadow of slavery*. P. E. Lovejoy, ed. London: Continuum, pp. 55–71.

Clifford, J. 1988. *The predicament of culture*. Cambridge, MA: Harvard University Press.

Crowley, T. 1990. That obscure object of desire: A science of language. In *Ideologies of language*. J. E. Joseph and T. J. Taylor, eds. London: Routledge, pp. 27–50.

Engerman, S. L., and B. W. Higman. 1997. The demographic structure of the Caribbean slave societies in the eighteenth and nineteenth centuries. In *General history of the Caribbean*, vol. III. *The slave societies of the Caribbean*. F. W. Knight, ed. London: UNESCO/Macmillan, pp. 45–104.

Fabian, J. 1978. Popular culture in Africa: Findings and conjectures, *Africa* 48:315–34.

Foner, E. 1983. *Nothing but freedom*. Baton Rouge, LA: Louisiana State University Press.

Gal, S., and J. T. Irvine. 1995. The boundaries of languages and disciplines: How ideologies construct difference, *Social Research* 62:967–1001.

Georgia Writers' Project. 1940. *Drums and shadows: Survival studies among the Georgia coastal negroes*. Athens, GA: University of Georgia Press.

Gillin, J. 1947. *Moche: A Peruvian coastal community*. Washington, DC: Institute of Social Anthropology, Smithsonian Institution Publications No. 3.

Gomez, M. 1998. *Exchanging our country marks*. Chapel Hill, NC: University of North Carolina Press.

Goveia, E. 1965. *Slave society in the British Leeward Islands at the end of the eighteenth century*. New Haven, CT: Yale University Press.

Gutman, H. 1976. *The black family in slavery and freedom, 1750–1925*. New York: Vintage.

Hall, G. M. 1992. *Africans in colonial Louisiana*. Baton Rouge, LA: Louisiana State University Press.

Hall, R. A. 1950. The African substratum in negro English: A review of Turner (1949), *American Speech* 25:51–54.

Hannerz, U. 1987. The world in creolization, *Africa* 57:546–559.

Harris, R., and B. Rampton. 2002. Creole metaphors in cultural analysis: On the limits and possibilities of (socio-)linguistics, *Critique of Anthropology* 22:31–51.

Herskovits, M. J. 1966. *The New World Negro*. New York: Minerva.

—— 1989. *The myth of the negro past*. Boston: Beacon Press.

Herskovits, M. J., and F. S. Herskovits. 1936. *Suriname folk-lore*. New York: Columbia University Press.

Higman, B. W. 1976. *Slave population and economy in Jamaica, 1807–1834*. Cambridge: Cambridge University Press.

—— 1984. *Slave populations of the British Caribbean, 1807–1834*. Baltimore, MD: Johns Hopkins University Press.

Holm, J. A. 1988. *Pidgins and creoles*. Cambridge: Cambridge University Press.

Isaacman, A. F. 1993. Peasants and rural protest in Africa. In *Confronting historical paradigms*. F. Cooper, A. F. Isaacman, F. Mallon, W. Roseberry, and S. J. Stern, eds. Madison, WI: University of Wisconsin Press, pp. 205–317.

Jourdan, C. 1991. Pidgins and creoles: The blurring of categories, *Annual Reviews of Anthropology* 20:187–209.

Joyner, C. W. 1979. The creolization of slave folklife: All Saints Parish, South Carolina, as a test case, *Historical Reflections/Reflexions Historiques* 6:435–53.

—— 1984. *Down by the riverside*. Urbana, IL: University of Illinois Press.

Khan, A. 2001. Journey to the center of the earth: The Caribbean as master symbol, *Cultural Anthropology* 16:271–302.

Kulikoff, A. 1986. *Tobacco and slaves*. Chapel Hill, NC: University of North Carolina Press.

Littlefield, D. 1981. *Rice and slaves*. Baton Rouge, LA: Louisiana State University Press.

Lovejoy, P. 1979. The characteristics of plantations in the nineteenth century Sokoto Caliphate (Islamic West Africa), *American Historical Review* 84:1267–1292.

—— 1997. The African diaspora: Revisionist interpretations of ethnicity, culture and religion under slavery, *Studies in the World History of Slavery, Abolition and Emancipation* 2:1–24.

—— 2000. Identifying enslaved Africans in the African diaspora. In *Identity in the shadow of slavery*. P. E. Lovejoy, ed. London: Continuum, pp. 1–29.

McWhorter, J. H. 2000. *The missing Spanish Creoles*. Berkeley and Los Angeles, CA: University of California Press.

Meillassoux, C. 1982. The role of slavery in the economic and social history of Sahelo-Sudanic Africa. In *Forced migration*. J. E. Inikori, ed. London: Hutchinson, pp. 74–99.

Mintz, S. W. 1970. Foreword. In *Afro-American anthropology*. N. E. Whitten, Jr., and J. F. Szwed, eds. New York: The Free Press, pp. 1–16.

—— 1971. The socio-historical background to pidginization and creolization. In *Pidginization and creolization of languages*. D. Hymes, ed. Cambridge: Cambridge University Press, pp. 481–496.

—— 1974a. *Caribbean transformations*. New York: Columbia University Press.

—— 1974b. The Caribbean region. In *Slavery, colonialism, and racism*. S. W. Mintz, ed. New York: W. W. Norton, pp. 45–71.

—— 1978. Was the plantation slave a proletarian? *Review* 2:81–98.

—— 1996. Enduring substances, trying theories: The Caribbean region as *Oikumene*, *Journal of the Royal Anthropological Institute* 2:289–311.

Mintz, S. W. 1998. The localization of anthropological practice: From area studies to transnationalism, *Critique of Anthropology* 18:117–133.

Mintz, S. W., and R. Price. 1992. *The birth of African American culture.* Boston: Beacon Press.

Morgan, P. D. 1982. Work and culture: The task system and the world of Lowcountry Blacks, 1700–1880, *William and Mary Quarterly* 39:563–599.

———— 1988. Task and gang systems: The organization of labor on New World plantations. In *Work and labor in early America.* S. Innes, ed. Chapel Hill, NC: University of North Carolina Press, pp. 189–220.

———— 1997. The cultural implications of the Atlantic slave trade: African regional origins, American destinations and New World developments, *Slavery and Abolition* 18:122–45.

Mufwene, S. S. 1997. Jargons, pidgins, creoles, and koines: What are they? In *The structure and status of pidgins and creoles.* A. K. Spears and D. Winford, eds. Amsterdam: John Benjamins.

Mullin, M. 1992. *Africa in America.* Urbana, IL: University of Illinois Press.

Muysken, P., and N. Smith, eds. 1986. *Substrata versus universals in creole genesis.* Amsterdam: John Benjamins.

Northrup, D. 1981. The ideological context of slavery in southeastern Nigeria in the nineteenth century. In *The ideology of slavery in Africa.* P. E. Lovejoy, ed. Beverly Hills, CA: Sage, pp. 100–122.

Olender, M. 1992. *The languages of paradise.* Cambridge, MA: Harvard University Press.

Pares, R. 1950. *A West-India fortune.* London: Longman, Green and Co.

Parkin, D. 1993. Nemi in the modern world: Return of the exotic? *Man* 28:79–99.

Parkvall, M. 2002. Cutting off the branch. In *Pidgin and creole linguistics in the twenty-first century.* G. Gilbert, ed. New York: Peter Lang, pp. 355–367.

Pearse, A. 1956. Carnival in nineteenth century Trinidad, *Caribbean Quarterly* 4:176–193.

Price, R. 1976. *The Guiana Maroons: A historical and bibliographic introduction.* Baltimore, MD: Johns Hopkins University Press.

———— 2001. The miracle of creolization: A retrospective, *New West Indian Guide* 75:35–64.

Price, R., and S. Price. 1972. Saramaka onomastics: An Afro-American naming system, *Ethnology* 11:341–367.

Rath, R. C. 1993. African music in seventeenth-century Jamaica: Cultural transit and transition, *William and Mary Quarterly* 50:700–726.

Reisman, K. 1970. Cultural and linguistic ambiguity in a West Indian village. In *Afro-American anthropology.* N. E. Whitten and J. F. Szwed, eds. New York: The Free Press, pp. 129–144.

Rose, W. L. 1964. *Rehearsal for reconstruction: The Port Royal experiment.* Indianapolis, IN: Bobbs-Merrill.

Scott, J. C. 1976. *The moral economy of the peasant.* New Haven, CT: Yale University Press.

Simmons, O. G. 1955. The criollo outlook in the mestizo culture of coastal Peru, *American Anthropologist* 57:107–117.

Smith, M. G. 1965. *The plural society in the British West Indies.* Berkeley and Los Angeles, CA: University of California Press.

Strathern, M. 1992. *Reproducing the future.* New York: Routledge.

Thornton, J. K. 1992. *Africa and Africans in the making of the Atlantic world, 1400–1680.* Cambridge: Cambridge University Press.

Trouillot, M.-R. 1998. Culture on the edges: Creolization in the plantation context, *Plantation Society in the Americas* 5:8–28.

Tschopik, H. 1948. On the concept of creole culture in Peru, *Transactions of the New York Academy of Sciences* 1:252–261.

Turner, L. D. 1949. Africanisms in the Gullah dialect. Chicago: University of Chicago Press.

Wagley, C. 1960. Plantation America: A culture sphere. In *Caribbean studies: A symposium*. V. Rubin, ed. Seattle, WA: University of Washington Press, pp. 3–13.

Walsh, L. S. 1997. *From Calabar to Carter's Grove*. Charlottesville, VA: University of Virginia Press.

Whitten, N. E., Jr., and J. F. Szwed. 1970. Introduction. In *Afro-American anthropology*. N. E. Whitten, Jr., and J. F. Szwed, eds. New York: The Free Press, pp. 23–60.

Wolf, E. 1966. *Peasants*. Englewood Cliffs, NJ: Prentice Hall.

Wood, P. 1974. *Black majority*. New York: W. W. Norton.

Woolard, K. A. 1998. Introduction: Language ideology as a field of inquiry. In *Language ideologies*. B. Schieffelin, K. A. Woolard, and P. V. Kroskrity, eds. New York: Oxford University Press, pp. 3–47.

Young, R. J. 1995. *Colonial desire*. London: Routledge.

10 Adapting to Inequality: Negotiating Nikkei Identity in Contexts of Return

Joshua Hotaka Roth

Return migration offers rich opportunities for examining the ways in which people conceptualize identity, difference, and transformation (Long & Oxfeld 2004). This chapter examines the case of Japanese immigrants and their descendants in Brazil, and their "return" migration to Japan.[1] Japanese Brazilians have often constructed Japan as the point of origin— the motherland (*bokoku*) or ancestral land (*sokoku*)—and source of identification, notwithstanding the tremendous social and cultural transformations Japan has undergone in the roughly one hundred years since the first Japanese migrated to Brazil. Do Japanese Brazilians feel they have retained some essential Japaneseness at their core, and what do Japanese say about this? If change is acknowledged, has it been positively evaluated or thought to be degenerative? Has "return" migration made Japanese of Japanese Brazilians? This chapter focuses on the contexts of interaction, and the discourses of migration and change, engaged in by Japanese and Japanese Brazilians alike. By focusing on specific contexts and discourses, we can understand transformation not just as the inexorable result of the passage of time but also as an active process of adaptation within limiting constraints (see Harris & Rampton 2002).

Recent approaches to diaspora and transnationalism have emphasized the concept of flexibility, turning our attention to the strategic innovations of which migrants are capable (Basch, Glick Schiller, & Szanton Blanc 1994; Hannerz 1996; Ong 1999). The focus on flexibility has provided an important counter to assumptions of inevitable change with the passing of generations such as those that undergirded earlier paradigms of cultural change and assimilation (Handlin 1951; Redfield, Linton, & Herskovits 1935). The concept of flexibility allows us to acknowledge that migrants have a degree of agency in deciding how they may identify and act depending on the contexts with which they are engaged. We must avoid the trap, however, of viewing migrants as completely autonomous agents. Immigration law, employment practices, and other constraints can to some degree shape the very subjectivities of migrants who must live with the stigma of illegality and marginality on a daily basis (Kearney 1991; Ong 1996; Rouse 1991). In this chapter, I argue that migrants adapt to, identify with, or resist the new social contexts through which they move. They do so not as completely autonomous individuals but as persons embedded within networks of social relations, cultures of adaptation, and political and economic institutions.

Unlike in some of the other contributions to this volume, the label "creole" does not apply to the group I consider. However, the analytical concept of "creolization," derived from Caribbean and other colonial contexts, is useful for thinking about the Japanese Brazilian case. Although the conditions that African slaves faced on Caribbean plantations were far more extreme than those that Japanese Brazilians have faced in Japanese factories, both cases involve adaptations that marginalized groups made under conditions of duress, in contexts of unequal power. While the condition of mixture described by the terms hybridity and syncretism presumes a process by which mixture occurred, "creolization" points directly to the process itself as it occurs under conditions of inequality. It is a useful concept, even in contexts beyond the Caribbean, when it encourages the examination of both agency and structure, of flexible strategies as well as the political policies and economic systems that shape and constrain choices.

Since 1990, Japanese immigration policy has generally provided three-year visas without any work restrictions for second-generation overseas Japanese (nisei) and just one-year visas for third-generation overseas Japanese (sansei), and requiring a much more burdensome and difficult application procedure for later generations. Hyperinflation in Brazil in the late 1980s and early 1990s, coupled with a still-booming Japanese economy, provided the backdrop for a sustained migration of overseas Japanese (Nikkei)[2] to Japan. By 2002, more than 300,000 Nikkei were living in Japan, roughly 75 percent from Brazil, 15 percent from Peru, and the rest from various other countries including Bolivia, Argentina, Chile, Paraguay, and Mexico (Kaigai nikkeijin kyokai 1998:43).[3] The new immigration policy was not merely a means to control immigration. The differential treatment of second-, third-, and later generations of Nikkei was also part of a discourse on the effects of migration. It contained the implicit understanding that the passing of each generation in overseas contexts involved a gradual degeneration from the yardstick of Japanese linguistic, cultural, and racial purity. Some Japanese Brazilians implicitly accepted this notion of degeneration. Others rejected it, a stance that became particularly pronounced among Japanese Brazilians in Japan.

MIGRATION, GENERATION, AND DEGENERATION DISCOURSE

In Brazil, some older Japanese immigrants have fretted over the loss of Japanese language ability from one generation to the next, and the increasing incidence of marriage to Brazilians of other ethnicities (Ishi 2003:87–88). They tended to characterize change negatively as loss of Japanese tradition. Some advocated a resumption of Japanese immigration to Brazil, to infuse the Japanese Brazilian community with fresh Japanese blood. When the return migration to Japan began in the late 1980s, these elderly Japanese immigrants were initially embarrassed, for they saw this return as an admission that they had failed to succeed in Brazil. This initial reaction wore off, as many of the return migrants were able to remit significant amounts of money to Brazil, which was invested in housing projects and other forms of conspicuous consumption. Elderly Japanese immigrants also began to see in the migration of younger Japanese Brazilians to Japan the possibility of reversing the process of cultural and linguistic loss. If adaptation to the Brazilian context had involved, in their view, a gradual process of degeneration from a previous cultural integrity, return to the motherland offered the possibility that the younger generations could be remade as more "authentic" Japanese.

There is no doubt some basis to the fears of elderly Nikkei about the loss of Japanese cultural traditions among younger generations in Brazil. But at the same time, Nikkei in São Paulo and a few other cities have expressed their Japaneseness in numerous public as well as private forums throughout the postwar era even as they have become ever more securely integrated within Brazilian society. In the 1970s, the business association of the Liberdade neighborhood, near the center of the city of São Paulo, where many Nikkei shops and restaurants are concentrated, installed Japanese-style red gates at the ends of several streets, demarcating the neighborhood as a distinctly Japanese space. Streets were lined with lantern-like streetlights. Restaurants and shops displayed signs written in Japanese characters. Japanese festivals now are held in the main plaza in Liberdade throughout the year, drawing tens of thousands of people,

Nikkei and non-Nikkei alike. More recently, Japaneseness has been cele-brated outside the ethnically marked neighborhood of Liberdade. The Festival of Japan, started in 1998, takes place in Ibirapuera Park, São Paulo's equivalent of New York's Central Park. Nikkei have also been allowed to build Japanese style croquet (gateball) courts in public spaces throughout the city, making them into "Japanese" spaces through the presence of large numbers of Nikkei, and by the planting of cherry trees, Japanese gardens, and other markers of Japaneseness around them (see Roth 2006: 595–96).

Whereas Nikkei of an older generation worry about the loss of trad-ition, some younger generation Nikkei, not surprisingly, express a degree of amusement about its persistence. Recently, a list of Japanese Brazilian ethnic characteristics was circulated on the Internet. The list of fifty characteristics included these:

- You know you are "japonês" if there's always some *tsukemono* [pickled vegetables] in your refrigerator.
- You know you are "japonês" if, in addition to salt, pepper, and olive oil, you keep a *shoyu* [soy sauce] dispenser on your dinner table.
- You know you are "japonês" if you have relatives named Mário, Paulo, or Jorge.
- You know you are "japonês" if there were farmers, launderers, or grocers in your family.
- You know you are "japonês" if your dentist, doctor, and optician are *nissei* [sic] [second-generation Nikkei].
- For men, you know you are "japonês" if you tried to grow a beard but gave up—your eyelashes being the hairiest part of your face.
- For women, you know you are "japonês" if you anticipate the de-sires and needs of men, even if they themselves don't know what they are. If you are second generation, you are capable of this, al-though you harbor some resentment about it. If you are third gen-eration, you don't have the slightest idea what all this is about. If you are fourth generation, you think it is the men who should be serving you.

This list represents a kind of self-reflection about the place of Japanese Brazilians within Brazilian society, the degree to which they have main-tained their Japanese identification, and the degree to which they have adapted to Brazilian circumstances. "Japonês" here refers to Nikkei. When Nikkei in Brazil refer to Japanese nationals, they most often use the Japanese term "nihonjin."

In the list of ethnic characteristics above, all but the last entry suggests that Nikkei identity involves the retention of Japanese cultural, social, and racial features, within a context distinct from that of Japan. The first two describe some of the foods that mark Nikkei ethnicity in Brazil. Pickled vegetables and soy sauce represent Nikkei comfort foods. The refrigerator is *always* stocked with pickled vegetables, and the soy sauce is ever present on the dinner table. But we must note that the soy sauce sits alongside the salt, pepper, and olive oil, representing Nikkei adaptation to the Brazilian context. The next entry also indicates adaptation, but by highlighting the popularity among Nikkei of extremely common Portuguese names such as Mário, Paulo, or Jorge, it suggests a facile attempt to assimilate that paradoxically further marks Nikkei difference. Likewise, the concentration of Nikkei in certain occupations (for example, farming, laundering, and running grocery stores) serves as an ethnic marker, and later on, so do certain higher status professions (for instance dentistry, medicine, and optometry). The entry about men's lack of facial hair refers to an immutable racial marker of difference. The final entry about generational changes among Nikkei women is the only one to suggest that Brazilian norms have replaced Japanese to the extent that younger Nikkei are hardly recognizable any more as Japanese.

The Nikkei friends who sent this list to me were not indignant about the stereotypes it contained. Rather, they appreciated it as a kind of inside joke, and they considered the qualities listed to be more endearing rather than embarrassing. For the most part, younger Nikkei today are secure in their status within Brazilian society. In superceding the humble agricultural origins of their immigrant parents and grandparents, many have become successful business owners, attended universities, and entered high status professions. If Nikkei are still perceived as distinctive within the Brazilian context, this has not kept them from being accepted as legitimate and desirable members of Brazilian society (Lesser 1999; Lesser & Mori 2001).

In the following sections, I explore the ways in which Nikkei have experienced "return" to Japan.

AMBIVALENT RETURNS

Since the 1970s, some older first generation Japanese immigrants to Brazil have returned to Japan for emotional and nostalgic reunions with family and friends. Return, however, had surprising effects. Some of these first-generation Japanese Brazilians had rather ambivalent feelings about the Japan they encountered upon their return. They hinted at these mixed feelings by referring to a figure from a famous Japanese folk tale, Urashima Taro. When I asked elderly Japanese Brazilians in Brazil about their trips back to Japan, some prefaced their remarks by saying, "I felt like Urashima Taro."[4]

Urashima Taro is the fisherman protagonist of a popular Japanese folktale. His kindness towards a sea turtle results in an invitation to visit the Kingdom of Ryugu at the bottom of the sea, where he passes the time in a succession of banquets and other festivities. Eventually, Urashima Taro decides he should return home, where he had left his aging mother without telling her of his travel plans. The Princess of Ryugu gives him a beautifully decorated box as a parting gift, but warns him not to open it. Much like Rip Van Winkle after his long sleep, on arriving in his village, Urashima Taro finds that things have changed. He cannot find his own home. Nor does he recognize anyone. When he asks an old man to point him to the Urashima home, the man recalls hearing a story as a child about an Urashima who had gone to the Kingdom of Ryugu and never returned. His mother had waited and waited for him, but eventually passed away. Lost in reverie, Urashima Taro opens the box, which releases a cloud of smoke that enshrouds him. When it dissipates, he is transformed into a white bearded and wrinkled old man.[5]

At one level, the story can be interpreted as a commentary on the fleeting nature of human life, which passes before one realizes it. When elderly Japanese immigrants referred to themselves as Urashima Taros, however, they clearly intended to emphasize the strangeness of the Japan they encountered when they returned after decades in Brazil. Like the protagonist of the tale, some no longer recognized their homeland. They had trouble identifying with the new postwar Japan. The younger generation of Japanese seemed to lack the older generation's work ethic. They spoke a corrupted form of Japanese, full of Americanisms. The elderly Nikkei returnees from Brazil were barely able to recognize many of Japan's urban centers, which had been completely rebuilt after the destruction of World War II. Return to Japan resolved the spatial displacement they had experienced while in Brazil, only to open up a temporal displacement from another Japan of their memories. If these elderly Nikkei did not identify with postwar Japan, they did identify with an older one, as is evident in their use of a folktale, symbolic of an older and more traditional Japan, to express these feelings of ambivalence on return.

Younger second- and third-generation Nikkei were aware of the folktale of Urashima Taro, even if it was not the important point of reference for them that it was for older first-generation migrants. In the early 1980s, Rosa Miyake, a second-generation Nikkei, recorded a Portuguese language musical version of the folktale. Varig, Brazil's national airline, adopted Miyake's song for a television commercial in the late 1980s to promote its flights between São Paulo and Tokyo. With Miyake singing in the background, an animated version of the folktale shows Urashima Taro opening the box and releasing the white smoke. What the viewer sees as the smoke clears is a pair of round trip tickets to and from Japan on Varig. This commercial was directed toward younger Nikkei, for many of whom the story of Urashima Taro held little significance except as a symbol of Japan.

Edgar was one of a handful of second-generation Nikkei I met who referred to the Urashima Taro folktale, although he used it to very different effect than did older immigrants. In Edgar's version, Urashima Taro does not just idly while away his time in the kingdom under the sea. Rather, he discovers a knowledge there that no one on land could have imagined, and dedicates himself to learning it. After a lifetime of study, he decides to return home to teach his people all he has learned. He has become old, however, and worries he does not have the energy to teach effectively, so as a parting gift, the princess gives him a magic box that turns him into a young man. While many Japanese in Japan consider Japanese Brazilians to have lost Japanese cultural knowledge over the decades, in Edgar's retelling of the story, Urashima Taro gains rather than loses knowledge. The paradise under the sea, read as Brazil, is the source of wisdom. Rather than being a story of loss, for Edgar, it represented all that Nikkei had learned in Brazil, raising them to the position of teachers in relation to the less sophisticated home village, read as Japan.

Just as returnees to Japan saw changes in their homeland, those who stayed in Japan saw changes in the migrants. From the perspective of many Japanese, Nikkei for the most part looked Japanese, yet did not speak or behave like them. Their very body language betrayed a fundamental difference in sense of self. The public displays of affection among Nikkei couples, the use of *fio dental* (literally, dental floss, that is, thong bikinis) by some Nikkei women at public swimming pools, the smells of barbequed beef and *linguiça* (Portuguese/Brazilian sausages), and the boisterous conversation and music that escaped the confines of cramped Nikkei apartments all presented Japanese with a jarring sensory presentation utterly different from what many had expected of the Japanese Brazilian returnees. Nikkei seemed to transgress the distinctions between *uchi* (inside) and *soto* (outside), public and private, which are inviolate to many Japanese (see Bachnick & Quinn 1994; Kondo 1990).

However, some older Japanese viewed Nikkei as preserving "traditional" qualities lost in a freaky young generation of Japanese youth who dyed their hair orange and blue and dressed in fanciful costumes spun out of the *manga/anime* (cartoon/animation) subcultures. Such differing opinions were not merely reflective of actual differences among Nikkei depending on their age, generation, gender, and where in Brazil they had grown up. Although such factors did make Nikkei quite a varied group, differing perspectives among Japanese arose at least in part from the different kinds of relationships they had been able to form with Nikkei. Relationships of mutual support or dependence predisposed them to find similarities, while those that were mediated through employment brokers predisposed them to find differences.

Mediating institutions such as strictly regimented workplaces and the larger employment system, classroom schedules, housing regulations, and immigration policies often have hindered the integration of migrant and native groups (Lamphere 1992:29) and have contributed to the emergence of oppositional identifications. For the most part, Japanese Brazilian migrants and the Japanese they encountered underwent a process of what I call "oppositional florescence," in which each group emphasized its difference from the other and discounted its similarities (Roth 2002:140–42). This oppositional florescence was not the inevitable outcome of return migration. Rather, it emerged under the very specific conditions within which second- and third- generation Nikkei migrants to Japan lived and worked. Many Nikkei, in opposition to Japanese, whom they began to assess more and more negatively, valorized their Brazilianness, much as Edgar did in his transformation of the Urashima Taro story (see also Roth 2002:92–117). Nikkei who had shunned samba and carnival in Brazil embraced them as a means of identifying with Brazil in Japan (Tsuda 2003:263–322). Eating Brazilian food in Japan was also a statement about their identity (Linger 2001:74–92). Brazilian flags adorned stores and restaurants opened by Nikkei in Japan. Similarly, Japanese managers and workers, in opposition to Nikkei, whom they characterized as lacking any consideration for their responsibilities toward the larger group, revalorized a Japanese work ethic that the long-lasting recession and economic restructuring of the 1990s had in many ways already made obsolete (see Roth 2002:37–63).

STRUCTURES OF MARGINALIZATION

The case of Sandra Fujimoto, a third-generation Nikkei from Brazil, brings out some of the structural constraints on interactions between Nikkei and Japanese. These constraints served to shape the way in which many Nikkei and Japanese thought about each other. Sandra was a *mestiza*— her grandparents on her father's side were Japanese, and on her mother's side, Russian. As such, her credentials as Nikkei were more open to question in Japan than were those of other Nikkei. Nonetheless, she shared many of the experiences of other Nikkei. Economic necessity drove her to Japan, rather than a strong identification with the land from which her Japanese grandparents had emigrated. Even if she did not intend to stay in Japan permanently, however, return could have allowed her to identify more with, rather than in opposition to, Japan. Sandra's developing dislike of Japan was not a foregone conclusion but the result of a specific set of conditions she experienced there.

Sandra represented the foreignness of Nikkei to some of the Japanese she encountered. She spoke little Japanese and did not seem inclined to learn much more than she already knew. In high school and college she had studied English and had taken up Persian and Arabic for about six months before going to Japan. She explained that she had many Syrian friends in Brazil and thought Arabic a very beautiful language, both spoken and written. In the two years that she had been living in Japan, Sandra dated an Iranian migrant whom she met every weekend at the benches along a wide, landscaped sidewalk in front of a downtown department store. Shortly after I got to know her, however, her boyfriend was fired from his job and returned to Iran. Like most Iranians in Japan, he had overstayed his tourist visa by several years (see Nishiyama 1994).

Sandra also violated Japanese sensibilities in the way she moved around from one job to another. She quit work at one auto factory after just one week because the speed of the assembly line was too great. All the workers there were "dead" by the end of the day, she said. She also worked for a couple of months at a firm that made pocket pagers but left because she was dissatisfied with the wages. She found a somewhat better paying job at a factory that manufactured compact disc players. Later, she regretted the move when her supervisors prohibited Brazilians from speaking to one another in Portuguese. Aside from Brazilians, most of the other workers were married Japanese women in their 40s and 50s. Her longest held job, for about eight months, was at an auto parts maker that hired Iranians, Peruvians, and Filipinos workers, as well as Brazilians.

In all but one case, Sandra was hired through employment brokers, as were the large majority of Nikkei in Hamamatsu. Relatively few were hired directly by manufacturing firms. Originally, this had not been the case throughout Japan. In the towns of Oizumi and Ota, in Gunma Prefecture, the number of Nikkei hired through brokers was initially somewhat smaller, because a consortium of manufacturing firms had formed to pool resources for the purposes of recruiting and maintaining Nikkei employees whom they hired directly. However, this consortium was dissolved in 2000, and employment brokers became increasingly dominant thereafter in Ota/Oizumi, as well as in Hamamatsu (Onai & Sakai 2001).

Brokers generally provided housing for foreign workers. In Hamamatsu, brokers procured one and two bedroom apartments scattered throughout the city, wherever landlords were willing to accommodate foreigners.

It was very difficult for foreigners to rent apartments on their own, since landlords required tenants to have guarantors (*hoshô-nin*). Occasionally, a Nikkei who had made friends with a Japanese could ask her to serve as her guarantor, but the vast majority had to rely on their employment broker to provide housing. Nikkei had to deal with a series of unknown roommates moving in and out, as well as occasional invasions of their privacy when their employment broker made unannounced inspections. Dependence on employment brokers for housing also meant that Nikkei could not change jobs without changing residences.

After moving through a series of apartments provided by her brokers, Sandra eventually moved in with a new Nikkei boyfriend and was able to secure a job directly with a manufacturing firm. She liked her coworkers and her boss, all of whom were women. This was one of the few places in her experience where Japanese and Nikkei workers socialized outside of work. Things did not last however, because a nasty fight with her boyfriend forced her to move out of their apartment. Since her employer at the time did not provide housing, she had to stay with friends until signing up with an employment broker that could place her in another apartment.

Japanese managers have frequently criticized Nikkei for lacking a sense of responsibility or solidarity at work (see Roth 2002:60–63; Watanabe 1995). From the perspective of Japanese managers, Sandra represented a kind of Nikkei who had lost all trace of Japanese qualities aside from her Japanese surname. Most Nikkei, not just *mestizas* like Sandra, frequently switched jobs. They did so, however, because there was little incentive to stay put, and not because of any cultural predilection to move or jump at the slightest offer of a better wage. Most Nikkei, after all, were hired through employment brokers and were not encouraged to develop any loyalty to a given workplace. Brokers pulled them from one factory and sent them to another at the convenience of Japanese managers, who considered brokered workers a cushion to ride over economic fluctuations rather than full-fledged members of workplace communities. In addition, structural limitations made it difficult for Nikkei to find situations that combined good housing and positive working conditions. The inability of Nikkei to live up to Japanese expectations was to a significant extent determined by mediating institutions such as the employment system and discriminatory housing policies that marginalized Nikkei in workplaces and neighborhoods (see Roth 2002:37–91).

The system of employment brokers had other negative consequences for the relationship between Nikkei and Japanese. Most significantly, it blurred the responsibility of employers to provide mandatory health and accident insurance. In cases of workplace accidents, brokers and managers of manufacturing firms tended to avoid taking any active measures to help injured workers get compensation. The rate of accidents among Nikkei was higher than among Japanese because Nikkei were concentrated in smaller subcontracting firms, which feel the greatest pressure from parent firms to cut costs. This often meant that such firms avoided following safety regulations (see Roth 2002:64–91). These circumstances fed into a growing oppositional florescence, in which more and more Nikkei in Japan began to represent themselves emphatically as Brazilian, rather than as Japanese.

MEANINGS OF MIXTURE

However, even as Nikkei wrapped themselves in the Brazilian flag, some began to incorporate Japanese elements into their speech, cuisine, and interactive styles as a result of more substantial interactions with Japanese. Many Nikkei who spoke little if any Japanese when they arrived in Japan began studying it at language schools and community centers. Likewise, some Japanese have started studying Portuguese. Japanese volunteers have helped Nikkei with a variety of work, housing, health, and immigration issues, and some Japanese and Nikkei coworkers and neighbors have gotten to know each other quite well. While most Japanese and Nikkei have interacted in workplaces, some have also sought each other out voluntarily in the context of language classes, discos, and the mini Brazilian-style carnivals that were held annually in many Japanese cities.

During the two years I conducted research in Hamamatsu, there were two community centers that regularly held Portuguese language classes. There were seven Japanese members of the Nambu (southern) community center language class. Their teacher was a Nikkei journalist who worked for one of the local Portuguese language newspapers. One of the students had lived in Brazil for about six months but had recently returned to Japan where he planned to work for the prefectural police department, which needed Portuguese speakers on staff to handle the growing Brazilian population. Another student worked for a small manufacturing company where about twenty Brazilians were working. One did volunteer work for the Catholic Church and a local nongovernmental organization (NGO) that helped foreign workers who had medical-, work-, or immigration-related troubles. Several were retirees interested in teaching Japanese to Nikkei.

At the Hokubu (northern) community center, Japanese and Nikkei gathered for less formal *batepapo* (chitchat) sessions. The members of this group met every Saturday evening to socialize and exchange Japanese and Portuguese classes and conversation. The leader of this social group was a Japanese employee of Yamaha who had been stationed in one of their Brazilian plants for about a year. In addition, there was another Japanese employee of a large auto parts manufacturer in Hamamatsu that employed over a hundred Nikkei workers. His wife and three daughters often attended meetings. Another regular, Kimata, was the very affable Japanese organizer of a samba group in town. His name made many Nikkei laugh, for it was pronounced exactly like the Portuguese *que mata* ("killer," "one that kills") and evoked an image quite contrary to Kimata's gentle persona. He had been a fan of Brazilian music for many years and was taking advantage of the recent migration of Nikkei to learn some Portuguese. Finally, there was a Japanese woman, Mariko, who came whenever she wasn't attending an Amway meeting.[6]

Among the seven or eight Nikkei were an older married man and woman who had been working in Japan for almost five years. There were several single men, ranging in age from eighteen to thirty. One had been in Japan for seven years with his family of seven siblings and both parents. Another had been in Japan for three years on his own. One, Edivaldo, had also been in Japan for three years and lived with two brothers and his parents. There were several single women in the group as well. One had four siblings working in Japan while their parents remained in Brazil. Another, Mirella, had a father who was initially working in Japan but who later returned to Brazil where his other children remained. Sandra, introduced earlier, was an occasional participant in this group. These Nikkei all worked in factories, except for Mirella, who worked as an interpreter and driver for one of the numerous employment brokers in town.

The *batepapo* group organized *churrascos* (Brazilian style barbeques) in the summer, short excursions to pick tangerines in the winter, *bônenkai* (end-of-year parties), and *despedidas* (farewell parties) for Nikkei moving to other parts of Japan or back to Brazil. More frequently, they would go out for an evening of *karaoke* or go to a restaurant for dinner after the Saturday evening meetings. This group intersected with several others, which provided their Nikkei and Japanese members access to broader communities. Mariko eventually succeeded in recruiting several Nikkei *batepapo* members to Amway. In addition, several Nikkei joined the samba group that the sweet and amiable middle-aged bachelor, Kimata, had organized. Several Japanese ended up taking trips to Brazil to visit Nikkei friends they had made in this group. One became a co-owner of a locally published Portuguese language newspaper and began importing Brazilian *propolis*, a health product collected from bee hives and derived from tree and flower resins that had become quite popular in Japan.

The activities of *batepapo* members led them to adopt certain mixed cultural forms. Many Nikkei were wildly enthusiastic about *karaoke*.

While some Brazilian restaurants with *karaoke* facilities stocked DVDs with Brazilian songs, many Nikkei seemed to enjoy singing Japanese songs with equal gusto. Several monthly journals were published in Portuguese to introduce Nikkei to popular Japanese songs, and *karaoke* was among the most popular courses at a Brazilian cultural center in Hamamatsu (see Roth 2002:92–117). The popularity of *karaoke* among Nikkei has to be seen in relation to enthusiastic Nikkei participation in amateur singing competitions in Brazil known as *nodo jiman* (lit., "throat pride") that highlighted popular Japanese songs known as *enka* (Hosokawa 1995). Despite the context of oppositional florescence, many Nikkei continued to enjoy *karaoke*, which, in the Japanese context, had also become for them a pleasurable means of learning Japanese.

Language was one obvious area in which Japanese forms were incorporated into Portuguese structures. Older second-generation Japanese Brazilians in largely Japanese settlements in Brazil had many decades ago already begun speaking dialects referred to as *koronia-go* (language of the *colônia* [settlement]) (Handa 1973; Kanazawa & Loveday 1988; Kuyama 1999). Such dialects involved the adoption of Portuguese lexical items into a Japanese syntactic framework, with speakers often infusing the Portuguese terms with nuances from the Japanese language (Handa 1973:503–06). Younger second- and third-generation Nikkei, especially those who had grown up in more mixed urban environments in Brazil, tended to speak a more conventional Portuguese. In Japan, however, many adopted a creole form that imported Japanese lexical items into a Portuguese syntactic framework, as in the following sentence:

Fiz quatro horas de *zangyo* ontem.[7]
(I did four hours of overtime yesterday.)

In this example, the Japanese term for overtime, *zangyo*, simply replaces the Portuguese *horas extras*. Sometimes, Japanese words would be conjugated as Portuguese verbs, as in the following participle construction:

Estou tudo *tsukareta*-da.
(I'm totally wiped out.)

Here, the speaker evokes the Portuguese *cansada* even as she replaced it with the Japanese term *tsukareta* by adding *da* to the end of it.

In addition to such mixed usages, Nikkei would often delight in puns for which apparently Japanese expressions had alternative meanings in the Brazilian context. They made use of such puns in playfully subversive ways. At work, many Japanese greeted one another and sometimes Nikkei at work in the morning with a routine *ohayô* or sometimes a more formal *ohayô-gozaimasu*. When a Japanese supervisor that Sandra particularly disliked greeted her, she often replied as follows:

> O raio . . . que mata você.
> (The lighting bolt . . . that killed you.)

In Portuguese, when the letter "r" appears at the beginning of a word it is pronounced much like the letter "h" in English. *O raio* ("the lighting bolt") in Portuguese is pronounced the same as *ohayo* ("good morning") in Japanese. Sandra would mumble *Que mata você* ("that killed you") softly and quickly in a way that roughly approximated *gozaimasu*, the Japanese formal form of the verb "to be."

A parallel situation arose in the use of the hand signal for "okay," which consisted of a circle formed by placing the tips of the thumb and forefinger together. In Japan, such a signal can mean money, but the American usage as "okay" is also often understood. When Japanese interact with foreigners, they often use this signal with this latter meaning in mind, although they chuckle to themselves in their knowledge of the signal's other meaning. In the Brazilian context, much the same signal held at waist level iconically represents an asshole and is used to flip someone off as one would with the middle finger extended in the United States. When Japanese and Nikkei signal each other thus, both parties chuckle to themselves about the alternate meanings being sent, although the Nikkei are likely laughing to themselves more loudly.

Such punning between languages is not used exclusively in confrontations between Japanese and Nikkei. Nikkei in Japan often take pleasure in such puns among themselves. One friend mentioned that he sometimes had the opportunity to do some seasonal agricultural work. He was once solicited to work harvesting Japanese radishes. This work was referred to as *daikon nuku*, literally, "radish pull out." Extracting these large white radishes, sometimes two feet in length and a couple of inches in diameter at the top, was hard work, but the main reason he refused it was that he didn't want any *daikon no cu*, in Portuguese, literally, "daikon up the ass." Although many Japanese view Nikkei to be linguistically handicapped, the examples above suggest that Nikkei were in some sense language virtuosos, adept at playfully code switching meanings across Japanese and Portuguese language contexts (see Paredes 1993).

Japanese slowly seeped into the language of many Nikkei in Japan, but this did not necessarily represent an expression of greater affinity with Japanese people or culture. Even if Japanese terms and expressions were used *ex*tensively among many Nikkei, it was less acceptable for any given Nikkei to use Japanese too *in*tensively. One member of the *batepapo* group, Mirella, who was particularly keen on perfecting her Japanese, came under a certain amount of criticism for her efforts at speaking in full, grammatically correct Japanese sentences. Over dinner, Edivaldo warned Mirella that her Portuguese would deteriorate to the level of Marcia, a mediocre Japanese Brazilian singer who had become a television personality (*tarento*) in Japan. To some extent, Marcia had become the public face of Nikkei in Japan. According to Edivaldo, how-ever, she seemed to have forgotten a lot of her Portuguese in the eight or so years she had lived in Japan. Turning to me, Edivaldo said "it's in-credible, she probably speaks [Portuguese] worse than you." For Edivaldo, language use indexed identity, and Marcia's disuse of Portuguese seemed to mirror her ignorance of Brazil. Edivaldo was disgusted by Marcia's in-ability to answer basic questions about Brazil, and even more about her nonchalant attitude toward her ignorance, as she shrugged it off as insig-nificant to her. He suggested that if Mirella didn't rein in her Japanese, her Portuguese might deteriorate to Marcia's level.

Edivaldo's jabs didn't phase Mirella, who, at the time, was excited about the prospect of moving in with a Japanese family. Before becoming an interpreter with an employment broker, Mirella had worked in a factory, where she had befriended Akiko, the factory owner's daughter who worked in the front office. Mirella's cheery butch persona contrasted sharply with Akiko's demure beauty. They got along very well, which led to some degree of kidding but also to some serious criticism from other Nikkei employees. While most of the Nikkei workers at the factory liked the boss and his family, their relationships were still defined in terms of their employment contract. When Mirella went beyond the boundaries that normally separated Nikkei workers and Japanese managers at the workplace, some other Nikkei read it as her attempt to curry favor, and as to their disadvantage (see also Tsuda 2003:323–54). It was an accusation that weighed heavily on Mirella for some time. Likewise, her ethnic alle-giance was frequently called into question in the context of her job as an interpreter for an employment broker. In this capacity, Mirella often had to negotiate the conflicting demands of Nikkei employees and Japanese managers. Nikkei workers made requests such as transfers to new apart-ments or better jobs that Mirella was not in a position to grant without asking her boss. If her boss turned them down, it was Mirella who bore the brunt of Nikkei resentment (Roth 2002:66–67).

Nikkei were comfortable mixing Japanese into their speech and inter-acting socially with Japanese in a range of contexts. But there was a point beyond which such mixing was sanctioned by the majority of other Nikkei who had begun to identify as Brazilians in opposition to Japanese. Although many Nikkei have made concerted efforts to learn Japanese and accommodate to the cultural expectations of the Japanese workplace, they were constrained by the realization that too frequent use of Japanese could lead others to suspect them of abandoning their Brazilian identity.

RESISTING DEGENERATION DISCOURSE

A discourse on degeneration has haunted Japanese migrants to Brazil since the early twentieth century. As the years have passed, fewer young Nikkei in Brazil have grown up speaking Japanese, and more and more have married non-Nikkei. Despite the continuing vitality of many Nikkei associations, newspapers, sports leagues, *karaoke* competitions, and discos, many elderly Nikkei have difficulty imagining a Nikkei society in which the newspapers are written in Portuguese rather than Japanese, and where *mestizos* eventually outnumber racially "pure" Nikkei. Some have called for renewed Japanese immigration to Brazil to rejuvenate Nikkei society. Others have pinned their hopes on the actual mass migration of Nikkei to Japan as a means by which Nikkei youth can learn about and gain greater appreciation for Japanese ways. Some young Nikkei who might otherwise have ended up marrying non-Nikkei married other Nikkei migrants they met in Japan. But as we have seen, Nikkei experiences in Japan have produced some unforeseen effects.

Nikkei may have learned about Japanese ways in Japan, but many ended up identifying more strongly there as Brazilians. Nikkei have not been decreolized, or quietly incorporated into Japanese society. Nor have many of those who have gone back to Brazil after a period of time in Japan taken with them a positive sense of Japanese values. Nikkei have resisted the discourse on degeneration that posited Japan as the original from which Nikkei had deviated, by turning it on its head. In the story of Urashima Taro, even older Nikkei travelers to Japan expressed their dismay about the extent to which Japan itself had deviated from its original state. In second-generation Edgar's telling of the story, Urashima Taro acquires great knowledge while in migration. Instead of lamenting the loss of tradition, Edgar's version valorizes the migration experience by focusing on the acquisition of new knowledge. Finally, Edivaldo's critique of the pop star Marcia's loss of Brazilian cultural knowledge overturns the degeneration discourse, putting Brazil in the place of the original culture and turning Japan into a destabilizing force.

The system of mediating institutions involving employment brokers and housing policies that have marginalized Nikkei within Japanese society helps explain the oppositional identification that has developed between Japanese and Nikkei. Similarly, in Brazil, political and economic circumstances shaped the ways in which Nikkei imagined their place within Brazilian society. To put it another way, Nikkei have adapted to specific contexts of interaction they have encountered in both Brazil and Japan. If they had creolized in the Brazilian context, they have not decreolized in Japan but rather creolized in another direction. In Brazil, they had adapted linguistically, culturally, and socially while maintaining some degree of identification as Japanese. And in Japan, they have again adapted linguistically, and culturally, but have dispensed with their identification as Japanese in favor of a stronger Brazilian one.

Adaptation may take the form of learning new linguistic and other cultural forms, relearning old ones, or creating hybrid forms with elements of both. Many Nikkei have accommodated themselves to Japanese workplace routines in limited ways, and learned enough Japanese to get by. But they have often done so with the understanding that there are limits to the ways in which they can use their knowledge without calling into question their Brazilian identification. Nikkei resistance to pressures to act Japanese liberates some to express a Brazilianness they may not have embraced as consciously while they lived in Brazil (Linger 2003). At the same time, their acts of resistance may condemn them to positions of marginality within the bottom rungs of the Japanese blue-collar sector (see Willis 1981), at least insofar as they decide to remain in Japan. It remains to be seen whether those Nikkei who seem to be settling in Japan will over many years inevitably become decreolized—assimilated linguistically and culturally as Japanese—or whether their adaptive strategies within the social contexts of workplaces and neighborhoods will preserve their Brazilian linguistic and cultural forms for much longer than expected. Sociolinguists and anthropologists have not sufficiently examined the relationship between conscious adaptive strategies such as code switching, specific social contexts, and long-term shifts in language and culture. Examining creolization as adaptation may help researchers recognize the series of contingencies that constitute what they often mistakenly assume to be inevitable processes of long-term change.

Notes

1. I put "return" in quotes because most Japanese Brazilians were born in Brazil and had never been to Japan before the late 1980s when thousands went to work in Japanese factories.
2. The category Nikkei encompasses nisei, sansei, and all subsequent generations. It can also include first-generation immigrants themselves. The characters for *Nikkei* literally mean "sun line" and refer to people of Japanese descent who live in countries other than Japan (see Roth 2002: 23–27).
3. Japanese had first migrated to Mexico in 1897, Peru in 1899, Bolivia in 1899 (via Peru), Chile in 1903, Brazil in 1908, Argentina in 1909 (via Brazil), and Paraguay in 1936 (Azuma 2002).

4. For a fuller treatment of the significance of this reference to Urashima Taro by elderly Japanese Brazilians, see Roth (2003).
5. A variant of the Urashima Taro folktale can be found in Seki (1963).
6. Amway is an American-based company that distributes health foods, vitamins, cosmetics, home appliances, and so forth by recruiting consumers as agents to sell to their friends and acquaintances. Bonuses are paid to recruiters for sales made by those they have recruited. It is a pyramid scheme, in which those sitting at the top of a network of sellers reap great rewards, while the majority of sellers lower down on the network hassle their friends for very modest gain. Amway was just one among a number of pyramid schemes that lured guileless and sometimes lonely Nikkei with promises of easy cash and social connection.
7. The Japanese term is written in italics in this and following examples.

References

Azuma, E. 2002. Japanese emigration timeline, 1868–1998. In *Encyclopedia of Japanese descendants in the Americas: An illustrated history of the Nikkei*. A. Kikumura-Yano, ed. Walnut Creek, CA: AltaMira Press.

Bachnik, J., and C. Quinn, eds. 1994. *Situated meaning: Inside and outside in Japanese self, society, and language*. Princeton, NJ: Princeton University Press.

Basch, L., N. Glick Schiller, and C. Szanton Blanc. 1994. *Nations unbound: Transnational projects, postcolonial predicaments, and deterritorialized nation-states*. Australia [Langhorne, Pa.]: Gordon and Breach.

Handa, T. 1973. O destino da língua japonesa no brasil. In *Assimilação e integraão dos Japoneses no Brasil*. H. Saito and T. Maeyama, eds. Petrópolis, RJ: Vozes.

Handlin, O. 1951. *The uprooted: The epic story of the great migrations that made the American people*. Boston: Little, Brown.

Hannerz, U. 1996. *Transnational connections: Culture, people, places*. London: Routledge.

Harris, R., and B. Rampton. 2002. Creole metaphors in culture analysis: On the limits and possibilities of (socio-)linguistics, *Critique of Anthropology* 22(1):31–51.

Hosokawa S. 1995. *Samba no kuni ni enka ga nagareru* [The Sounds of *Enka* in the Country of Samba]. Chuukou Shinsho 1263. Tokyo: Chuuou Kouron-sha.

Ishi, A. 2003. Searching for home, wealth, pride, and "class": Japanese Brazilians in the "Land of Yen." In *Searching for home abroad*. Jeffrey Lesser, ed. Durham, NC: Duke University Press.

Kaigai nikkeijin kyokai [Association for Overseas Japanese]. 1998. *Nikkeijin hongu shurosha doko chosa hokokusho*. Tokyo: Kaigai nikkeijin kyokai.

Kanazawa, H., and L. Loveday. 1988. The Japanese immigrant community in Brazil: Language contact and shift, *Journal of Multilingual and Multicultural Development* 9(5):423–435.

Kearney, M. 1991. Boundaries of state and self, *Journal of Historical Sociology*, 4(1):52–74.

Kondo, D. K. 1990. *Crafting selves: Power, gender, and discourses of identity in a Japanese workplace*. Chicago: University of Chicago Press.

Kuyama, M. 1999. O empréstimo lexical no japonês falado pelos imigrantes—a integração do português ao japonês. In *Anais do 9º encontro nacional de professores universitarios de lingua, literatura e cultura japonesa*. Brasilia: Universidade de Brasilia, pp. 176–183.

Lamphere, L. 1992. Introduction: The shaping of diversity. In *Structuring diversity: Ethnographic perspectives on the new immigration*. L. Lamphere, ed. Chicago: University of Chicago Press.

Lesser, J. 1999. *Negotiating national identity: Immigrants, minorities, and the struggle for ethnicity in Brazil.* Durham, NC: Duke University Press.

——— ed. 2003. *Searching for home abroad: Japanese Brazilians and transnationalism.* Durham, NC: Duke University Press.

Lesser, J., and K. Mori. 2001. *The new face of discrimination.* São Paulo: Centro de Estudos Nipo-Brasileiros.

Lie, J. 2001. *Multiethnic Japan.* Cambridge, MA: Harvard University Press.

Linger, D. 2001. *No one home: Brazilian selves remade in Japan.* Stanford, CA: Stanford University Press

——— 2003. Do Japanese-Brazilians exist? In *Searching for home abroad.* J. Lesser, ed. Durham, NC: Duke University Press.

Long, L. D., and E. Oxfeld, eds. 2004. *Coming home? Refugees, migrants, and those who stayed behind.* Philadelphia: University of Pennsylvania Press.

Nishiyama, T. 1994. *Tokyo no Kyababu no Kemuri* [Tokyo Kebab Smoke]. Tokyo: Keishobô.

Onai, T., and E. Sakai. 2001. Nikkei burajirujin no teijuka to chiiki shakai: Gunmaken Ôta/ Ôizumi chiku o jirei toshite [Nikkei Brazilians, permanent residence, and local society: Ôta/Ôizumi region, Gunma Prefecture, as case study]. Tokyo: Ochanomizu Shobô.

Ong, A. 1996. *Cultural citizenship* as subject-making, *Current Anthropology* 37(5): 737–762.

——— 1999. *Flexible citizenship: The cultural logics of transnationality.* Durham, NC: Duke University Press.

Paredes, A. 1993. On ethnographic work among minority groups. In *Folklore and culture on the Texas-Mexican border.* R. Bauman, ed. and introduction. Austin, TX: CMAS Books, Center for Mexican American Studies, University of Texas at Austin.

Redfield, R., R. Linton, and M. J. Herskovits. 1935. Memorandum for the study of accultur-ation, *Man* 35:145–48. (Reprinted 1936 in *American Anthropologist* 38(1):149–152.)

Roth, J. 2002. *Brokered homeland: Japanese Brazilian migrants in Japan.* Ithaca, NY: Cornell University Press.

——— 2003. Urashima Taro's ambiguating practices: The significance of overseas voting rights for elderly Japanese migrants to Brazil. In *Searching for home abroad.* J. Lesser, ed. Durham, NC: Duke University Press.

——— 2006. A mean spirited sport: Japanese Brazilian croquet in Saõ Paulo's public spaces,' *Anthropological Quarterly* 79(4):581–604.

Rouse, R. 1991. Mexican migration and the social space of postmodernism, *Diaspora* 1(1):8–23.

Seki, K., ed. 1963. *Folktales of Japan,* translated by Robert J. Adams. Chicago: University of Chicago Press.

Tsuda, Takeyuki. 2003. *Strangers in the ethnic homeland: Japanese Brazilian return migra-tion in transnational perspective.* New York: Columbia University Press.

Watanabe M. 1995. Nikkei burajiru-jin no koyou o meguru mondai [Problems faced in hiring Japanese Brazilians] In *Dekasegi nikkei burajiru-jin vol. 1,* [Japanese Brazilian migrant workers]. W. Masako. Tokyo: Akashi Shoten.

Willis, P. 1981 [1977]. *Learning to labor: How working class kids get working class jobs.* New York: Columbia University Press.

11 The *Créolité* Movement: Paradoxes of a French Caribbean Orthodoxy

Mary Gallagher

Among the "end products" that could be expected to issue from the process of creolization are languages, people, and cultures definable not just as creolized but as creole. What does it mean, however, to be creole? One of the most lively approaches to this ontological question has been articulated over the past couple of decades by a number of French Caribbean writers and thinkers, and in this chapter I outline certain paradoxes associated with their work.[1]

The polemical vigor of the *créolité* (or "creoleness") movement that emerged in the late 1980s from Martinique, the more French of the two French Caribbean islands, is proportionate to the movement's controversiality. Although the term had made a brief appearance in Haitian writer René Dépestre's *Bonjour et adieu à la négritude,* in which he refers to the "essential *créolité* of the Caribbean and of Latin America" (Dépestre 1980:157), the ideology of identity that has accreted around it in Martinique cannot be compared with any identity movements elsewhere in the Caribbean, even in Haiti. Although some might argue that the Haitian *noiriste* ("blackism") or *indigéniste* ("indigenism") movements demonstrate a comparable ideological investment, twentieth-century Haitian theories of cultural identity have been almost exclusively local. They eschew extrapolation, if not from the Haitian condition, then at least from the Caribbean condition. The theoretical ambition of anglophone Caribbean writers has been similarly circumscribed and circumspect.

Thus, although Edward Kamau Brathwaite, Wilson Harris, and Derek Walcott have authored important speculative studies on Caribbean identity and culture, they have not attempted to articulate—much less prescribe in the French Caribbean manner—an overarching, tentacular poetics, that is, a pan-Caribbean—and even global— program of culture that welds an aesthetics and an ethics to an epistemology and an ontology.

A PECULIARLY FRENCH
(CARIBBEAN) MOVEMENT

Given that Martinican and Guadeloupean authors write in French, publish with French publishers, compete for French literary prizes, and attract a readership that is largely based in Metropolitan France, the programatic impulse described above could be read as an effort to preempt accusations of a sell-out. It could be seen, in other words, as a compensatory strategy, reinforcing a literary project with a discourse of cultural differentiation and resistance. The particularly acute "separation anxiety" afflicting Martinican as opposed to Guadeloupean intellectuals no doubt explains why the impulse characterizes Martinican rather than Guadeloupean writing. That anxiety is a consequence of the particular (perceived) political and economic emasculation of Martinique, or what J. Michael Dash calls that island's "overwhelming context of adaption and acquiescence," its "culture of consent" (Dash 1998:19). It would be understandable, then, if Martinican writing were to be simultaneously more drawn toward, and more anxious to differentiate itself from, Metropolitan France.[2] Certainly, Martinique appears to have provided even more fertile ground than Guadeloupe for dissemination of the ideational, universalizing tropism widely regarded as characterizing Metropolitan French culture, in contrast, for example, to the more empirical spirit of "Anglo-Saxon" thought. This is precisely the implication of Derek Walcott's open letter to Patrick Chamoiseau, which first appeared in 1996 in the *New York Review of Books*.[3] Walcott observes that the polemical tone of the co-authored pamphlet credited with launching the *créolité* movement, *Éloge de la créolité*,[4] flaunts that faith in new movements and theories that marks the history of aesthetic thought in France. He considers the tract as part of the peculiarly French obsession with "publishing manifestos," observing that "nothing is more French than [its] confident rhetoric." In its "emphatic isolation" Walcott hears the echo of "all those pamphlets outlining programs for a new painting, a new poetry, that erupt from metropolitan ferment, and that, reaching out to embrace a public, baffle it by their vehemence" (Walcott 1998:223–24).

The *créolité* movement is not alone among French Caribbean movements in its marked association with France. The *négritude* movement was, after all, conceived in Paris, and the seminal moment in Édouard Glissant's conceptualization of Caribbean consciousness also took place in France,[5] just as *Éloge de la créolité* began life as a talk presented in the Paris suburbs. Certainly, such exogenous (Metropolitan—and therefore less than immaculate) conceptions are a little misleading given the fact that these writers, with the exception of Glissant, have written almost exclusively in and from Martinique. Yet they reflect the fact that French Caribbean writing has been published and promoted primarily in Metropolitan France. Indeed, Martinican theory bedazzles Paris to such an extent that, in a highly unusual move, and one that underlines the French publisher's recognition of the international and indeed transcontinental importance of the writing, Gallimard brought out a bilingual edition of the *créolité* manifesto, featuring the American English translation alongside the French text. It is surely paradoxical that the English translation was thus favoured over a possible Creole translation.

A SUSPECT TELEOLOGY?

Over the final two decades of the twentieth century, that body of French Caribbean writing associated with the *créolité* movement sedulously promoted a certain narrative of Caribbean identity. The first section of *Éloge de la créolité,* for instance, recounts the gradual twentieth-century movement of the Caribbean psyche toward self-discovery and self-acceptance, a progression leading via the putative self-alienation of Aimé Césaire's *négritude* and the supposed sybilline remoteness of Édouard Glissant's *antillanité* (Caribbeanness) to the ultimate authenticity and self-possession claimed for *créolité*. This narrative locates the *créolité* movement within a historicist frame; it describes Caribbean identity as moving from the program of *négritude,* where the principal concern is said to be with essence, through *antillanité* or "Caribbeanness," where concern with the contingencies of existence or *l'étant* predominates, to "creoleness," in which notions of essence vie with notions of process (*créolité* versus *créolisation*). Such a teleology leaves, however, the more recent work of Édouard Glissant out of the frame, although this work in fact goes further and deeper in its exploration of creolization than does the *créolité* movement. I am thinking here of Glissant's wide-ranging poetics of relation or "creolisation," central to his hallmark visions of the *tout-monde,* that is, his whole-world poetics. Already, however, in *Le Discours antillais* (1981), the collection of essays centered on Glissant's notion of *antillanité,* the world is seen "in terms of ceaseless cultural transformation [that] subverts the old temptation to essentialist and exclusivist strategies" (Dash 1995:147).[6]

The authors of the *créolité* pamphlet do allow that "it was Césaire's Negritude that opened to us the path for the actuality of a Caribbeanness which from then on could be postulated, and which itself is leading to another yet unlabelled degree of authenticity" (*Pr.* 80). Depicted as incipiently committed to the geographical and the local, a perspective that is acknowledged as central to Glissant's *antillanité, négritude* is thus identified in the *créoliste* manifesto, as it already had been by Glissant, as a necessary stage in the teleology of Caribbean self-recovery and indeed self-discovery. It is nonetheless criticized for having aggravated what the *créolistes* term "our identity instability" (*Pr.* 82). This is because it was founded on the illusion of return to the sustaining womb of Africa and also, as Frantz Fanon had recognized, because its universalizing tendencies collapsed the past and present problems specific to the Caribbean within those of black alienation in general. *Négritude* is also viewed by the *créolistes*, however, as only challenging colonization and racism in the name of a characteristically Western, universalizing or homogenising concept, thus reinforcing the effects of assimilation or frenchification. Hence, although the authors of *Éloge de la créolité* claim Césaire as an ante-Créole rather than an anti-Créole, *négritude* is held to have led its disciples toward an anticolonial struggle "outside any interior truth, outside any literary aesthetics" (*Pr.* 82). This comment is damning insofar as the authors of the *Éloge* equate inner depth with authenticity and identify art as the only means of approaching these inner depths.

Articulated in the slipstream of *négritude* writing, Édouard Glissant's *antillanité*—elaborated in the author's essays, poetry, and novels of the 1960s and 1970s—focuses explicitly on place and positionality. Etymologically, the name "Antilles" is derived from the Latin "*ante*" and "*illum*," meaning "before the continent" (Chamoiseau 1997:234–45). Although the preposition can function both temporally and spatially (meaning "in front of" as well as "prior to"), the temporal reference is the primary one here and refers to the historical fact that the Caribbean islands were reached by the European explorers before the latter located the American continent (in the etymology, the monolithic singularity of the pronoun can refer only to the continental landmass anticipated by the "explorers"). The relational resonance of this etymology is reinforced by the consistent emphasis within Glissant's "Caribbean discourse" on the importance of seeing the Caribbean in positional terms. Relationality is, indeed, one of the lynchpins of Glissant's thinking, finding its way into the title of his third major essay collection.

In suggesting that their vision and writing supersede Glissant's *antillanité* in a teleology of Caribbean self-realization, the *créoliste* pamphleteers can be seen—retrospectively at least—to distort the integrity of Glissant's thinking. They also appear, however, to fall into the very trap that they seek to neutralize. On the one hand, in an echo of Glissant's emphasis on the value of opaqueness, they insist that their reflective inwardness does not aim at transparency; that is, at the reduction of the Creole to an impoverished self-identity. Rather, they prescribe an aesthetic and epistemology that will allow Creoles not just to accept their complexity (*Nous accepter complexes*) but to discover, know, and explore it: "Exploring our creoleness must be done in a thought as complex as Creoleness itself [. . .] that is why it seems that, for the moment, full knowledge of Creoleness will be reserved for Art" (*Pr.* 90). Only art, it is suggested, can register the impacted yet dynamic complexity of *créolité*. On the other hand, however, the very notion of exposure suggested by the expression "full knowledge" surely threatens the complexity and opaqueness that Glissant's poetic writing is intended to protect (see Glissant 1969). The *créolistes* indeed explicitly distinguish their own vision from Édouard Glissant's *antillanité* in terms of heuristic "added value." *Antillanité*, they insist, is too remote a vision to enable or map the journey inward toward authenticity—in the manifesto, the authors refer to the relative difficulty of locating the "paths of penetration in [sic] Caribbeanness" (*Pr.* 84).

Although the authors of the manifesto construct themselves as Glissant's heirs and as seeking to facilitate the full implementation of his vision, their program effects in reality a considerable shift of emphasis. For, in addition to turning "Glissant's ideas into ideological dogma" (Dash 1998:23), and, even more problematically, hypostatizing or foreclosing his thinking, the factor that most clearly demarcates *créolité* from *antillanité* is the whole hinterland of connotation surrounding the two terms. Both movements distance themselves from *négritude* by insisting on the particular rather than the general: but whereas *antillanité* stresses immediate geographical relationality, the proponents of *créolité* focus more on culture. It is in great part through its defense and occasional illustration of Creole and of creolised French that the literature of the *créolité* movement opposes the Caribbean legacy of alienation. Whereas Glissant's vision is held to counter the generality of *négritude*'s reference by anchoring his thinking in the geocultural specifics of the Caribbean, *créolité* is claimed to have a deeper, more tangible or approachable cultural reach by virtue of its emphasis on language rather than space.

Having registered some of the more programmatic aspects of the *créolité* project, one might be surprised to find that its authors explicitly deny the theoretical status of their thinking. On the very first page of the *créolité* manifesto, they caution: "these words we are communicating to you here do not stem from theory" (*Pr.* 75). Glissant, too, in the glossary to *Le Discours antillais* was unwilling to identify *antillanité* as a theory: "*Plus qu'une théorie, une vision.*"[7] Clearly, both *Le Discours antillais* and *Éloge de la créolité* are concerned with cultural definitions and positionings. But, for Glissant, there cannot be a theory of *antillanité* because the reality to which it would refer is—and will always remain—virtual; it is this projective inflection that leads him to prefer the more aspirational term "vision".[8] It is, no doubt, the combined aspirational and resistant intent behind Glissant's *antillanité* that accounts for what Chamoiseau and Confiant criticize as the remoteness of this notion. In other words, the inaccessibility or opaqueness of Glissant's "vision" is related to his rejection of the transparency associated with conceptualization. There is thus a certain irony in the *créolistes*' repudiation of the reductive nature of "Western universalising concepts," given their critique of Glissant's impenetrability.

A PARADOXICAL APPROACH
TO THE TERM "CREOLE"

Having briefly presented the problematic teleology in which the *créolistes* situate their movement, I would now like to outline some of the other paradoxes of the movement. The first of these concerns the term *créolité* itself. The movement's chief authors draw attention in their manifesto to the derivation of the term *créole*, an expression long overshadowed by what Chris Bongie aptly calls "resisting memories" of exclusionist racial classification. Characterized by Bongie as a "shifting signifier,"[9] as "slippery" and "resolutely unstable," it has always been a locus of considerable semantic confusion. To begin with, its etymology is complex and opaque. That complexity is, however, startlingly short-circuited in the footnote that the authors of *Éloge de la créolité* devote to philological considerations. They state there that the word *créole* seems "to come from the Spanish word *crillo* [sic], itself derived from the Latin verb *criare* [sic] which means "to raise, to educate." The creole is the person who was born and raised in the Americas and who is not a native like American Indians" (*Pr.* 121). The *créolistes*' appeal to etymology, which highlights displacement as the chief criterion of creoleness and makes no reference to race, is paradoxically both tentative and dismissive, for the same footnote ends with the following observation: "etymology is, as everybody knows, a dangerous and uncertain field. There is, therefore, no need to refer to it in order to approach the idea of creoleness" (*Pr.* 121). Now, without embracing the fundamentalism of Heidegger, for whom etymology seems to constitute the condensed "wisdom of the tongue," the etymological and philological trajectory of the term *créolité* would appear to be, contrary to its dismissal by Chamoiseau and Confiant, particularly pertinent. After all, usage of the term that the *créolistes* mobilize in a narrative of identity based on displacement has itself formed a complex pattern of variation (or, one might say, "creolization"), based on its dissemination and naturalization in different geographical and cultural contexts.[10]

French lexicologists broadly agree that the term *créole* derives via the Spanish *criollo* from the Portuguese *crioulo,* meaning a slave born in his master's house, from the Portuguese verb *criar* ("to breed," but also "to bring up"), itself derived from the Latin verb *creare* (meaning "to create" or "to beget"). However, in *Éloge de la créolité,* Portuguese usage is not mentioned at all, although the Portuguese *criar* seems to be conflated with the Latin *creare* in that fictitious hybrid (or simple solecism?) of the *créoliste* footnote—*criare*. In bypassing the Portuguese usage, the *créolistes* erase principally, of course, the discrepancy or shift between the Portuguese and the Spanish meanings—that is, between reference to the displaced African slave population and reference to persons of Spanish or European origin born in the New World. Clearly, neither Iberian usage refers exclusively or even principally to racial or hereditary considerations; on the contrary, the primary or agreed reference, given the discrepancy regarding racial identity, might be taken to be the reference to exogenous birth, that is, to transportation or migration. No doubt the difference between the two Iberian usages reflected the differing nature of these initial colonies: unlike the Portuguese, the Spanish favored large-scale settlement by whole battalions of European colonists. Robert Chaudenson confirms that, while seventeeth-century French lexicographers followed the Spanish sense of the term, defining the *Créole* as a *Européen né aux Isles,* up until the mid-eighteenth century the term was deployed in France's "New World" colonies to designate both Europeans and Africans, both whites and blacks, the only significant criterion being birth in the colonies.[11] From the middle of the eighteenth century onward, however, the French Caribbean followed Metropolitan French usage, reserving for the unqualified term the exclusionist meaning of white European born in the colonies.

The inclusive contemporary usage promoted by the *créolistes*, whereby the term is taken to refer to all those who share common "New World," secondary, or adventitious origins, is not a new extension of reference within the French-speaking American colonies. It is, rather, a reversion to local usage up to the mid-eighteenth century. Moreover, in French Guyana, for example, that inclusiveness—as foreign to the original

Portuguese usage as it was to the original Spanish usage—was never surrendered. As the *créolistes* point out, the black Guyanese have always called themselves *Créoles*. Furthermore, the term served in French Guyana less to indicate displacement or transplantation than to indicate the degree of perceived cultural assimilation into European ways. To be creole was not just to have adapted to a new geographical environment but also to have been integrated into the colonial cultural system. In this context, the Guianese maroon communities would not have been regarded, for example, as Creoles.

Another subtle shift, this time away from a notion of displacement and adaptation to a notion of a newly forged culture, is reflected in the definition of *Créolité* by the *créolistes* as "the interactional or transactional aggregate of Caribbean, European, African, Asian, and Levantine cultural elements, united on the same soil by the yoke of history" (*Pr.* 87). In this promotion of creoleness as an open and inclusive mixing and relationality, the term *créole* that had been—despite dramatic semantic fluctuations in space and in time—widely defined primarily and invariably with respect to displacement or relocation, finds its historical, geographical, and cultural polysemy canceled, its relation to location or relocation attenuated, and its connotations of exclusion by race replaced by connotations of inclusion by culture. In the *créoliste* creed, to be *créole* is to belong to a creolized culture, defined not just as displaced, but also—even primarily—as adjusted, relational, or even mixed. But what is paradoxical about the *créolistes'* mobilization of this term is that, in an apparent failure of memory, they fail to harness its shifting history, its aura of indeterminacy, and immense semantic variability in space and time, an aura that could itself be said to be the apotheosis of "creolization."

CRÉOLITÉ: CULTURAL RETROSPECTION AND POLITICAL LIMBO

A central paradox of the *créolité* movement concerns the tension between its visionary claims and its revisionist perspective, between its particularistic retrospection and its globalist pretensions. For the principal authors of the movement, creole culture is first and foremost the product of the process of creolization enabled by the plantation system endemic over several centuries in the American South, Central America, Brazil, the Indian Ocean, and the Caribbean. However, they do assert that the entire world is approaching a state of creoleness in that every people and every culture is increasingly entering into relation with others. Hence they do not simply theorize Caribbean cultural identity, since creoleness is said to be emblematic of the global, postmodern present and future. Its postmodern model of emergent identity is held, indeed, to prefigure the future of all culture:

> The term "creole" is eminently modern. It is not *passé* and colonial as some might think. Indeed it is even postmodern in the sense that it indicates the emergence of a new model of identity that we could term multiple or mosaic, in the process of being elaborated under our noses, especially in Western megapolises. Over three centuries, creolisation prefigured, as it were, this irreversible phenomenon.[12]

And yet, the creoleness that these writers contemplate and recommend is resolutely rooted, unambiguously located in a specific, mourned past, and the relation between that past, on the one hand, and the celebration of the present and future of creoleness on the other hand, is by no means clear.

In *Lettres créoles,* Patrick Chamoiseau and Raphaël Confiant date *créolité* from 1635, that is, from the inception of plantation culture. However, the phenomenon is injected by its "authors" with a latent, perhaps compensatory temporal depth and with infinite spatial complexity or density. It is, after all, rather elliptically identified as "our primitive soup," "our primeval chaos," and "our mangrove swamp of virtualities" (*Pr.* 90). Apart from stressing the tangled or blended texture claimed for creoleness—by analogy with the mangrove swamp and with soup—these metaphors evoke a "primeval" or "primitive" time. On the one hand, then, the *créolistes* acknowledge a belated cultural big bang, around 1635; on the other, they evoke a primitivity and virtuality designed perhaps to compensate for this relative belatedness. The tension between the idea of a new beginning—or "New World"—and notions of temporally indefinite, primeval latency is reinforced by the definition of *créolité* as an "open specificity" (*Pr.* 89)

Although the *créolité* vision is inherently programatic and future-oriented, the aesthetic outlined in the main body of the manifesto is strikingly retrospective. After all, the first factor of *créolité* to be singled out is the oral tradition, identified as the principal vector of continuity with the culture of the Plantation past; indeed, it is said of the writing of *créolité* that it can achieve authenticity only insofar as it is inseminated by the past via creole orality. And in effect, the literary writing of Chamoiseau and Confiant copiously confirms this self-conscious transcription into French of spoken Creole constructions and rhythms. The second factor of creole authenticity to be highlighted, namely *la mémoire vraie* ("true memory") is even more explicitly retrospective and revisionist. It is characterized as a careful attentiveness to the voices of the past, even—or especially—when their scream has been swallowed into the gaps of the colonial version of history. The novels of Confiant and Chamoiseau are—in fact—entirely devoted to remembering this lost and emphatically local past. After orality and counter-history, the third element of the creole aesthetic is an inclusivist desire to embrace the creoleness of each aspect of Caribbean reality and history: "We are part and parcel of our world. We want, thanks to Creoleness, to name each thing in it, and to declare it beautiful" (*Pr.* 100–01). It rapidly emerges, however, that this inclusiveness is also deeply revisionist, since the *créolistes* endorse the rehabilitation of various key elements of colonial culture, including the "*béké* ethnoclass" (*Pr.* 90). The final elements to be prescribed are openness to the outside world—a corrective to insularity and stagnation—and linguistic plurality: both Creole and French are to be embraced, but neither is to be idolized; rather both languages are to be valued and creatively renewed.

In the writing of the *créolité* movement, what passes for creole cultural authenticity is overwhelmingly predicated, then, on the colonial past; indeed, the *créolité* aesthetic is fundamentally an attempt to recover elements of a resistant cultural model held to have been conceived and to have thrived in that past. *Lettres créoles* (Chamoiseau & Confiant 1991), for example, idealizes the distinctiveness of the smaller-scale version of the Plantation that reigned in the Petites (or Lesser) Antilles, its relative compactness being held to explain the peculiar intensity of the French Caribbean cultural interaction. The collapse of the plantation system is lamented as a cultural catastrophe that precipitated the decline of creoleness, in that the cultural magic of *créolisation* or *métissage* was gradually replaced by a "system of global consumption of things from outside . . . and we began, starting with the mixed race, to confuse freedom and assimilation, urban culture and civilisation, freedom and frenchification" (Chamoiseau & Confiant 1991:67).

The reluctance to address and interpret the yawning gap between a dissymetrical historical model of creolization (based on colonization and/ or slavery), on the one hand, and an idealized, mutualist, "interactional" contemporary and futurist model, on the other, is not unrelated to the failure to acknowledge—much less harness—the complicated etymology and complex philology of the term "creole." It is also related to the temptation to foreclose Édouard Glissant's attempt to imagine creolization as process without end, and to the presentation of that foreclosure as progress. All of these apparent *impensés*, or neglected questions, betray perhaps a desire to freeze-frame "creoleness," leaving time out of the reckoning.

CREOLE EXCLUSIONS

Although the spatiocultural reference of *créolité*, unlike that of *antillanité*, "theoretically" includes Louisiana and the Indian Ocean, in practice, *créoliste* discourse refers almost exclusively to the Caribbean. For example, in what is apparently an afterthought required by some notion of political correctness, the authors of the *créolité* manifesto claim that they are in sympathy with the French Caribbean independence movement. Even if they reject the ideologies that have hitherto underpinned this movement, specifically Marxism, they rather quixotically propose an ideal political evolution based on cultural affinities. That is, they envisage a preliminary association of creolophone islands (here there is no pretence at inclusion of non-Caribbean or non-island space, since only Martinique, Guadeloupe, Haiti, Dominica, and Saint-Lucia are mentioned) as a prelude to wider pan-Caribbean federation with the anglophone and hispanophone islands and, ultimately, with Central and South America. However, the Indian Ocean is entirely omitted from this aspirational confederation.

While the authors of the *créolité* manifesto claim to speak for and about creole cultures everywhere, their discourse usually refers by implication to one creole space only: that is, the Americas, and in particular the Caribbean arc.[13] From a movement priding itself on its defense of an interactive diversity, such deficient recognition of the heterogeneity of creole "space" is unexpected. Before claiming to envisage "*notre monde en pleine conscience du monde*" (*Pr.* 13)—that is, our world in full consciousness of the whole world—without problematizing the deictic reference, the authors of *Éloge de la créolité* could profitably have pondered Homi Bhabha's belief that the "other" is never outside or beyond us; it emerges forcefully, within cultural discourse, when we *think* we speak most intimately and indigenously "between ourselves" (1990:4).

It is in this same context that the stereotyping of women and of gender relations in general in the writing of the *créolité* movement has been criticized (Arnold 1995), its allegedly oppressive and *passéiste* representation of gender clashing with the *créolistes*' claims to an open, inclusive, creative, and complex model. Again here, it is as though the architects of *créolité* found it impossible to break free from a model constrained by the past.

Despite Patrick Chamoiseau's conviction that what will prevail of *créolité* is the rendez-vous with global diversity and relationality,[14] Richard and Sally Price have noted the rigid insularity of the movement, demonstrated by its failure to relativize itself even within the local Caribbean context. Beyond the Caribbean, the Prices cite, among others Homi Bhabha,

Tzvetan Todorov, and Anthony Appiah, Sidney Mintz, and Simon Gikandi as intellectuals who have built up a body of work on creolization, hybridity, and so on. Where, they wonder, is the *créolistes'* awareness of this kindred intellectual work? A further related contradiction is noted by the same critics in relation to the question of maroon culture. Again, according to the Prices, the *créolistes* underestimate the "tremendous diversity of African cultures and languages represented in any early Caribbean colony," a diversity that made of the early maroon communities "the most thoroughly (and earliest fully) "creolized" of all New World communities." Instead, the maroons are depicted as "uncultured isolationists" (Price & Price 1999:130). This criticism is borne out by the evocation of the maroon in *Lettres créoles* as an inarticulate figure confined to the wordlessness of the scream and of silence and positioned outside the economy of creolization, to which he converts only after 1848 when he abandons the hills, bringing with him intact the "Africa of his memories, mythical and unreal" (Chamoiseau & Confiant 1991:34).

In line with most particularisms, especially nationalisms, the writing of the *créolité* movement is accused of being antimodern and anticosmopolitan. Certainly, in Chamoiseau's first three novels and in virtually every line of Raphaël Confiant's work, the writing is moved by what Timothy Brennan calls the "populist undercurrents of national thought" (1990:54). Indeed, much *créolité* writing confirms Bruce King's view that "nationalism is an urban movement which identifies with the rural areas as a source of authenticity, finding in the 'folk' the attitudes, beliefs, customs, and language to create a sense of national unity among people who have other loyalties. Nationalism aims at [. . .] rejection of cosmopolitan upper classes, intellectuals, and others likely to be influenced by foreign ideas" (cited in Brennan 1990:53). It is all the more difficult not to read the *Éloge* as a fundamentally nationalist tract given that it holds, fundamentally, a discourse of identity or distinctiveness. Again, what is remarkable here is that the *créolistes* do claim that their thinking transcends nationalist boundaries and aspirations, attaining to that higher level of authenticity associated with acceptance of a constant dynamic of complexity, a shifting, open-ended inclusiveness. In other words, they do appear to endorse the "antinationalist, ambivalent nation-space" that looks toward the "new transnational culture" of which Homi Bhabha makes so much.[15] What many critics might consider as involuntary self-contradiction is regarded, however, by others as motivated intent. Michel Giraud (1997), for example, believes that the absence of political sovereignty in the French Caribbean creates a vacuum, by virtue of which cultural legitimacy or supremacy becomes the prize. In other words, in a society in which culture, not politics, confers authority and power, cultural schools and not political movements exclude or marginalize. Giraud studies in some detail the paradoxical orthodoxy of creole authenticity on the basis of which the cultural hegemony of *créolité* is imposed and policed.

It should be said, however, that the critical debate around "*créolité*" has involved excesses on both sides. Faced with accusations, for example, of bad faith in their double role as "social critics railing against French domination and beneficiaries of lucrative literary prizes from Paris, both the champions of a fast-disappearing "traditional" Martinique and unchallenged masters of the modern media" (Price & Price 1999:139), the *créolistes* have understandably defended themselves with some animus. However, the tenor of some of this defensiveness (the verbal manhandling reported by Richard Burton, for example)[16] exposes contradictions between the facts of *créoliste* relational practice, on the one hand, and, on the other, claims to a culture "*qui ne domine pas mais qui entre en relation*" ("that does not seek to dominate but rather to relate") and that is governed by a "*désir convivial*" (*Pr.* 113–14).

AESTHETIC DOGMA AND CREATIVITY

Predictably, the *créolistes* roundly refute the indictment of *créolité* in the glossary of Glissant's *Discours antillais*, which decries it as the obsessive intent to establish monoglot, Creole linguistic supremacy. In fact, one detects nowhere in the manifesto or indeed in any other writings by Chamoiseau or Confiant the slightest will to impose or even to promote Creole monolingualism. On the contrary, for all the pious words in praise of Creole, the subtext of *Éloge de la créolité* bespeaks a lucid realism in relation to the language (although the dedication is bilingual, the body of the text and the epigraph are monolingual). None of these writers sees his attempt to remain faithful to the spirit only of Creole (namely, the creolization of French) as betrayal or defeat. And each would roundly refute Michel Giraud's indictment of the irony involved in "saying in French—so as to have a readership—that Creole is the cornerstone of Caribbean cultures." Not only would these writers point to the fact that Creole is more systematically foregrounded in the *créolistes*' texts (either directly, or by the use of creolized French) than in the writing of many other Caribbean writers, but they would also argue that the frequent use of translation into French, of glossaries, and of periphrastic footnotes means that their use of language is always highly relational. Nonetheless, the defense and illustration of the vernacular—essentially by the ongoing "creolization" of French—does seem to be held by the *créolistes* as being virtually coterminous with the fundamental creativity of creole culture and as being a measure of the creoleness of this or that writing practice. Unfortunately, however, this dogmatic prescription (the *Éloge* reads like a five-point plan) has produced in many cases predictably formulaic rather than creative results.

PHILOSOPHICAL APORIA

Precipitating some of the paradoxes outlined above, and bringing us back to the notion of teleology, a deep philosphical faultline underlies the whole notion of "creoleness." Inevitably, of course, the very words *antillanité* and *créolité* suggest a certain essentialist nostalgia. As Chris Bongie puts it, commenting on *Éloge de la créolité*:

> the authors' praise of an *"identité créole"* remains trapped within and committed to a foundationalist politics of identity grounded in claims of authenticity. The opening words of the document—"neither Europeans, nor Africans, nor Asiatics, we proclaim ourselves Creoles" (p.1 3)—clearly affirm a New World identity that is logically equivalent to the Old World identities that are being denied [. . .]. (Bongie 1997:165)

Despite the manifest continuities between them, Édouard Glissant distinguishes himself from his heirs not just by having rapidly jettisoned the notion of *antillanité* for that of creolization but also by meticulously distinguishing between state and process and by promoting creolization as insistently as he rejects creoleness. The "particularistic logic" that Bongie discerns even within the "inevitable return to what Glissant's vision of creolization is purportedly bent upon undoing" is nicely redeemed by the critic, however, who holds it up as a perfect example of the creolization process itself.

> This apparently paradoxical co-existence of two differing logics is, I believe, actually fundamental to the creolising process, rather than an anachronism that must eventually be bypassed in [a] sort of "epistemic" leap . . . it is the attenuated prolongation of memories, rather than their transcendence, that characterises this "process of mutation and adaptation." (Bongie 1997:167)

As we have seen, in the *créoliste* narrative the French Caribbean sense of self follows a monolinear, evolutionist temporal logic culminating less in a creolization without end (that is, an endless process of mutation and adaptation) than in the state of grace that is creoleness. Moreover, in ignoring synchronic relations with other New World thinking, this narrative is locked into a narrow and incestuous plot—filiation or dialectic. However, several factors at work in *créoliste* writing, in particular the reverberations of intertextual dynamics, fortunately combine to subvert that impression of closure and constraint. It is undoubtedly in the processes and crossings among different times, spaces, texts, cultures, languages, and so on that the creole dynamic most clearly finds expression. And yet the paradoxes that we have seen to be inherent in the *créolité* movement—chiefly, perhaps, a distrust of, or disregard for the effects of time, tend to militate against the full play of these processes and crossings and to reduce the scope of the dynamic involved. And, whereas the *créolité* movement does not provide answers to the most important questions posed by creolization—especially since it short-circuits so many of them, its principal paradoxes do quite successfully point up many of those questions.

Notes

1. Some of the points developed in this article have been adumbrated, usually with a different emphasis, in Mary Gallagher (2002).
2. This is the view expressed by J. Michael Dash (1998:11): "It is no coincidence that Martinique is a prolific producer of theories of difference. Envisioning opacity at all costs is the only form of resistance open to Martiniquans, and to this extent one is never in doubt as to the political implications of what Glissant is proposing."
3. Reprinted in Walcott (1998:213–32).
4. References to this work, first published in 1989 by Gallimard, are to the subsequent bilingual edition: Jean Bernabé, Patrick Chamoiseau, Raphaël Confiant, *Éloge de la créolité/In Praise of Creoleness* (Paris: Gallimard 1993), identified hereafter in the text by the abbreviation *Pr*.
5. As recounted in Glissant's (1956) *Soleil de la conscience*.
6. Glissant's (1981) *Le Discours antillais* has been translated into English by Betsy Wing as *Caribbean Discourse. Selected Essays* (1989).
7. See Glissant (1981:495/1989:261): "More than a theory, a vision. The force of it is such that it is applied to everything. I have heard *antillanité* proposed on a few occasions (without further details) as a general solution to real or imagined problems. When a word acquires this kind of general acceptance, one presupposes that it has found its reality."
8. As early as the mid 1950s in *Soleil de la conscience*, Glissant expressed a certain squeamishness about having his work interpreted as theoretical generalization: on the first page of that work, he stresses the personal texture of his views, their strictly positional value: "*Cas très individuel dont nul ne saurait, à des fins diverses, faire un usage d'orientation plus général*" (Glissant 1956:11). This caution is also apparent in the disavowal of systematic thinking ("*pensée de système*") in Glissant (1997:18).
9. Chris Bongie (1997:153–78). A considerably amplified version of this article features under a similar chapter title in Bongie (1998), the fourth chapter of which is entitled "Resisting Memories: Édouard Glissant and the Medusa of History."
10. Chaudenson (1992:8). This work has been translated as Robert Chaudenson, *The Creolisation of Language and Culture* (London: Routledge, 2001).

11. Chaudenson observes that dictionary usage (which, until very recently, applied the term "creole" to whites only) can be very misleading and that French lexicography does not take account of regional French and creole usage, or of usage variations in place and time (Chaudenson 1992:9).

12. My translation. *"Le terme 'Créole' est donc éminemment moderne, et non passéiste et colonial comme d'aucuns pourraient le croire, et même post-moderne dans le sens où il signale l'émergence d'un nouveau modèle d'identité qu'on pourrait appeler 'multiple' ou 'mosaïque,' en train de s'élaborer sous nos yeux partout à travers le monde, notamment dans les mégalopoles occidentales. La créolisation a été en quelque sorte la préfiguration, au cours des trois derniers siècles, de ce phénomène irréversible"* (Confiant 1993:266).

13. See the criticisms enunciated from an Indian Ocean perspective by Réunionnais critic Jean-Claude Carpanin Marimoutou (1991:95–98).

14. *"[. . .] ce qui est indépassable, c'est le positionnement de la diversité, l'identité relationnelle"* ("what will endure is the positioning around diversity, the relational quality of identity"). See Chamoiseau (2001).

15. This critique takes on added historical resonance and irony when one recalls that, according to Timothy Brennan, "if one discounts the civil wars of England and France, the first nationalists are not Frenchmen, Spaniards, or Englishmen, but the creole middle classes of the New World,—people like Simon Bolívar, Toussaint l'Ouverture, and Ben Franklin" (1990:58–59).

16. See the final pages of Burton (1997).

References

Arnold, A. J. 1995. The gendering of *créolité:* The erotics of colonialism. In *Penser la créolité*. M. Condé and M. Cottenet-Hage, eds. Paris: Karthala.

Bhabha, H., ed. 1990. *Nation and narration*. London: Routledge.

Bongie, C. 1997. Resisting memories: The creole identities of Lafcadio Hearn and Édouard Glissant, *Sub-Stance* 84:153–178.

——— 1998. *Islands and exiles: The creole identities of post-colonial literatures*. Stanford, CA: Stanford University Press.

Brathwaite, E. K. 1984. *The voice: The development of nation language in anglophone Caribbean poetry*. London: New Beacon.

Brennan, T. 1990. The national longing for form. In *Nation and narration*. H. Bhabha, ed. London: Routledge.

Burton, R. 1997. *Le Roman marron*. Paris: L'Harmattan.

Chamoiseau, P. 1997. *Écrire en pays dominé*. Paris: Gallimard.

——— 2001. *The creolisation of language and culture* (translation of Chaudenson 1992). London: Routledge.

Chamoiseau, P., and R. Confiant. 1991. *Lettres créoles: Tracées antillaises et continentales de la littératures 1635–1975*. Paris: Hatier.

Chamoiseau, P., and M. McCusker 2000. De la problématique du terroir à la problématique du lieu: Un entretien avec Patrick Chamoiseau, *The French Review* 73(4):724–733.

Chaudenson, R. 1992. *Des îles, des hommes, des langues: langues créoles—cultures créoles*. Paris: L'Harmattan.

Condé, M., and M. Cottenet-Hage, eds. 1995. *Penser la créolité*. Paris: Karthala.

Confiant, R. 1991. *Aimé Césaire: Une traversée paradoxale du siècle*. Paris: Stock.

Dash, J. M. 1995. *Édouard Glissant*. Cambridge: Cambridge University Press.

——— 1998. *The other America: Caribbean literature in a New World context*. Charlottesville, VA: University of Virginia Press.

Dépestre, R. 1980. *Bonjour et adieu à la négritude*. Paris: Robert Laffont.

Gallagher, M. 2002. *Soundings in French Caribbean writing since 1950: The shock of space and time*. Oxford: Oxford University Press.

Giraud, M. 1997. La créolité: Une rupture en trompe-l'oeil. In *Cahiers d'études africaines*, 148:795–811.

Glissant, É. 1956. *Soleil de la conscience*. Paris: Seuil.

———— 1969. *L'intention poétique*. Paris: Seuil.

———— 1981. *Le Discours antillais*. Paris: Seuil.

———— 1989. *Caribbean discourse: Selected essays*. B. Wing, tr. Charlottesville, VA: University of Virginia Press.

———— 1990. *Poétique de la relation*. Paris: Gallimard.

———— 1997. *Traité du tout-monde*. Paris: Gallimard.

Harris, W. 1983. *The womb of space: The cross-cultural imagination*. Westport, CT: Greenwood.

Marimoutou, J.-C. 1991. Créole et créolité, *Notre Librairie*, 104:95–98.

Price, R., and Price, S. 1999. Shadowboxing in the mangrove: The politics of identity in post-colonial Martinique. In *Caribbean romances: The politics of regional representation*. B. Edmondson, ed. Charlottesville, VA: University of Virginia Press.

Walcott, D. 1998. *What the twilight says: Essays*. London: Faber & Faber.

12 Creolization Moments

Aisha Khan

This chapter is a further reflection on a discussion I embarked upon some years ago (Khan 2001, 2003a, 2004b), where I queried and critiqued the concept of "creolization," which had been lately reinvigorated by new manifestations of long-standing questions in anthropology, history, cultural studies, and literary theory, as well as in popular discourse in the Americas and elsewhere in the world. The abiding questions about creolization have to do with the nature of cultural change, the expressions and consequences of cultural encounters among diverse groups within certain regimes of power, and the character of, and relationships among particular social formations, notably regions and nation-states. Manifestations of the creolization concept have come in the form of such varied concepts as "plural societies," "miscegenation," and, more recently, "hybridity" and "multiculturalism."

The recent florescence of the creolization concept can be explained in a number of ways. For one, important late twentieth-century turns in scholarship have deemed it particularly applicable to the increasing globalization of culture (for example, Clifford 1997; Hannerz 1987). Second, the creolization concept lends itself well to revisionist approaches to cultures as unbounded, fluid, contingent, and articulated within various "-scapes" (Appadurai 1996) that constitute today's world. Third, the concept is understood to be a means of revealing the successful and creative agency of subaltern or deterritorialized peoples, and the subversiveness inhering in creolization, which contradicts earlier notions of cultural dissolution and disorganization (for instance, Fernandez Olmos & Paravisini-Gebert 2003; Glissant 1995).

One important point to foreground at the outset is that conscious and unconscious dimensions are simultaneously captured under the rubric of creolization. On the one hand, certain practices and transformations come about out of our awareness, as people respond to the unfolding events of their lives as they make them. On the other hand, new or differently configured practices, or those that are perceived as such by practitioners, are consciously reflected on, generally in terms of the direction and meaning of cultural change. Because it entails both conscious and out of awareness aspects, creolization serves scholars, intellectuals, politicians, and activists, from within the Caribbean region and outside it, as both a model that *describes* historical processes of cultural change and contact and a model that *interprets* them, exemplifying (as I have earlier pointed out [Khan 2001: 274]) what Clifford Geertz (1973) distinguished as "a model of" and "a model for." Too often in academic analyses (and arguably particularly in recent treatments) these two aspects become conflated. This double burden of ideological work that the concept of creolization thus carries requires more explicit attention than offered in the vast amount of scholarly literature that relies on it. This lacuna is likely due in part to the concept's functioning as what Pierre Bourdieu and Loic Wacquant (1999) identify as the "commonplaces" of public discourse, or "presuppositions of discussion which remain undiscussed . . ." and thus all the more convincing (1999:41). There is, then, the tendency of models, such as creolization, to become overdetermined. Such overdetermination, I argue, obfuscates creolization's key aspect: its quotidian contingency, or the meaning and significance that are derived from its everyday expression. Not only does "creolization" entail both out of awareness processes and those discerned by practitioners, it requires deconstruction into its "model of" and "model for" dimensions.

Given its positive, affirming emphasis on cultural resilience, subversive agency, and theoretical usefulness, and its prevalence in academic and other discourse, it is incumbent on us to take a closer look at the concept of creolization and the ideological work to which it has been put toward the representation of certain lived realities. What is at stake, in other words, in the recent (re)appearance of interest in creolization is the distinction between creolization as process (empirical, historical, cultural, transformative) and creolization as concept (the theoretical models developed to account for and understand those processes)—and the consequences of conflating process and concept. In this chapter my closer look consists of a focus on what I call *creolization moments*. These are empirical contexts of creolization's emergence as a problematic of cultural identity and social structure and organization. The chapter considers two of these moments: (1) the ideology of creolization as it emerged in connection with colonial rule and post World War II "callaloo" cultural politics in the Republic of Trinidad and Tobago, and (2) the ideology of creolization as it emerged in connection with the broader, academic study of Caribbean societies from the early twentieth century to its mid-point.

CREOLIZATION MOMENT 1:
THE TRINIDADIAN PROBLEMATIC

As colonial projects, Caribbean societies have tended to treat creolization as a central problematic, construed not simply as a natural, unmarked process of cultural (and biogenetic) development but as an object of cultural (and biogenetic) derailing, one that produces certain kinds of ambiguous, disruptive embodied consequences. These results are generally construed either as potentially socially liberating oppressed or exploited constituencies within the society or as socially destructive of order, norms, and legitimacy, depending on the point of view. Hence, on the one hand, interactions among populations of the same "type," however that type is defined, would be deemed normative. Whereas, on the other hand, putatively different types are what cause social comment. Reified and rather fetishized, the concept of creolization in the Caribbean has been subject to numerous interpretations; and in Trinidad across two centuries, from colony to nation-state.

As I have discussed in greater detail elsewhere (for example, Khan 1993, 2004a), Trinidad has been conventionally characterized as a social class-color pyramid consisting of three increasingly expanding strata: upper/"white," middle/"colored" or "brown," and lower/"black." This foundational social pyramid more or less recognized subsequent mid-nineteenth-century influxes of Indian, Chinese, and Syrian-Lebanese labor migrants through the vector of class rather than through the local imaginary of shared biocultural nexus of Afro-Euro social and sexual relations. Indian indentured laborers, for example, were typically incorporated, in both symbolic and material terms, as part of the pyramid's lower stratum, though not necessarily (or consistently) labeled "black"; successful Indian entrepreneurs would likely be included in the middle range, though not simultaneously labeled "colored" or "brown," given the black-white ancestral theme that cannot accommodate foreign (that is, non-Euro, non-Afro) others. As a heuristic device, then, the class-color pyramid identified Trinidadian society as possessing a white-brown-black constitution. Ideologically, "exotic" immigrants could not be mixed, as in absorbed, into the black-white continuum of race and color (Segal 1993). This model of Trinidad, and Anglophone-Caribbean societies in general, as resting on a black-white axis is to an extent out of fashion today, given new scholarly approaches to understanding identities and the construction of difference, for example, as not being static or bounded. Another factor is the rise of revisionist nationalist narratives that emerged from the political developments of the mid-twentieth-century emphasizing ethnoracially distinct local groups nonetheless together constituting the "callaloo" nation, as opposed to the "creole" colony. The decades-long imprimatur of the black-white axis and the tricolored pyramid, however, played a part in the relatively slow momentum of the perception of "mixed" as more than "colored"/"brown," and "creole" as a harmonious, callaloo "rainbow" of ethnocultural difference (rather than gradations of color), to take hold in the region. Arguably today, still, the tension between these two models, one might say the one of society and the other of nation, works to exclude in some key respects Indo-Trinidadians from the nationalist narrative and thus from state policy. I will return to this momentarily.

If we think in historical terms, Trinidad's hierarchical continuum of race and color, racial designations, class position, and notions of femininity and masculinity always have been mutually constitutive. This is because creolization as process (history) and creolization as concept (ideology, theory, metadiscourse) are never completely distinct. For example, in eighteenth- and nineteenth-century Trinidad (and much of the rest of the Caribbean) the importance of color as an ostensibly literal description of phenotype was its ideological work in signaling class position and the conduct and values appropriate to each. "Colored middle class" or "brown" populations in the Anglophone Caribbean attested to the social meaning of color, whereby the intermediacy of "brown" was negotiable according to level of education, occupation, comportment, and other signs of the ability to claim membership in the middle class, irrespective of alleged darkness of skin color or other indications of a "black" phenotype.

These sorts of articulations apply to "whiteness" as well. For example, as explained above, a creole person is generally viewed in the Caribbean as possessing local biology, that is, a combination of European and African, white and black, that derives from sexual reproduction ("creole" deriving from the Spanish word, *criollo*, or "locally born"). Hence, local culture locates the "white"/European creole individual within a New World—that is, Caribbean—context as well as raises some doubt as to the purity of his or her origins. In Trinidad, creole "whites," then, were

Europeans born in the colony rather than in the mother country. Allegedly produced only in the European homeland, "white" identity becomes culturally as well as biologically suspect, parsed in Trinidad as "Trinidad white" and "French Creole" to designate degrees of dubiousness about purity. The source of the problem of taint was gendered and classed throughout the Caribbean, typically laid at the doorstep of women, particularly those who fraternized too closely with the subordinated. The diary of Lady Maria Nugent, for example, the (American) wife of a nineteenth-century governor of Jamaica, attests to this misgiving, with its criticism of Jamaican "white" women. Their laxity in speech and behavior was due, Lady Nugent surmised, to degradation resulting from too much interaction with Afro-Jamaicans (Bush 1981). As she wrote in her journal, "Many of the ladies speak a sort of broken English, with an indolent drawling out of their words, that is very tiresome if not disgusting" (quoted in Knight 1997:275). Almost a century later, the wife of the governor of Trinidad, Lady Young, "wrote privately to Secretary of State Malcolm McDonald that: 'local white creoles have no conception of manners, loyalty or any other civilized virtue. They simply do not live in the same box as ordinary human beings . . . they are as strange and remote as the Africans and low-caste Indians who have, as everything tends to sink[,] much influenced the whole trend of life in these islands" (quoted in Samaroo 1974:xi).

Compounding this disturbing, creolizing production of ambiguous boundaries distinguishing cultures, gender (femininity), and classes (and their mutual constitution) was the perception of Trinidad as the benchmark of diversity. From its earliest days after the British annexed it from Spain (in 1802), and particularly after the mid-nineteenth-century's influx of "foreign" immigrants from India and China, Trinidad has been characterized by observers as a phenomenally heterogeneous place, filled with remarkable contrasts. As just one example of many, Lady Anne Allnutt Brassey, a widely traveled British baroness who wrote a two-volume memoir of her Caribbean voyage (Brassey 1885; see also Khan 2003b), remarked about Trinidad that "strange were the objects that met our view. There were negroes with their funny merry faces, . . . graceful little brown coolies [Indians] of every caste and sect; and representatives of the large mulatto and yellow-faced population, of no particular race . . ." (Brassey 1885:103, v.1). It is interesting and, I think, not coincidental, that Brassey does not count the European population as among those "strange objects," even though European presence on the island was greater at this time than it would become, greatly diminished, in successive generations (Brereton 1998). She also leaves out the Chinese, who, unlike Europeans, would certainly have fit her bill for unusual alterity, but this may simply be from her lack of exposure to them during her brief stay. What is also noteworthy, for our purposes, is that in her phenotypic kaleidoscope, Brassey casually includes those who have "no particular race"—the "mulatto," the "yellow," the "creole" (in the sense of "mixed"). Like most European and North American observers of the day, her characterization is of a "heterogeneous" society, but this heterogeneity represents, as it did for most of her contemporaries (and many decades beyond), cacophony rather than some form of social order, whether dysfunctional or dependable. "Creole societies" may be sites of curious heterogeneity ("strange objects") but "creolization," the processes of various mixings within societies that give them a certain internal logic, is a different kind of image. That is, creolization as a process lends method, if an unfortunate one within the Victorian gaze, to the madness of those ostensibly random cultural and biological assemblages known as colonies. As we will see shortly, the discourse of creolization in Trinidad will alter significantly when processed through interests and agendas other than colonial, notably those of the post-independence, callaloo nation-state.

In Trinidad's origins as a colonial possession, its system of stratification based on a class-race-color hierarchy laid the foundations for a post-independence society whose hallmark has been "racial" group competition, fostered by class inequalities and state control of certain resources, and couched in terms of antipathies between Indo and Afro populations. Although it was not until the 1946 Trinidad census that a "racial question proper" was first posed (Kuczynski 1953:339), this mid-century period was one in which anticolonial sentiment and agitation for independence (not just in Trinidad but throughout the British West Indies) stirred a spirited public discourse. After World War II nationalist sentiment became more diffuse, emphasizing constitutional reform and universal suffrage. Cultural nationalism also blossomed at this time: as the "black" and "colored" middle class became more prominent, "it increasingly sought new symbols with which to define itself" (Stuempfle 1995:78–79; see also Thomas 2004). Increasingly, attention was given to Afro-Trinidadian folk culture as the standard-bearer of the nation. On the part of the Afro-Trinidadian middle-class intelligentsia who assumed control of the state upon political independence from Britain (in 1962), as well as among other sectors of the population, among the most commonly adopted anti-imperialist, anti-Western stances entailed a turn toward precolonial cultural forms, optimistic correctives to Eurocolonial hegemony. The idiom of cultural identity as a crucial element in resistance to colonialism was a key aspect in the racial consciousness that transcended other potential forms of communal cohesion, notably unity across classes, despite that the period between 1919 and 1945 saw the development of middle-class sectors among both Afro- and Indo-Trinidadian populations, a concomitant increase in Indo-Trinidadian middle-class political participation, and the heightened politicization and representation of the Afro-Trinidadian working class, expressed particularly as labor unrest (MacDonald 1986:45–47). The period of 1946 to 1956 in Trinidad "was a time of bourgeois experimentation with governing the nation" (MacDonald 1986:72). It was particularly after WWII that Afro- and Indo-Trinidadians would "clash politically" (Majid 1988:19). Within the "semiotics of colonialism" (Hintzen 1997:54) in Trinidad, the mutually constitutive relationship between "culture" and "race" helped to reify these into terms that seemed objective and self-evident. Keeping constituencies antithetical on the basis of perceived racial interests helped contain the number of competing political factions to two—Afro and Indo. It also buttressed "race" as a central idiom in Trinidadian society— the discourse and the imagery according to which identities, configured against a particular anticolonial ideology, continued to be constructed. Thus even while the creole colony, separate and hierarchical, became the callaloo nation, united and democratic, the emergent forms of constituency representation, both symbolic and political, retained an emphasis on the Afro-Euro foundational axis, where Indo voting blocs, stimulated by the historically ever-present "Indian opposition parties," press the state for recognition and opportunity on the basis of an ethnocultural distinctiveness that resonates alterity in a kind of Catch 22: that is, in order to be counted one must be differentiated, and that differentiation necessarily draws on noncreole (that is, nonlocal) traditions and practices that carry a racial valence expressed as ethnocultural identities.

If we take the claim that "Trinidadians are very open to multiple forms of identity" (Crowley 1957; Stoddard & Cornwell 1999:339) as a rhetorical position rather than a national character trait, we have entered into the Trinidadian nationalist narrative of harmony and "unity in diversity" (for example, Harney 1996).What we need to bear in mind, however, is that this narrative, or discursive strategy, is peculiar to the historical moment of the Republic's struggles for independence and creation of a new Caribbean nation-state. Indeed, Indo-Trinidadians have for the majority of their history in Trinidad critiqued in various fashion what they see as the national silence about their own, particularly valuable, contributions to the nation and their consequent political and cultural invisibility within it (see, for example, Khan 2001, 2004a; Munasinghe 2001).

One notable effect of the rhetoric of harmony and tolerance is that it actually limits public discourse to affirmations of goodwill and optimism (Harney 1996; see also Prashad 2001; Segal & Handler 1995). Such apparent promotion of freedom and equality is difficult to challenge, since it masks "deep economic and political stratification" (Harney 1996:54). When race is substituted for class as both the organizing principle of political culture and the explanatory representation of the nation, an all-encompassing *cultural* callaloo becomes the diversity touchstone: only certain images in the national culture portrait are accommodated, as any Indo-Trinidadian can recite, irrespective of whether she or he personally subscribes to this critique. Thus, for example, Indo-Trinidadian religious festivals such as Divali are generally (if only relatively recently) included in state representations of the culturally all-inclusive callaloo nation, Indo-Trinidadian indentured labor history generally is not (except in the broadest of strokes), and the figure of the *dougla* (an Indo-Afro "mix") only ambivalently, and therefore inconsistently, so. True diversity in the sense of including any, and unanticipated, forms of alterity is not possible.

In his discussion of U.S. ideology, Vijay Prashad (2001) points out, with startling relevance to Trinidad, that when the state holds the differences within civil society to be "nonpolitical distinctions" (for example, "cultural," and "racial" as in heritable), it can hold itself above those distinctions, as if decrying them, and manage difference with such strategies as "unity in diversity" (2001:57). In other words, the state does not "emancipate people from distinctions (or undermine the power embedded in certain social locations), but it emancipates itself from them" (2001:58). The overall cultural schema of the state purports to equally protect the cultural heritage of its constituent social groups but does not undermine the material structures of privilege on which the state rests. Thus an anticolonial project of sovereignty "devolves into the state logic of management of difference" (2001:58). Two related consequences derive from this: one, state priority becomes the alleged protection of (certain forms of) cultural difference for its own sake; and two, other distinctions become negated or eclipsed, notably those of class, an outcome that protects the foundation of inequality on which the state depends.

Creole heterogeneity thus is limited to certain designated permutations and, as Nigel Bolland (1998) has pointed out, it rests on a premise of collective individuality constituting a society rather than a dialectical model of structural oppositions defined in relation to one another within particular historical moments (1998:25–26). These factors produce an impasse that most discussions of creolization miss or ignore: creolization is neither the template for a society's achieving social, cultural, and political equality nor the harbinger of discord. Confined to its own discursive strategy, the concept of creolization cannot, so to speak, be thought outside its own narrative box. The example of Trinidad highlights that "creolization" is as much about conscious, political orchestration of notions of culture and cultural change as it is about what happens to local culture on the ground; as such, it functions in Trinidad to an important extent as a "model for," that which interprets, leading the "model of," that which describes, toward particular descriptive agendas, in the colonial and post-independence imaginaries about their respective social structures and organization.

CREOLIZATION MOMENT 2: THE SOCIAL SCIENCE PROBLEMATIC

In the first decades of the twentieth century, Franz Boas and his students concerned themselves with what would be known as "salvage ethnography," the documenting of traditions, practices, and lifeways in North America viewed as disappearing or, as Ruth Benedict put it, "broken" (Benedict 1934). Melville Herskovits, among the most influential of Boas's students, would seek African cultural continuities in the Americas, succumbing to the "romance of the 'jungle' and of the 'negro'" that had permeated the cultural climate of the United States (and parts of Europe) by the 1920s (see Herskovits 1941; Herskovits & Herskovits 1934; Price & Price 2003:17).

Broadly interested in processes of cultural change, Herskovits identified the problem of acculturation as central to these processes. In his concept of "socialized ambivalence," developed during his fieldwork in Haiti (for instance, Herskovits 1937), Herskovits attempted to explain the relationship between the two constituent cultures he delineated there, "African" and "European." In an intellectual project that certainly falls within a "creolization" problematic, Herskovits saw Haitian culture as consisting not of a combination of African and European but of two distinct sets of values or behavioral alternatives (Mintz 1964:46), which he exemplified in contrasts such as polygyny versus monogamy, or obligations toward ancestral deities versus eternal damnation (Mintz 1977:76). This contradictory pull demonstrated that Haitians evinced "ambivalence"—the condition of simultaneously holding positive and negative feelings for the same thing, such as esteem with disdain (Bourguignon 2000:104). This ambivalence was "socialized" because it was not expressed as idiosyncratic inner turmoil but rather as normative (Herskovits 1937). The source of this norm was the incomplete union of African and European ancestral cultures (Bourguignon 2000:104), which produced a basic cultural conflict: the underpinning of Haiti's political and economic precariousness. Herskovits surmised that it was "entirely possible" that socialized ambivalence underlay much of Haiti's economic and political instability, "so that, arising from a fundamental clash of custom within culture, [socialized ambivalence] is responsible for the many shifts in allegiance that continually take place . . ." (Herskovits 1937:295). The implication is that cultural blending produces harmonious acculturation in contrast to the precarious social situation that Herskovits observed among Haitians, which was allegedly produced by discordant cultural heterogeneity within the society. Indeed, Erika Bourguignon suggests that in Mirebalais, where Herskovits conducted his field research, there is not much evidence of "incomplete fusion of cultures," that the ethnographic data on creolization as a process "is full of examples of the integration or syncretism of African and Catholic elements in religion and other aspects of culture" (Bourguignon 2000:104). In ignoring the conflict fundamental to Haiti's structure of social stratification, and shifting his focus to acculturation, Herskovits abandoned an exploration of conflict and ambivalence to emphasize harmony, a condition that derived from cultural continuities and maintenance of African traits (Bourguignon 2000:107).

The historical and scholarly context of his research significantly shaped Herskovits's conclusions. During the mid 1920s to 1930s, the validity of studying acculturation was still being debated among anthropologists, but by 1936 the *American Anthropologist* published "A Memorandum for the Study of Acculturation," coauthored by Robert Redfield, Ralph Linton, and Herskovits. Although acculturation was formally "defined as a two-way process, most subsequent acculturation studies stressed the impact of western [sic] civilizations upon non-western ones, so that acculturation soon received the connotation of 'westernization'" (Malefijt 1977:85), that teleological propulsion toward a certain direction (at times both cultural and phenotypic, as in Latin America's ideology of *blanqueamiento* ("whitening") or *mestizaje* ("mixing"). Furthermore, Herskovits formulated Haitian "socialized ambivalence" during the end of U.S. military occupation there, when a cultural renaissance was flourishing, involving in part a rejection of North American and European hegemony—cultural and otherwise. Not being a place where cultural changes were perceived to be headed toward westernization, Ann Marie de Waal Malefijt (1977:86) drolly observed that "[c]learly, then, Haiti was not the place to study 'acculturation'" (1977:86). With "socialized ambivalence" Herskovits ultimately relied for explanation on the necessarily tenacious conflict found in cultural difference. Although Herskovits surely did not view it in these terms, one might argue that, here, the energy of creolization is implicitly located in the force of abrasion, that is, the contrariness of opposites together but not much attracting.

Thus until about the late 1920s in the regional Caribbean, "creole" largely signified "heterogeneous" and sometimes "hybrid" (in the modern, not postmodern sense), with internal social compatibility more or less possible. As the Caribbean's period of intense labor unrest, trade union activity, and economic decline associated with the Great Depression emerged by the beginning of the 1930s, a variation of "creole" took center stage: the cognate "plural," as in "plural societies." A major question now for academics and policymakers (both local and external) would be how these "powder keg" countries managed to hang together, deflecting the centrifugal forces of social unrest and cultural dysfunction.

Indeed, after World War I, such philanthropic organizations as the Rockefeller Foundation, who were interested in, among other things, academic research and institution building, significantly shaped the development of the social sciences. Particularly during the 1920s and 1930s their aim was to make the social sciences "more scientific in order to promote social and economic stability" and to "develop more effective methods of social control" (Fisher 1983:215, in Patterson 2001:73). In this same period, a wider concern in American anthropology in the 1930s was with the problem of acculturation, or "what happened when groups of individuals with different cultures came into continuous contact resulting in changes in the original cultural patterns of one or both groups" (Patterson 2001:86). Scholars not necessarily committed to ethnographic research, as was Herskovits, were nonetheless concerned with questions about the kinds and consequences of transformations cultures underwent when exposed, perniciously or fortuitously, to "cultural contact, migration, and conquest" (Park 1950:5) that produced what were thought of as heterogeneous societies. As Robert Park, a forefather of American sociology, observed, under these influences, "cultural complexes" fracture into smaller units, transmitted and diffused independently of their original cultural context. "One of the first and most perplexing problems of cultural anthropology and sociology," he deduced, "is to discover the conditions and the processes by which cultural traits have been diffused and modified" (1950:5)—analogous to what we might today call "creolization." In a sense recognizing the problem of process, Park argued that the "dynamic character" by which cultural traits "interact and modify one another" is due to their being rooted in the "instincts and habits of human beings"; traits "are not merely diffused" as static units, they are, instead, "transformed, recreated" (1950:7). His characterization of "culture" as representing the *activity* that brought into existence the products which are assembled in museums and described in books (1950:7) suggests a counterposing of practice and product that acknowledges the dynamism of production and transformation. Yet evident, as well, is that Park is himself a product of his time, assuming the fixity of cultural *traits*, and that cultural reproduction followed, more or less, a "one-way transfer" model of change (as Buisseret [2000:3], in a different context, phrases it), from dominant to subordinate cultures.

Grappling with the problem of power, Park wished to "formulate a few general hypotheses" about "hybrid peoples" (1950:133, 132), who command our attention because they "offer the most obvious and tangible evidence" of European cultural contact, and because their numbers and their respective social roles indicate the character of race relations and cultural assimilation (1950:132). Through these roles and relationships, hybrid peoples constitute a "miscegenation map of the world," by which miscegenation and assimilation can be studied comparatively—along with the "social and political consequences which accompany them" (1950:132). Park's hypotheses are that "miscegenation" is most common on "frontiers," among "primitive people when their tribal organizations have been undermined by slavery or by sudden incorporation, in some other way, into the industrial systems of more highly civilized peoples" (1950:133). In other words, colonialism's labor projects (that is, slavery, indenture, free wage labor) bring far-flung peoples together, but also, colonialism's legal and moral projects (that is, colonial "society") reified and fetishized miscegenated "types." Hybridization, or miscegenation (which Park uses interchangeably), takes place where "people of divers cultures" mingle with unusual freedom, and where custom is thus "relaxed and the traditional distinctions of class and caste not rigorously enforced" (1950:377). From these kinds of comments we can infer a presumption that social boundaries such as class are more fluid in frontier settings, suggesting in turn that class stratification is less relevant in these (indistinct) "creole" or "hybrid" contexts. One possible reason for this association is that under conditions of radical (extreme) heterogeneity, all elements of social structure are viewed as breaking down and thus being minimally effective or important in social organization.

Building on his ideas about frontier hybridity, as well as on, by then, a well-entrenched supposition about colonial cities, towns, and ports—known also as "plural societies"—being centers of cosmopolitan social and economic traffic, Park asserted that the "common market place has always been the natural meeting place of peoples of different races and cultures" (1950:378). Jamaican sociologist Michael G. Smith (for example, 1965) was among the most influential scholars to articulate a model of "plural societies" for understanding the Caribbean as a locus of colonized cultural heterogeneity, where the marketplace was the necessary locus of social intercourse. Building on the work of J. S. Furnivall (1948) in Southeast Asia, Smith described colonial societies as being held together by the political dominance of a ruling minority rather than cohering through values shared among the diverse ethno-cultural segments brought together in these societies. For Smith, each of these segments that together made up a "plural society" possessed deep-seated cultural differences rooted in norms and values. While the various segments interact with one another, they maintain social institutions that continue to be mutually exclusive and inherently incompatible. In these allegedly artificial settings, social interaction principally takes place within the context of the marketplace, where transactions do not require value compatibility.

If the plural society model was unable to accommodate cultural and social change over time, its poor fit for creolization models also lay in its assumption about the necessary antinomy among different norms and values. More viable in creolization theory is the work of British anthropologist Raymond T. Smith (for example, 1967), who espoused a view of "creole society" that emphasized the centripetal force of elite values. Rather than consisting of ethnocultural segments hanging together by the pull of dominant authority (a "conflict" model, a "plural society"), Caribbean societies cohere, he argued, according to Eurocolonial values that legitimate an all-encompassing hierarchy of privilege in which all social sectors were in accord (a "consensus" model, a "creole society"). Common values about the "moral and cultural superiority of things English" (1967:235), rather than coercion, kept these societies, and their hierarchies, intact. As Diane Austin (1983:226) notes, Raymond Smith's ideas reflect North American sociologist Talcott Parsons's approach, in which a basic principle is that societies are value-integrated. While agency in the form of social and cultural change can be accounted for by Raymond Smith's "creole society" model in ways not possible in Michael Smith's "plural society" model, the emphasis on integration does not deal as well with tensions between creolization as model of and as model for, as that which descriptively recounts and that which theoretically predicts.

A major underlying question of these approaches, shared by many academics and policy makers of the early to mid-twentieth century, is one of social cohesion—"the social and political consequences" of hybridity/creolization, or, what happens when heterogeneous cultures are brought together. One of Robert Park's interests, as part of the Chicago School of sociology, was the question of what happens "when people of divergent cultures come into contact and conflict" (Steinberg 1981:47). This was put into practice, for example, in June of 1923, when the *East Indian Patriot*, a local Trinidadian newspaper, reported that

> Our colony was recently visited by Professor Robert E. Park of the Chicago University, and Professor N.G. Weatherly of the University of Indiana, who, we understand, were deputed by the Rockefeller Institute to study the question of Socialism [sic], as obtains among the different races of the world. They were greatly interested in our cosmopolitan population, and hoped, during their brief visit here, to acquire sufficient information on the subject allotted to them. (*EIP* 1923)

While we do not learn more about Park's and Weatherly's Trinidadian research, we can infer from the newspaper's reportage that state and research institution interests converged over anxieties about socialist (and communist) movements, multicultural diversity (and allegedly consequential racial conflict), and what were rapidly becoming waning imperial regimes in colonial contexts of growing labor unrest. Never entirely simply an academic matter of charting cultural change, cultural continuities, or cultural areas, "creolization" for these inquirers indicated deeper issues of potential social (and cultural) *dis*integration and dysfunction.

This second example of a creolization moment, from the social sciences operating in the region, again points to the fact that the creolization concept has been deeply embedded within larger narratives of governmentality and the scholarly objectives, both commendable and suspect, that accompany, as support or as contradiction, those regimes and their concerns about social structure and organization. Nor surprisingly, perhaps, once again we encounter the problem of conflating the "model of" and the "model for" in creolization processes (whether it is a moment that is consciously reflected upon by practitioners or not), where the latter (model for) speaks for the former (model of), rather than consisting of an on-going dialogue between the two.

A NOTE TO END ON

Aijaz Ahmed (1995) correctly points out that the "cross-fertilization of cultures has been endemic to all movements of people . . . and all such movements in history have involved the travel, contact, transmutation and hybridisation of ideas, values and behavioural norms" (1995:18). The rub, of course, is our desire to glean patterns (of power, of change, of meaning) from all this busy and protracted human activity that will help us make sense of it. As Arif Dirlik (1994) recognizes, the spatial and ideological jumble we know the globe to be today means that "the flow of culture has been at once homogenizing and heterogenizing; some groups share in a common global culture regardless of their location . . . while others are driven back into cultural legacies . . . to take refuge in cultural havens that are as far apart from one another as they were at the origins of modernity . . ." (1994:352–353). In the context of creolization, the problem of power, in other words, is quotidian. I have proposed that a direction we might pursue is to interrogate more acutely why we seek certain patterns, possibilities, and prescriptions in human experience, specifically, in relations of power. These questions still require probing, interrogating what and whose ends they serve. Making an effort to disaggregate and complicate the "whose" as well as the "when" and the "why" will advance us toward discouraging the romanticization and overdetermination of theory, which ultimately are not conducive to understanding the nuances, polyphony, and complexities of all that is contained within the rubric "creolization."

References

Ahmed, A. 1995. The politics of literary postcoloniality, *Race & Class* 36(3):1–20.

Appadurai, A. 1996. *Modernity at large: Cultural dimensions of globalization*. Minneapolis: University of Minnesota Press.

Austin, D. 1983. Culture and ideology in the English-speaking Caribbean: A view from Jamaica, *American Ethnologist* 10(2):223–240.

Benedict, R. 1934. *Patterns of culture*. Boston: Houghton Mifflin.

Bolland, N. 1998. Creolisation and creole societies: A cultural nationalist view of Caribbean social history, *Caribbean Quarterly* 44(1 & 2):1–32.

Bourdieu, P., and L. Wacquant. 1999. On the cunning of imperialist reason, *Theory, Culture and Society* 16(1):41–58.

Bourguignon, E. 2000. Relativism and ambivalence in the work of M. J. Herskovits, *Ethos* 28(1):103–114.

Brassey, Lady A. A. 1885. *In the trades, the tropics, and the roaring forties*. Vols. I and II. Leipzig: Bernhard Tauchnitz.

Brereton, B. 1998. The white elite of Trinidad, 1838–1950. In *The white minority in the Caribbean*. H. Johnson and K. Watson, eds. Kingston, Jamaica: Ian Randle, pp. 32–70.

Buisseret, D. 2000. Introduction. In *Creolization in the Americas*. D. Buisseret and S. G. Reinhardt, eds. College Station, TX: Texas A & M Press, pp. 3–17.

Bush, B. 1981. "White ladies," "colored favorites," and "black wenches": Some considerations on sex, race, and class factors in social relations in white creole society in the British Caribbean, *Slavery and Abolition* 2(3):245–262.

Clifford, J. 1997. *Routes: Travel and translation in the late twentieth century*. Cambridge, MA: Harvard University Press.

Crowley, D. 1957. Plural and differential acculturation in Trinidad, *American Anthropologist* 59(5):817–824.

Dirlik, A. 1994. The postcolonial aura: Third world criticism in the age of global capitalism, *Critical Inquiry* 20:328–356.

EIP (East Indian Patriot). 1923. Vol. II, no.10.

Fernandez Olmos, M., and L. Paravisini-Gebert. 2003. *Creole religions of the Caribbean*. New York: New York University Press.

Fisher, D. 1983. The role of philanthropic foundations in the reproduction and production of hegemony: Rockefeller Foundations and the social sciences, *Sociology* 17(2): 206–233.

Furinvall, J. S. 1948. *Colonial policy and practice*. Cambridge: Cambridge University Press.

Geertz, C. 1973. Religion as a cultural system. In *The interpretation of cultures*. New York: Basic Books, pp. 87–125.

Glissant, E. 1995. Creolization in the making of the Americas. In *Race, discourse, and the origin of the Americas*. V. L. Hyatt and R. Nettleford, eds. Washington, DC: Smithsonian Institution Press, pp. 268–275.

Hannerz, U. 1987. The world in creolization, *Africa* 57(4):546–559.

Harney, S.1996. *Nationalism and identity: Culture and the imagination in a Caribbean diaspora*. London: Zed Books.

Herskovits, M. J. 1937. *Life in a Haitian valley*. New York: Knopf.

——— 1941. *The myth of the negro past*. New York: Harper and Brothers.

Herskovits, M. J., and F. Herskovits. 1934. *Rebel destiny: Among the bush negroes of Dutch Guiana*. New York: McGraw-Hill.

Hintzen, P. 1997. Reproducing domination identity and legitimacy constructs in the West Indies, *Social Identities* 3(1):47–75.

Khan, A. 1993.What is "a Spanish"? Ambiguity and "mixed" ethnicity in Trinidad. In *Trinidad ethnicity*. K. Yelvington, ed. Knoxville, TN: University of Tennessee Press, pp. 180–207.

——— 2001. Journey to the center of the Earth: The Caribbean as master symbol, *Cultural Anthropology* 16(3):271–302.

——— 2003a. Isms and schisms: Interpreting religion in the Americas, *Anthropological Quarterly* 76(4):761–74.

——— 2003b. Portraits in the mirror: Nature, culture, and women's travel writing in the Caribbean, *Women's Writing* 10(1):93–117.

——— 2004a. *Callaloo nation: Metaphors of race and religious identity among South Asians in Trinidad*. Durham, NC: Duke University Press.

——— 2004b. Sacred subversions? Syncretic creoles, the Indo-Caribbean, and "cultures in-between," *Radical History Review* 89:165–84.

Knight, F. 1997. Pluralism, creolization, and culture. In *General history of the Caribbean,* Vol 3. F. Knight, ed. London: UNESCO/Macmillan, pp. 271–86.

Kuczynski, R. R. 1953. *Demographic survey of the British colonial empire,* Vol. 3, *West Indian and American territories*. London: Oxford University Press.

MacDonald S. B.1986. *Trinidad and Tobago: Democracy and development in the Caribbean*. New York: Praeger.

Majid, A. 1988. *Urban nationalism: A study of political development in Trinidad*. Gainesville, FL: University of Florida Press.

Malefijt, A, M. de Waal. 1977. Commentary, *Boletin de Estudios Latinoamericanos y del Caribe* 22:83–91.

Mintz, S. 1964. Melville J. Herskovits and Caribbean studies: A retrospective tribute, *Caribbean Studies* 4(2):42–51.

——— 1977. North American contributions to Caribbean studies, *Boletin de Estudios Latinoamericanos y del Caribe* 22:68–82.

Munasinghe., V. 2001. *Callaloo or tossed salad? East Indians and the cultural politics of identity in Trinidad*. Ithaca, NY: Cornell University Press.

Park, R. E. 1950. *Race and culture*. Glencoe, IL: The Free Press.

Patterson, T. C. 2001. *A social history of anthropology in the United States*. New York: Berg.

Prashad, V. 2001. *Everybody was Kung Fu fighting: Afro-Asian connections and the myth of cultural purity*. Boston: Beacon Press.

Price, R., and S. Price. 2003. *The root of roots or, how Afro-American anthropology got its start*. Chicago: Prickly Paradigm Press.

Samaroo, B. 1974. Foreward. In *Through a maze of colour*. A. Gomes, ed. Port of Spain: Key Caribbean Publications.

Segal, D. 1993. "Race" and "colour" in pre-independence Trinidad and Tobago. In *Trinidad ethnicity*. K. Yelvington, ed. Knoxville, TN: University of Tennessee Press, pp. 81–115.

Segal, D., and R. Handler. 1995. U.S. multiculturalism and the concept of culture, *Identities* 1(4):391–407.

Smith, M. G. 1965. *The plural society in the British West Indies*. Berkeley and Los Angeles, CA: University of California Press.

Smith, R. T. 1967. Social stratification, cultural pluralism and integration in West Indian societies. In *Caribbean integration: Papers on social, political, and economic integration.* Rio Piedras, Puerto Rico: Institute of Caribbean Studies, pp. 226–258.

Steinberg, S. 1981. *The ethnic myth: Race, ethnicity, and class in America.* New York: Atheneum.

Stoddard, E., and G. H. Cornwell. 1999. Cosmopolitan or mongrel? Créolité, hybridity, and "douglarization" in Trinidad, *European Journal of Cultural Studies* 2(3):331–353.

Stuempfle, S. 1995. *The steelband movement.* Philadephia: University of Pennsylvania Press.

Thomas, D. 2004. *Modern blackness: Nationalism, globalization, and the politics of culture in Jamaica.* Durham, NC: Duke University Press.

About the Contributors

Philip Baker has published extensively on pidgin and creole languages since the 1970s. He is currently Senior Research Fellow in the Department of English and Linguistics at Westminster University.

Jorge Cañizares-Esguerra is Professor of History at the University of Texas at Austin. He is the author of the prize-winning *How to Write the History of the New World: History, Epistemology, and Identities in the Eighteenth-Century Atlantic World* (2001); *Puritan Conquistadors: Iberianizing the Atlantic 1550–1700* (2006); *Nature, Empire and Nation: Explorations of the History of Science in the Iberian World* (2006); and (co-edited with Erik Seeman) *The Atlantic in Global History, 1500–2000* (2006).

Joyce E. Chaplin is Professor of History at Harvard University. She received her Ph.D. at Johns Hopkins University. She is the author of *An Anxious Pursuit* (1993), *Subject Matter* (2001), and *The First Scientific American* (2006).

Thomas Hylland Eriksen is Professor of Anthropology at the University of Oslo and the Free University of Amsterdam. His research has focused on cultural complexity, identity politics, and globalization. His recent books include *Globalisation—Studies in Anthropology* (2003) and *Engaging Anthropology* (2006).

Mary Gallagher teaches French at University College Dublin. Her main publications are *La Créolité de Saint-John Perse* (1998); *Soundings in French Caribbean Writing Since 1950* (2002); and *Ici-Là: Place and Displacement in Caribbean Writing in French* (2003).

Aisha Khan teaches Anthropology at New York University. Her research interests include New World diasporas, Atlantic studies, postcolonial societies, and the construction of identities. She has published widely on her research among South Asians in Trinidad and among the Garifuna

(Black Carib) in Honduras. Her most recent book is *Callaloo Nation: Metaphors of Race and Religious Identity among South Asians in Trinidad* (2004).

Peter Mühlhäusler has worked on pidgin and creole languages of the Pacific area since 1972 and lectured on this topic in Berlin (Technische Universität) and the University of Oxford. He is the Foundation Professor of Linguistics at the University of Adelaide. He has published about two hundred articles and four books in creolistics, including *Pidgin and Creole Linguistics* (1997).

Stephan Palmié is Associate Professor of Anthropology at the University of Chicago. He is the author of *Das Exil der Götter: Geschichte und Vorstellungswelt einer afrokubanischen Religion* (1991), *Wizards and Scientists: Explorations in Afro-Cuban Modernity and Tradition* (2002), and editor of *Slave Cultures and the Cultures of Slavery* (1995).

Joshua Hotaka Roth is an associate professor of anthropology at Mount Holyoke College. He is author of *Brokered Homeland: Japanese Brazilian Migrants in Japan* (2002). His research interests include migration, minorities, risk, urban space, and car cultures.

Charles Stewart teaches in the Department of Anthropology at University College London. He has conducted long-term field research in Greece. He is the author of *Demons and the Devil: Moral Imagination in Modern Greek Culture* (1991), editor (with Rosalind Shaw) of *Syncretism/Anti-Syncretism* (1994), and also editor (with Eric Hirsch) of a special issue of *History and Anthropology* (vol. 16, 2005) on "Ethnographies of Historicity."

Miguel Vale de Almeida, anthropologist, is associate professor at ISCTE-Lisbon, Portugal. He has conducted research in Portugal, Brazil, and Spain, on issues of gender, "race," ethnicity and postcolonialism in the Lusophone world, and sexual orientation. In addition to books in Portuguese, he has published two books in English: *The Hegemonic Male* (1996) and *An Earth-Colored Sea* (2004). He is editor of the journal *Etnográfica*.

Françoise Vergès, Reader, Centre for Cultural Studies, Goldsmiths College, London, is the author of *Monsters and Revolutionaries: Colonial Family Romance and Métissage* (1999). Forthcoming: Project for a Museum of the Present, Maison des Civilisations et de l'Unité Réunionnaise.

Subject Index

Name Index